SULTANS OF ADEN

By the same author

LAYARD OF NINEVEH
John Murray 1963
MORNING WILL COME
John Murray 1943
WHAT HAPPENED TO FRANCE
John Murray 1940
LUCIE DUFF GORDON
John Murray 1937
EGYPT
Thames and Hudson 1967
Edited new edition of
FIRST FOOTSTEPS IN EAST AFRICA
by Sir Richard Burton
Routledge 1966

SULTANS OF ADEN

Gordon Waterfield

JOHN MURRAY

Printed in Great Britain for
John Murray, Albemarle Street, London
by William Clowes and Sons, Limited
London and Beccles
7195 1793 1

FOR HAROLD INGRAMS, C.M.G., O.B.E.

Contents

Contents

Part Two: THE FALL OF CAPTAIN HAINES

Illustrations

Illustrations

x

Illustrations

* *Reproduced by permission of the Trustees of the National Maritime Museum, Greenwich*
† *Reproduded by courtesy of the Mansell Collection, London*
‡ *Reproduced from* The Route of the Overland Mail to India *by T. Grieve and Robert Moresby, London 1852; by permission of the Trustees of the British Museum*

xi

Preface

I have dedicated this book to Harold Ingrams, the expert on South Arabia, because he has long had an affection and admiration for Captain Stafford Bettesworth Haines of the Indian Navy and encouraged me to write about him. There is very little published about him and the main story is based on the contemporary despatches from the India Office Records. I wish to thank the following: Mr. S. C. Sutton, the Librarian and Keeper of Records of the India Office, for the great help given by him and his staff, especially Mr. Martin Moir, Assistant Archivist; the staff of the invaluable London Library, of the Fulham Public Library, members of the Print Room of the National Maritime Museum at Greenwich and Mr. R. G. Searight for his knowledge of nineteenth-century prints. For advice and research, my wife, Mr. John Murray, Miss Jane Boulenger, Mrs. Joan St. George Saunders, Mr. Murray Graham, and Miss Dorothy Liptrap for work on the illustrations.

The spelling of Arabic names is at times unusual since it is influenced by their rendering in the original despatches, and Mrs. Doreen Ingrams, who kindly did the Index, should not be held responsible by the experts.

Fulham, 1968

Introduction

The Arab members of the South Arabian Delegation, who negotiated their independence with the British at the end of November
1967, argued that they were owed large sums of money in aid,
because for nearly one hundred and thirty years the British had
exploited Aden, ever since they captured it in 1839. It has, indeed,
become a popular doctrine to set out an adverse balance sheet
against colonialism which was not, of course, done when Arabs and
others had their empires. Besides, the early history of British relations with Aden is not only dramatic but also complicated.

Commander Stafford Bettesworth Haines of the Indian Navy was
sent to Aden by the East India Company in 1838 and purchased the
Peninsula from Sultan Mahsin of Lahej and Aden; he was then
nearly kidnapped by the Arabs and the final outcome was the
capture of Aden by storm on January 19 1839. It is not intended to
make a study of the rights and wrongs of the British occupation of
Aden, though the question of imperialism in its good and bad aspects
will probably be at the back of the reader's mind. Sultan Mahsin
was prepared to sell Aden to the British because he wanted money
and feared that the Egyptians, then occupying the coastal region of
the Yemen, would take Aden without paying him anything. Having

sold Aden to the British it was not long before the Sultan began to protest that it was better to sell one's mother than one's country and organised three major attacks to retake Aden. Was he an Arab nationalist or an unreliable and avaricious man? In 1839 Aden was a derelict village of six hundred inhabitants and from this Haines created a thriving market-place of twenty thousand inhabitants bringing prosperity to the Arabs and considerable expense to the British. Was he an imperialist exploiting the country? Was he depriving Arabs of their freedom or creating opportunities for a new freedom?

The Egyptians, if they had seized Aden, would not have shown any interest in or respect for Arab freedom; in 1840 Mohammed Ali Pasha, Viceroy of Egypt, withdrew his armies from the Yemen because of a Middle East crisis—much in the same way as President Nasser did nearly one hundred and thirty years later. The Arabs were then no better off under a rapacious Sherif of Mocha who ruined trade, or under the Ottoman Turks who would have taken Aden if the British had not been there; Turkish imperialism was particularly hated because of its ruthless interference with the lives of the Arabs.

The Arabs of South Arabia have always been passionate individualists. 'Every Arab considers himself worthy to rule and it is rare to find one of them submitting to another, be it his father or brother or head of his clan', wrote Ibn Khaldun, the famous Arab historian of the fourteenth century whose family came from the Hadhramaut. In Haines' time, five hundred years later, the Arabs had changed little. They clung to a Beduin freedom to carry on tribal fighting, plunder the settled farmers and rob or extort high transit dues from the caravans trading between Aden and the Yemen—a good life for the strong but not for the weak. They were excessively proud, remarked Haines, regarding themselves as a chosen race because they had accepted Islam voluntarily in the seventh century and therefore considered themselves 'blessed'.

In the middle of the present century a Sayyed remarked: 'the tribes live today as they have done for centuries, valuing above all their freedom and abusing it by perpetual indulgence in tribal and family vendettas.'[1] Harold Ingrams, the expert on South Arabia, has described the Arab way of life as a 'system of anarchy', but has argued that there is a 'system' though most English people cannot see it. There is another factor which induces pride among the Arabs of South Arabia; they regard the beautiful and fertile Yemen as the birthplace of the Arab race where, it is considered, expression was first given 'to that mystical concept of unity which lies at the root of the disputed nature of the Arab Nation'. Today the conflict continues between the desire for unity and the insistence on the rights of unfettered individualism—'the essence of Arabism'.[2]

Haines during his administration of Aden from 1839 to 1854 interfered as little as possible with the way of life of the Arabs, except when it affected trade with Aden, for he knew that individual freedom was their passion. During the next hundred years or so the British seemed to understand the 'separateness' of Beduin Arabs and realised that it was better to leave them to their own devices and to win friendship by the payment of annual stipends. Harold Ingrams writes that the British did not impose their rule in a form which aroused Arab 'defensive reflexes' and that until about the 1950's the British were accepted as valued friends by the people of Aden and of the Protectorate.[3] After that there was a change. The desire to improve conditions by British methods began to assert itself under the Colonial Office, which took control in 1937, and later Federalism was planned. British Government policy was 'to bring the Federal structure as close to representative Government as possible,' explained Sir Charles Johnston, who was Governor of Aden and then High Commissioner during the critical years from 1960 to 1963.[4] Arab nationalists objected that it was a foreign concept and that it was intended to separate South Arabia from the Yemen.

Throughout history this had been regarded as one area even though individual Arab chiefs from time to time established their independence when there were weak Imams of Sana, the capital of the Yemen. Haines wanted to treat the Yemen and South Arabia as one area. Aden was the 'Eye of the Yemen' and its natural port; 'if once a safe communication for commerce be opened with Sana', wrote Haines, 'Aden would flourish.' He wanted Aden to be not only a great port where ships of all nations came to refuel, but also the market-place for trade from the fertile lands of the Yemen with Britain, India and the countries of the East. If Haines' recommendations to take up the many friendly overtures from the Imams of

Sana had not been rejected by the East India Company, it is possible that there would not have ensued the hostility which kept the Yemen separate from Aden and South Arabia. 'Had we been on friendly terms with the House of Sana', wrote Colonel Harold Jacob, a well-informed Political Officer in South Arabia at the beginning of the century, 'the course of the Great War had been far different and we should have no jarring sects warring for supremacy over Turkish remains.' He would have handed over the Arab chieftains of South Arabia to the Imam of the Yemen who would have been pleased to annex them and he argued against the Government of India's viewpoint that Aden should be nothing more than a military fortress. 'Haines was right. Aden is pre-eminently a commercial centre. Its growth has been retarded by militarists who style it a fortress only!'[5]

The British Government had no desire to extend its empire in the first half of the nineteenth century after its failure to retain the American colonies. But a secure place was needed for coaling in the age of steam navigation and Aden was chosen. It was argued that it was an enclave which had to be defended but that there should not be any close relations with others in the Yemen and South Arabia. It was a policy of 'passive imperialism', which was a contradiction in terms and very difficult for a Political Agent to carry out effectively. The presence of the British in Aden had already embroiled them with the neighbouring chiefs, with the Yemen, with Egypt and with the Ottoman Empire. Haines understood the importance of Aden in the event of war—'a valuable brilliant in the British Diadem requiring only a European war to develop its true value'—but he also realised that it was a great mistake to maintain Aden only as a military outpost.

The military pattern was set after Haines left Aden in 1854 when the Government of India laid down that 'the military importance of Aden is to be considered paramount to its commercial improvement, and should be the first object in view'. Haines' plans were overruled and Aden declined as a real commercial port for the interior. It grew, indeed, eventually into a city of nearly three hundred thousand people with shops catering for servicemen and civilians and for passengers from ships; small industries were set up and the large British oil refinery established in Little Aden, but that was not the development that Haines had envisaged for much of it

4

was not germane to the area. With the departure of British troops
and Indian merchants there was, of course, a great reduction in local
trade, but given security, Aden should retain some of its prosperity.
Ships would then continue to bunker there, passengers buy
cheap cigarettes and cameras in a free port—if it is kept so—and
perhaps once more Yemeni agriculture will prosper and trade with
the interior develop, unless the Russians in the meantime have made
Hodeida into a rival up-to-date port. If there is no security Aden
could be destroyed and even return to the derelict village it was one
hundred and thirty years ago.

'There is no tradition of peace', wrote Mr. David Holden in September 1967. 'There are shifting patterns of regional, tribal and
personal alliances, submerged beneath the British presence of one
hundred and thirty years, and now re-emerging in new, and many old,
forms. . . . Beside the façade of modern nationalism, with all its
imperialist jargon, the old divisions are still discernible in some, if
not quite all, of their traditional bitterness.'[6] Haines would have
agreed. The tribesmen he knew were very similar to the ones I had
to deal with at the beginning of the 1940 war when I was sent out
from London to help raise an irregular Arab-Somali force to take
part in the recapture of Somaliland from the Italians. Arabs from
the hills flocked to our camp at Shaikh Othman when they heard
that they could earn a rupee a day and have a rifle. They were
delightful characters, handsome, well-made, with white teeth, flash-
ing eyes, long black hair hanging in ringlets and their bare chests
blue with woad; they were gay, amusing and irresponsible. They
took an oath on the Koran that they would cross the sea to Somaliland and fight the Italians and we trained them for several months,
but when the expedition was planned they faded away and only the
Somalis, eager to fight, and one platoon of Arabs crossed over.
Haines would have known that an oath on the Koran would not be
binding. 'Yes, we have broken our promises but it is our custom',
they used to say to him. 'Fear alone will control them for a while
until they become familiar with European laws and pay ordinary
attention to their word of honour', reported Haines who often
chided them on their failure to follow the precepts of the Koran
which he knew better than many of them. He was convinced that the
British were bringing order, justice and a better way of life to the

Arabs who had been enclosed in ancient traditions for many centuries.

Haines' liking for Arabs, knowledge of their language, history, ways of thought and intricate tribal organisation enabled him to gain his ends against the hostility of neighbouring tribes who were encouraged by the intrigues of Egyptians and Turks. In spite of frustrations, resulting often from the attitude of the Government of Bombay, he held to his course because of his optimistic view of the port's future. He thought that perhaps the Arabs could be reminded that they had a long tradition as successful traders going back thousands of years when South Arabia was well populated and prosperous.

In the times of Ancient Egypt, of Rome, Byzantium and the early Ottoman Empire, Aden had been a flourishing trading centre because of its natural harbours, where ships could anchor from the monsoon winds bringing silks from China, spices from Ceylon and the Malay archipelago and frankincense from Somaliland and Southern Arabia. The trade routes across Arabia and through the Gulf of Aden and the Red Sea made the Arabs very wealthy, but the trade withered after the Portuguese in the fifteenth and sixteenth centuries had opened up new routes round the Cape of Good Hope. Trade moved again to the Red Sea area when Yemen coffee began to be popular in America and Europe and when steam navigation in the 1830's made it possible to maintain regular communications between India and Suez at all seasons. Haines was inspired by his knowledge of the past history of the area to believe that once Aden was given security it would regain something of its former prosperity, otherwise the heat and lack of vegetation in the bare plains and volcanic mountains discouraged Arabs, Indians and Somalis from settling there.

As Political Agent Haines had a large area to deal with—South Arabia, the Yemen, the lands of the Somali and Danakil along the African coast and the hinterland of Abyssinia. Much of this area had remained for many centuries virtually isolated from developments in Europe and America, though with India and the Far East the Arabs retained closer contacts. The Nizam of Hyderabad formed his bodyguard from the people of the Hadhramaut and there were Arab colonies in Java, Singapore, Sumatra, southern India and China.

Introduction

With the improvement of communications European ideas and techniques began to infiltrate into remote areas to the great resentment, at first, of the inhabitants whose ancient traditions and ways of life were assailed. The resentment felt by the neighbouring Muslim tribes at the coming of the infidel English to Aden was one of Haines' main problems, and the bitter inter-tribal feuds distressed him because they interfered with trade and prosperity for all.

The attitude of the Arabs towards the British became more favourable even in Haines' time and continued to improve with the years. His Highness Sir Ahmed Fadhl, Sultan of Lahej, who died just before the outbreak of the First World War, still resented the fact that the British had taken Aden, but wrote to the British Representative: 'Time has passed and ill-feeling has given place to affection towards you. Aden in your hands is as if it were still in mine. Aden has become an important fortress in your hands, the centre for trade and the port is rich. We rejoice at its progress.'[7]

Certainly Aden progressed from the turmoil and suffering in the Yemen and in much of the Arabian peninsula, and the British helped the Arabs to become more prosperous in spite of nationalist arguments that they had been exploited. A greater knowledge of the world through education, radio and newspapers and a realisation of the advantages of security will, it is hoped, save the Arabs from reviving their self-destructive vendettas which might be continued under cover of political affiliations.

There could be other problems. The Russians might show interest in Aden as they have already done in the Yemen and Somalia. The Gulf of Aden and the Red Sea, leading to the Suez Canal and the Gulf of Aqaba, are today even more important trade routes than they were in the eighteenth and nineteenth centuries when there was rivalry between the British and the French, each wanting to control ports so that they would be in a position to interfere with each other's trade. It is also an important strategic area where planes from airfields in South Arabia or the Horn of Africa could control the Red Sea and the Persian Gulf denying oil to the West. The Chinese, too, are active in East Africa, so that the Arabs of South Arabia may have to continue to be on the alert to retain their independence.

This story of the re-creation of Aden by the British makes use of the contemporary despatches, most of them unpublished, to describe the important fifteen years of Haines' administration followed by his disgrace and unjust treatment by the Honourable East India Company. It is not intended as a full biography for Haines' private papers have not so far been found and may never be, but the despatches 'disclose many interesting side-lights into that great man's character' and reveal his extensive knowledge of human behaviour and his varied labours.[8]

Haines died at the age of fifty-eight on June 16 1860 and is buried in Colaba cemetery, Bombay, where a tombstone records only his name and date of death. 'This', wrote Harold Ingrams, 'is the only memorial to the man who secured Aden for the far-trading Britons, the first conquest of Victoria's reign. Long after he had been forgotten elsewhere, those who worked in Aden believed that the true memorial was the place itself. . . . There was a memorial, too, in the hearts of the people, for, as late as the nineteen twenties, the people of the surrounding interior called those who lived there The Children of Haines'.[9]

PART ONE

The Rise of Captain Haines

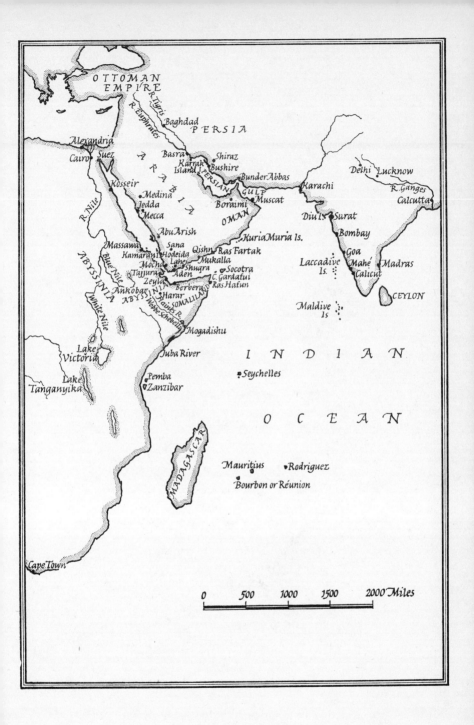

OTTOMAN
EMPIRE

R. Tigris
R. Euphrates
Baghdad
PERSIA

Alexandria
Cairo
Suez
ARABIA
Basra
Karrak
Island
Shiraz
Bushire
PERSIAN
Bunder-Abbas
Karachi
Delhi
Lucknow
R. Ganges
Calcutta

Kosseir
R. Nile
GULF
Muscat

Medina
Jedda
Mecca
Boraimi
OMAN
Diu I.
Surat

Abu Arish
Bombay

Massawa
Kamaran I.
Hodeida
Sana
Mukalla
Qishn
Kuria Muria Is.
Ras Fartak

ABYSSINIA
Blue Nile
Mocha
Lahej
Shugra
Aden
Socotra
C. Gardafui
Ras Hatun
Laccadive
Is.
Goa
Mahé
Madras
Calicut
Tajjura
Zeyla
Ankobar
ABYSSINIA
Berbera
Harar
SOMALILAND

White Nile
Webe-Shebeili
Tarres R.
Maldive
Is.

Mogadishu

Lake
Victoria
Juba River
I N D I A N

Lake
Tanganyika
Pemba
Zanzibar
Seychelles

O C E A N

MADAGASCAR

Mauritius
Rodriguez
Bourbon or Réunion

Cape Town

CEYLON

0   500   1000   1500   2000 Miles

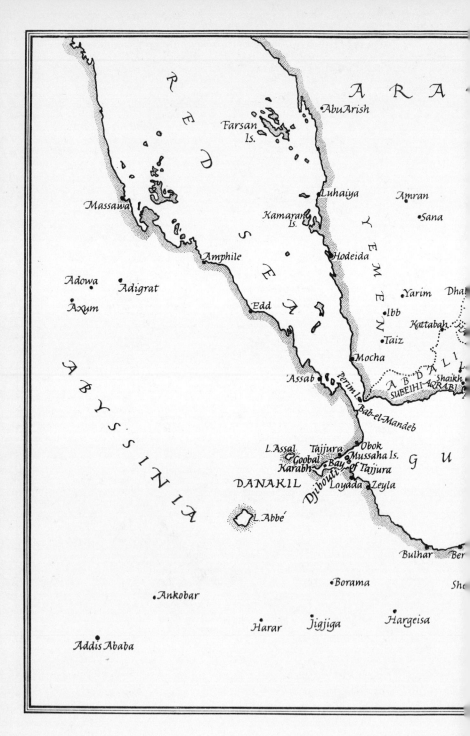

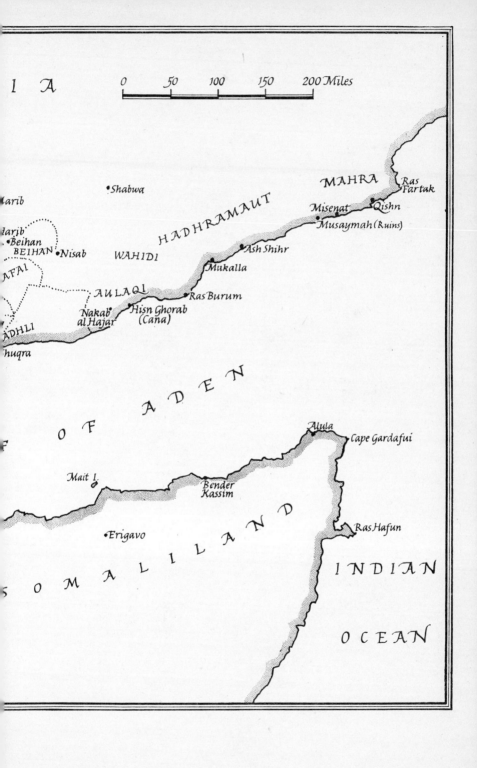

1 A

0   50   100   150   200 Miles

•Shabwa

MAHRA   Ras
                         Fartak
                    Misenat •Qishn
                  •Musaymah (Ruins)

HADHRAMAUT

Marib

larib
•Beihan
BEIHAN •Nisab   WAHIDI   •Ash Shihr
AFAI
                                    •Mukalla
        AULAQI
                      •Ras Burum
      Nakab •Hisn Ghorab
ADHLI al Hajar   (Cana)

huqra

O   F   A   D   E   N

                                    •Alula
                                         •Cape Gardafui
        Mait I.
F   •Bender
                          Kassim

                                         •Ras Hafun
        •Erigavo
                                    I N D I A N

S O M A L I L A N D

                                    O C E A N

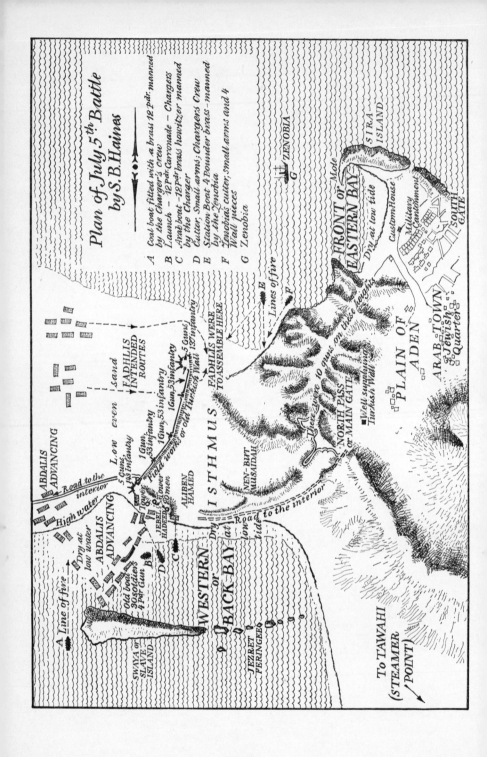

Plan of July 5th Battle by S.B. Haines

A Coal boat fitted with a brass 12 pdr. manned by the Charger's crew
B Launch — 12 Pdr Carronade — Chargers
C Arab boat — 12 Pdr brass howitzer manned by the Charger
D Cutter, Small arms; Chargers Crew
E Station Boat 4 Pounder brass — manned by the Zenobia
F Zenobia's cutter, small arms and 4 Wall pieces
G Zenobia

→ Lines of fire

← A Line of fire

FRONT OR EASTERN BAY

☩ ZENOBIA
G

SIRA ISLAND

Mole

Dry at low tide

Custom House

Military Cantonment

PLAIN OF ADEN

ARAB TOWN
Jewish Quarter

SOUTH GATE

ABDALIS ADVANCING

Road to the interior

High water

Dry at low water

ABDALIS ADVANCING

SWAYA OR SLAVE ISLAND

Old boat 30 Soldiers 4 Pdr Gun B

D C

WESTERN OR BACK BAY Dry at low tide

JEZIRET PERINGEE

To TAWAHI (STEAMER POINT)

Low even sand

FADHLIS INTENDED ROUTES

5 Guns, 193 infantry

1 Gun, 53 infantry

Tower JEBEL HADEED 50 men

ALI BEN HAMED

Field work

1 Gun; 53 infantry

5 Guns, 193 infantry

1 Gun, 53 infantry

16 Gun, 53 infantry

5 Guns 137 infantry

old Turkish Wall

FADHLIS WERE TO ASSEMBLE HERE

E

F

There were 10 guns on these heights

NORTH PASS or MAIN GATE

NEN-BUT MUSAIDAH

Road to the interior

Well supplying Turkish Wall

ISTHMUS

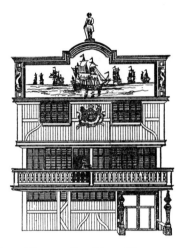

The East India Company
and steam navigation

(1600 to 1857)

It was the increase of the price of pepper from three to eight shillings a pound, as a result of the Dutch monopoly of the East India spice trade, which first brought together a number of merchants in London and led to the formation of the East India Company and eventually to India becoming part of the British Empire.

In 1600 Queen Elizabeth issued a Charter to 'the Governor and Company of Merchants of London trading into the East Indies' giving them a monopoly of trade and the right to control their own affairs. The ships built by the Company at Deptford, which became famous as 'East Indiamen', had not only to carry cargo but to be well armed to meet Dutch, Portuguese and French war vessels whose governments and merchants were fighting for the valuable trade of the Far East.

In order to trade the Company found it was necessary to establish centres or factories on the coast of India—the first one was at

Surat, north of Bombay—and these had to be protected by forts, soldiers and armed vessels. In spite of the attempts of other British merchants and sea-captains to break its monopoly—profits could be as much as one hundred per cent—the East India Company prospered and gradually built up an empire of its own. Its Charter gave it the right to acquire territory, to employ armies (which came to number as many as twenty-four thousand soldiers), form alliances, make war and peace and exercise civil and criminal jurisdiction. By 1689 the Company was thinking as much in terms of revenue from India as of trade. The Court of Directors of the Company laid down rules to be followed by the Governors of the three Presidencies of Bengal, Madras and Bombay: 'The increase of our revenue is the subject of our care, as much as our trade . . . it is that that must make us a nation in India.'

As the Mogul Empire, which had ruled northern India since the beginning of the sixteenth century, began to disintegrate after the death in 1707 of the great Aurungzeb, the Company found, in the disorder which followed, that it was taking the place of the Mogul Empire and had to fight land wars to protect its installations and government. In this the Company had a rival, Joseph Dupleix, the Governor-General of French India, who was determined to drive the English from India and set up a French Empire within the framework of native rule. A French squadron under La Bourdonnais arrived in 1746 from East Africa and the British surrendered Madras. One of the fugitives was Robert Clive, a young clerk in the East India Company, who became a soldier and defeated the French and Indian troops in a series of battles which made him Governor of Bengal twelve years later. French power was broken in 1761 with the capitulation of Pondicherry, later restored to the French. Clive was followed by Warren Hastings who became the first Governor-General of India from 1774 to 1785.

The East India Company had by then become so powerful that the British Government decided, through Pitt's Act of 1784, to bring the Company to a great extent under its authority. That was done through the institution of a Board of Control, a department of the British Government, consisting of a President, five other Privy Councillors, including the Chancellor of the Exchequer and a Secretary of State.

The East India Company and steam navigation

The East India Company's main business was carried on from East India House in Leadenhall Street, where Charles Lamb worked as a clerk and Joseph Hume, who had made a fortune in India, joined in the great debates when the Court of Directors had to face questions on policy and finance from the General Court of Proprietors. In the City of London the Company's warehouses covered ten acres of land but it was decided that it must have its own docks and warehouses near the river. In August 1806 the East India Docks were opened.

Several thousands were present and the *Globe* newspaper gave a stirring account of the flags flying and the guns firing. 'The elegant little yacht of the Trinity House, decked to her masthead in the naval finery of flags and streamers of all nations, led into the basin in a very elegant style, followed by the *Admiral Gardner*, East Indiaman. . . . As she passed in, she answered the salute of the Regimental Artillery by firing her minute guns, while the company's band on her quarter-deck played "Rule Britannia" with full chorus from the ladies and gentlemen who crowded her decks.' The newspaper remarked that among the innovations for the greater security and better convenience of the trade through the dock there were sixty covered wagons each able to carry fifty chests of tea from the landing to the stores at India House 'which will place the whole trade under the immediate care of their own servants.'

In recent years a power station has been built on part of the East India Docks and perhaps in the next few years the rest of it will be covered with flats or offices. But the main dock is still in use with its warehouses surrounding a great expanse of water fed with ships through the huge gates of the lock. Looking out on the broad reach of the Thames towards Woolwich Reach it is possible to imagine the departure of the famous East Indiamen of seven hundred and fifty tons, the largest ships in the port of London in their time, leaving for the long journey to India loaded with goods and passengers, such as the Company's soldiers, clerks, bankers and merchants, or bringing back rich cargoes from India, China and Ceylon. These cargoes were so valuable that the Company built a high wall round their mile of warehouses (which still stands by the Blackwall tunnel) and it kept a large staff, including Company soldiers, to guard against thieves.

On important policy matters the functions of the India House administration were taken over more and more by the Board of Control. It might have been expected that instructions from the British Government concerning the East India Company's territory would have been issued to the Governor-General of India through the Court of Directors, but the British Government did not always want the twenty-four businessmen, who composed the Court, to know of secret decisions which might have been made in Cabinet discussion. The Court of Directors was, therefore, frequently side-stepped through a new committee consisting of three members of the Court who were sworn to secrecy. This Secret Committee, as it was called, was used by the Board and the Governor-General of India when they wished to communicate without the knowledge of the Court of Directors. Even so the Court continued to be a powerful body since it was able to appoint and dismiss Governor-Generals, subject to the agreement of the Crown, and since it held the patronage of appointments throughout India including those of consuls in certain areas outside India of interest to the East India Company. The Court retained considerable political influence; when, for instance, Sir John Cam Hobhouse, afterwards Lord Broughton, was President of the Board of Control, his political opponent in the House of Commons was Sir James Hogg, Chairman of the Court of Directors and member of the Secret Committee. If the latter objected to a despatch being sent or received from India through the Secret Committee, which he thought should have been seen by the Court of Directors, he was able, on occasions, to reach a compromise with the Board of Control by threatening to raise the matter in Parliament or to take it up with the Prime Minister.

The Secret Committee was an ingenious device but not a satisfactory method of dealing with the affairs of India, since the Court of Directors of the East India Company were the experts and continued to deal on their own with the Governor-General and the Governors of the three Presidencies, Bengal, Bombay and Madras. 'Had a committee been assembled from the padded chambers of Bedlam', wrote Lord Curzon, 'they could hardly have devised anything more extravagant in its madness, or more mischievous in its operation. To it must be attributed many of the astounding errors and contradictions that characterised our Indian policy at that time. . . . In England for nearly three-quarters of a century there were Homeric contests between the Court of Directors and Board of Control. When both the Court and the Board had disappeared [in 1858] the rival antagonists were sometimes the Secretary of State for India and his Council.' *

This rivalry in England sometimes led to confused orders being issued to India and there were also differences between the Bombay Government and the Supreme Government of India in Calcutta. The former, consisting of a Governor and three or four members of Council, controlled the Bombay Marine which became the Indian Navy in 1830. It looked outwards to the Persian Gulf, East Africa, the Gulf of Aden and the Red Sea, where it had Political Agents in strategic places such as Bushire, Basra and Mocha. When the Indians became British subjects the Government inherited the wide and valuable trading interests in these areas, established as a result of the enterprise through many generations of Indian merchants or Banians; this meant that the Government had the responsibility of protecting them at places as far apart as Mocha, Zanzibar and Basra.

The Supreme Government of India with its Governor-General and Council of three or four members in Calcutta was more expert on the many problems of the huge land mass of India with its millions of people speaking about ninety different languages. There were at times, therefore, conflicts of views between Bombay and Calcutta as well as with London. The Government of the Bombay Presidency had had the power of framing their own laws and dealing with their own affairs until the British Act of 1833 which placed supreme power in the hands of the Governor-General and his Council in Calcutta. Everything had to receive the sanction of the Supreme Government, even details such as the granting of a new salary or allowance. This extreme degree of centralisation was much criticised in view of India's diversity of races and language, and because the Company was in contact with many other quite different peoples, such as the Persians, the Arabs, Egyptians, Turks, Somalis and Abyssinians who were better known to Bombay than to Calcutta. Besides that, it took from ten to fifteen days for despatches to

* *British Government in India*, by Marquis Curzon of Kedleston, Cassel and Co., 1925.

go between Bombay and Calcutta—and longer if the Governor-General was at his summer residences of Simla or Ootacamund.

The Company had developed from a trading organisation to a government administering a vast territory. The Charter Act of 1813 deprived the Company of its monopoly of the Indian trade and the Act of 1833 removed its China trade privileges; the British Government ordered that there should be more concern with the interests of the people governed than with profit and loss. During the nineteenth century the Government of India was involved in a series of wars in India, Burma, Afghanistan, Persia and elsewhere, which affected the various Presidencies in India—Bombay, Madras, Calcutta—and the poorer they grew the more dependent they became on the British Government 'so circumstanced, so impoverished, they cannot be generous—they can barely afford to be just.'[1]

Considering how unfairly a number of the East India Company's servants were treated their remarkable loyalty, initiative and bravery is much to their credit. Young naval officers, for instance, carried out valuable surveys and quasi-diplomatic missions in hot and unfrequented parts of the Persian Gulf, the Red Sea, Somali and Arabian coasts and islands of the Indian Ocean, dealing with tribes who had sometimes had no contacts with Europeans except to plunder their ships when wrecked on the coast; army officers, too, went on long treks in wild country.

One of the most important problems was to improve communications between England and India. It took a year to eighteen months for the Governor-General of India to receive a reply to a despatch sent to London via the Cape route and sometimes it was too late for the Board of Control, through the Secret Committee, to veto an action of which it disapproved; sometimes the Governor-General had the embarrassment of having to reverse policy when instructions finally arrived. Merchants in England and in India also urged better communications as trade developed. During the periods of warfare with France in the eighteenth and nineteenth centuries quick communication became essential. James Baldwin, who acted as British Consul in Cairo, got into serious trouble with the British Government for sending despatches by a native boat to India at a cost of £4,500 though he did it again on January 31 1793 when he learned that war had been declared between Britain and France and

16

thus enabled the British in India to recapture Pondicherry before the French knew that war had been declared.

At the end of the eighteenth century Lord Wellesley, the Governor-General of India, started a fortnightly post along the Euphrates route—from Bombay to Basra, then to Aleppo by Arab postmen on fast dromedaries, to Constantinople and across Europe by men on horseback. This was better than the Suez route while Britain was at war with France and Bonaparte held Egypt from 1798 to 1801.

By the 1820's steam navigation was becoming a practical possibility, and Egypt had been made safe for foreign travellers under the determined rule of Mohammed Ali Pasha, the Viceroy, who owed nominal allegiance to the Ottoman Sultan at Constantinople. In 1823 Mr. Mountstuart Elphinstone, Governor of Bombay, proposed that communication by steamships should be established by way of the Red Sea, and a steam vessel named the *Hugh Lindsay* of four hundred and eleven tons was built in the Bombay dockyards and launched in 1829. Strong support for this scheme was given by the British and Indian merchants who formed the 'Bombay Steam Committee'; while a 'Steam Navigation Fund' was started in Calcutta and Mr. Thomas Waghorn was asked to go to England to raise money for a steamer service. Then there were also the growing number of British officials, soldiers and clerks who demanded a better service for despatches, mails and newspapers than was afforded by the Cape route and sailing ships.

By the 1830's in Britain the mercantile class, which was seeking to expand their trade abroad and was beginning to have more political power through the Reform Bill of 1832, were in a position to make their influence effective in their demands for better communications to the East. But the Court of Directors of the East India Company resisted pressure for a long time, being satisfied with the Cape route, since the East Indiamen could sail direct to India without danger of mails being interfered with by oriental governments or Arab tribes on the overland routes, nor did passengers run so much risk of contracting cholera or smallpox.

There were difficulties, too, with the Porte for the Ottoman Sultan claimed sovereignty in the Red Sea area and many other places, and when Turkey was strong enough to make its influence felt Christian vessels were forbidden to sail further north than

Mocha (sometimes Jedda was allowed) since it was argued that their presence might endanger the holy Muslim cities of Medina and Mecca. But more effective than Turkish influence was the strong northerly wind in the Red Sea which made it impossible for sailing ships from India to reach Suez except during a few months of each year.

The Government of Bombay, in charge of important operations to protect trade in the Persian Gulf against Arab sea-pirates and responsible for the protection of Indian merchants trading in Mocha and the Gulf of Aden, was determined that steam navigation should be developed. In this it was supported by the Supreme Government of India which considered that more rapid links of communication with the British Government were essential. Experiments were carried on with steam despite discouragement from the East India Company's Court of Directors.

It was decided to send the *Hugh Lindsay* on an experimental voyage to Suez by way of Aden, Mocha and Jedda. She left Bombay on March 20 1830, overloaded with coal, under Commander John Wilson, an enthusiast for the Red Sea route. She reached Aden on March 31 and Suez on April 22—thirty-two days and sixteen hours including stops—which was considered a sufficient success to make the Bombay-Suez route feasible. Aden was the most conveniently placed staging place as it was halfway between Bombay and Suez, but owing to its poverty there was insufficient labour and it took over six days to put one hundred and eighty tons of coal on board. The next year the little steamer made the voyage in twenty-one days and six hours against heavy winds and seas, 'perhaps the greatest exploit of steam power up to that time'.[2] The Court of Directors was not prepared to play any part in these experiments. In fact it had sent despatches to the Government of India in 1830 stating that no more steam experiments were to be carried out, but as the despatches were sent by sail by the Cape route the Bombay Government was able to carry out a number of experiments before the orders were received. Commander Hawkins, in the *Clive*, had been sent to the island of Socotra and had reported that it would be suitable as a coal depôt. It was decided that there should be a detailed survey.

The East Indiaman, *Edinburgh*, being launched in the London Docks

East Indiamen rounding the Cape of Good Hope

Drawing of a scene in Socotra by J. R. Wellsted

Haines recommends Aden as a coaling station

(1830 to 1836)

The Government of Bombay, therefore, decided to have Socotra properly surveyed and looked through the list of the Indian Navy to see who would be the best officer to send. He needed to be not only a good surveyor but also a diplomat as he would have to treat with the Sultan of the Mahra tribe, on the South Coast of Arabia, who was reported to own the island of Socotra. Their choice fell on Commander Stafford Bettesworth Haines. He was born in 1802 of a Sussex family and joined the Bombay Marine as a Midshipman, becoming one of its ablest surveyors. He was highly thought of by Sir Charles Malcolm, Superintendent of the Indian Navy from 1827 to 1838, under whose direction the Navy acquired a high reputation for the detailed and difficult surveys carried out by enterprising young officers in the Indian Ocean, China Seas, Persian Gulf, Red Sea and the coasts of Africa and South Arabia.[1]

Haines' talents had led to his appointment as a young officer to be President of the Standing Committee of Survey and Draughtsman to the Indian Navy. He had shown himself as a determined commander of ships in the Persian Gulf and a disciplinarian who was able to keep on good terms with his subordinates. The general impression he gave was of a rather formidable but likeable man, thick-set and energetic, with a broad forehead denoting a good intelligence; a full beard and moustache almost hid a large and determined mouth but the most striking feature were his eyes which were light in colour, set well apart conveying determination and intensity which could be very intimidating when he was angry or resolved to have his way.

After Commander Moresby* and Captain Elwon had surveyed the Red Sea to determine the best course at all seasons for steamers proceeding to and from Suez, Haines had been instructed in 1832 to carry out the survey of the south coast of Arabia for five hundred miles from Bab-el-Mandeb, at the entrance to the Red Sea. He was in command of the survey ship *Palinurus* served by officers who were nearly all to have distinguished careers in the Indian Navy—Lieutenants T. G. Carless, J. R. Wellsted and J. P. Sanders; Midshipmen Felix Jones, J. S. Grieve, C. J. Cruttenden, J. Rennie and A. Ford. Haines inspired several of them with his interest in the Arab world and encouraged his officers to make explorations inland when the opportunity offered. A number of valuable accounts of areas unknown to nineteenth-century Europeans were published by these and other young naval officers.

In the autumn of 1833, Haines received instructions from Bombay to interrupt his survey and to sail for Qishn, a port of the Mahra tribe on the South Arabian Coast and to obtain permission from the Chiefs to carry out a survey of Socotra. On December 31 Haines reached Qishn and had a conference with two young chiefs who

---

* While on this survey Robert Moresby painted a number of watercolours of the Red Sea area, two of which are among the illustrations on another page. He was an able officer, brother of Admiral of the Fleet Sir Fairfax Moresby, and carried out a number of excellent surveys. He left the Indian Navy in 1841 because he was annoyed at the treatment he had received, and joined the Peninsular and Oriental Company, commanding the Company's first steamship of two thousand tons which sailed for India round the Cape of Good Hope with eighty passengers in September 1842.

gave him permission to do what he liked at Socotra; the Sultan of the Mahra was away at the time. The *Palinurus* arrived at Tamarida, the chief town of the island, in January 1834; the officers worked hard at the survey in difficult conditions. Wellsted and Cruttenden went on an expedition to explore the mountains of the island and an account is given in Wellsted's *Travels*,² though he did not acknowledge his debt for the information obtained from Cruttenden, who knew Arabic, or for the use he made of Haines' survey.³

After completing the survey Haines sailed for Bombay and in October, 1834, was told to return in the *Palinurus* to Qishn to negotiate with the chiefs for the purchase of the island of Socotra; he was given 10,000 German crowns (dollars)* but the Governor-General of India hoped that he would be able to buy the island 'for a much smaller sum, and the less money you pay the more credit you will derive'. So confident was the Government that there would be no difficulty that he was told to proceed from Qishn to Socotra and take formal possession of the island in the name of the Honourable East India Company; it was possible, he was informed, that troops would have already been sent from Bombay and in that case he was to hand over charge to the commanding officer.⁴

When Haines returned to Qishn he was received by the young chiefs he had met before and also by the Sultan, who had been away during his previous visit. The Sultan, Omar ibn Tawari, who was deformed and quite blind, was led in; his voice was strong, 'and in manner he was extremely frank and energetic', reported Haines. 'I wish I could see you,' said the Sultan, 'your voice is young and strong. Have you been long away from your home?' Haines was then thirty-two years old and, as he told the Sultan, had served his Government for many years. He explained that to carry on steam navigation between India and England a depôt under British control

---

* The dollar was worth about 4 shillings or 2 rupees. It was also called the German, Austrian or Maria Theresa crown or thaler. It is a large silver coin, current throughout South Arabia and the Yemen; in Abyssinia the Maria Theresa dollar is the main currency as the head of the Empress was considered to represent the Virgin Mary. (See also note 21, chapter 15.)

These thalers were originally struck from a rich silver mine in Bohemia called Joachimsthaler. They were accepted in England and Spain and introduced in 1787 as the unit in North America (though altered) and they were current in Germany until 1873 when the mark was introduced.

was needed; the island, useless to the Sultan at present, would bring him profit from the trade which would develop under the British flag. He was attentive and after a pause said in a firm and decided manner; 'Listen, Captain Haines. As sure as there is an only God and He in heaven, I will not sell so much ground (making a span with his hand). It was the gift of the Almighty to the Mahras and has descended from our forefathers to their children over whom I am Sultan.' Haines admired the character of the old chief; 'a cripple, and deprived of his eye-sight, he never forgot that he was the patriarch of his tribe—and avarice (that Arab vice) failed to tempt him to barter his birthright for money. He evinced no anger throughout; was polite but firm, telling me that he knew we could take his country by the strong arm, but that he believed our principles of justice would not permit us to do so.' On parting the Sultan said, 'God is witness we have both endeavoured to fulfil our respective duties: you to your Government, and I to my tribe, as their father.'

Haines sailed for Socotra to see whether there had been any developments; to his embarrassment, in view of the conversation he had held with the Mahra Sultan, he found that the troops had arrived off the island, the Bombay Government having been confident that he would obtain agreement to British possession.

Socotra is an attractive mountainous island but is very exposed to the violence of the monsoon winds of the Indian ocean; the surf comes thundering in and the palm trees bend to the ground. During the landing of the British troops from Bombay one of the boats capsized and many were drowned. Captain R. A. Bayly, in command of the first detachment which occupied the island, expressed his gratitude to Haines for the help given in disembarking stores and provisions—'a smart and excellent officer'.

Before leaving in the *Palinurus* to resume work on the South Arabian coast, the officers who had carried out the survey of Socotra recommended that the military should make their camp in the mountains near Tamarida, but they remained on the coast, were decimated by fever and all troops had to be withdrawn in April 1835. 'Ere the island was abandoned', wrote an officer, 'scarce a man could be found with strength sufficient to dig a grave for his companions. At one time every man was prostrate with fever except the doctor and he eventually died. Several officers had their health permanently ruined and few survived to tell the tale of the Socotra expedition.'[5]

With the abandonment of Socotra the search continued for a coaling station. In England the movement in favour of steam navigation was growing. A Committee of the House of Commons had been set up in 1834 and resolved 'that a regular and expeditious communication with India by means of steam vessels is an object of great importance to Great Britain and India'. Colonel Chesney, who had surveyed the Euphrates route connecting the Mediterranean with the Persian Gulf, gave evidence and £20,000 was voted to carry out an experiment with river steamers on the Tigris and Euphrates. The Governor of Bombay, Sir Robert Grant, in April 1837 urged that both lines of communication must be carried on to guard against any sudden interference 'should war or plague render one or the other line impossible for a season'.

The Egyptian line through Suez was considered the fastest for the mails and the pleasantest for travellers but was more expensive to maintain. The Court of Directors were worried at the high price of coal which cost £20 a ton at Suez and took fifteen months travelling round the Cape, though the enterprising Thomas Waghorn later arranged for coal to be carried by camel from the Nile to Suez making the total cost only a little over £4 a ton. The Governor of Bombay was distressed that the Court of Directors still wished to carry on communication by sailing vessels, since for eight months in the year the Red Sea could be considered as closed to sailing vessels, nor was it possible to keep up a regular communication through the Persian Gulf without steamships. It was pointed out that the London Committee's letter of December 1 was received in Bombay on March 29 by sail but that, by steam, letters of the same date had arrived in Bombay from London by February 5—that was sixty-six days instead of over a hundred days.[6]

Then there was the question of competition from Russia whose pressure on Turkey was causing some alarm in Britain. The Russians were using steam-boats on the Volga and the Caspian Sea and, commented Thomas Love Peacock, Chief Examiner of the India House, they would probably be using them on the Euphrates and Tigris: 'they will do everything in Asia that is worth the doing, and that we leave undone'.

The British Government decided it would bear half the cost of both lines of communication if the Government of India paid the other half, and the Court of Directors were persuaded to support the development of steam navigation. A number of armed steamers were built at Bombay and in Britain for the Indian service. They were all paddle-steamers and the engines were used as an auxiliary to sail. In 1836 the *Atalanta* steam sloop of a little over six hundred tons with four guns was launched in London; another armed steamer, the *Berenice*, of seven hundred and fifty-six tons was built at Glasgow and sailed for India in February 1837. In the summer of that year a monthly service of mails by steamship was established between Bombay and Suez with these two ships and the *Hugh Lindsay*, and the following year a record was set up with the mails reaching Bombay from England in forty-one days and Calcutta in fifty-four.[7]

It was decided to convert the Indian Navy into a 'steam marine'. Captain Robert Oliver, R.N. replaced the much respected Sir Charles Malcolm as Superintendent of the Indian Navy, and was to offend many officers including Haines. 'Those only were to blame who placed over such men as Ross, Moresby and Haines, an officer their inferior in every acquirement necessary for the occupant of such a post, save seamanship and a knowledge of steam.'[8] The officers and crews did not like the grime of the steamers cluttered up with coal, baggage and passengers.

Haines was saved from the sufferings of those commanders who were being transferred to steamships, for he continued to work on his own in command of the *Palinurus* along the coast of southern Arabia. His account of the survey shows the detail with which it was done and reveals his interest in the peoples and the past history of the areas visited. He was sorry for the Arabs in their poverty: 'It is melancholy to find this interesting coast, which in former days was probably fertile and prosperous, now almost entirely desolate and the few inhabitants that remain nearly always at strife with their neighbours.'[9]

The officers of the *Palinurus* visited such interesting sites as Nakab al Hajar and Hisn Ghorab which had not been visited in modern times. 'At whatever time the buildings around Hisn Ghorab were erected', wrote Haines, 'I consider their discovery of great importance; the fort having, doubtless, been intended to protect the harbour on its eastern side, independently of the town beneath, which, judging from the size and extent of the ruins, must have been considerable. Its position would point it out as a sea-port of some consequence, and the citadel on the hill might be the grand depôt for its commercial resources.' [10] Inland from Ras Burum the valleys were rich and beautiful, producing large quantities of millet and above them rose the purple-streaked mountains whose summits in the cold season were said to be at times covered with snow.

Mukalla was a busy port of about 4,500 inhabitants with foreigners from nearly every part of the globe and many boats in its sheltered bay. 'Traffic in slaves exists to a frightful extent', wrote Haines. 'I have seen 700 Nubian girls exposed at once in the slave-market here for sale, and subject to the brutal and disgusting inspection of the purchasers; the price varies from £7 to £25 a head.' He was favourably impressed by the people of the Hadhramaut he saw in Mukalla—'handsome features, slight made, active men, well-armed with matchlock and kris, ornamented with gold or silver' and regretted that there was insufficient time and money to visit the inland towns of the fertile Hadhramaut which would have been a journey there and back of about a fortnight. The coastal Arabs lived by fishing and trade; frankincense, aloes and sharks' fins were their main exports; they caught an abundance of sharks and the fins fetched a good price in the Chinese market via Muscat and Bombay.

Aden, however, in spite of its lack of trade and its few inhabitants, interested Haines more than any other place in South Arabia. It was the extraordinary formation of this volcanic cape with its two good harbours which attracted him and, indeed, had attracted others before him such as Lord Valentia, at the beginning of the century, who had described it as 'the Gibraltar of the East'.[11] Its desolation and utter barrenness, with jagged hill-tops contorted by volcanic disturbances of the past and Jebel Shamshan rising abruptly to over 1,700 feet above the sea, did not deter Haines. His knowledge of its history made him optimistic about the possibilities for the future. Though the hills were naked and barren and the valley but little better he considered that it had a grand and picturesque appearance. 'On the east side of this cape the town of Aden is situated, near the sea, from whence to the hills there is a plain of gradual ascent. Surrounding it are the mountains forming an amphitheatre. In the reign of Constantine Aden was called the Roman Emporium owing to its commercial celebrity.'

Aden's fame was mentioned in the Bible and its trade described in the *Periplus*,[12] it was fought for by the Portuguese in the fifteenth and sixteenth centuries after having been captured in 1538 by the armed forces of the Sultan of Turkey, Suleiman the Magnificent (1520–1566). The Sultan's great aqueduct stretched for eight miles in a north-westerly direction into the interior built of red brick and stone. Tanks had been made and the gullies dammed to catch the heavy rain which fell at times, each overflowing to the one below, but all were silted up, and there were the remains of about three hundred wells, some of them from sixty to one hundred and twenty-five feet deep, which needed cleaning. There were also the remains of fortifications, walls and baths. Haines was especially impressed by the magnificent road near the top of Jebel Shamshan, 'built of large loose stone so beautifully laid that in some places it appears as if three centuries had not misplaced a stone . . . it is an undertaking that would do credit to any engineer of the present day'.

'But there is now', wrote Haines, 'not more than ninety dilapidated stone buildings in the town, the rest are common or *cadgan* huts— the whole huddled together without the slightest regularity and built of the old and once flourishing city. A visitor when looking over the remains of this once opulent mercantile emporium cannot but regret the causes that have led to so great changes in the course of a few centuries.' The Sultan of Lahej, Hussein Fudthel abd-el-Karim, generally known as Sultan Mahsin, had imposed high taxes on everything so that the merchants had been driven away 'and it is now a mere miserable village without trade, and but seldom visited except by passing vessels, who anchor for protection in its splendid harbour. . . . The Chief here disables himself by oppressing all, the poor in particular.' There were no more than six hundred persons; of these two hundred and fifty were Jews, fifty were Indian merchants (Banians) and the other half were Arabs. Aden had a governor, a customs-master with one or two assistants and a guard varying from ten to fifty Beduins. A few boats from India on their way to Mocha put in to sell cotton cloths, rice, small quantities of iron and lead, while boats brought dates from the Persian Gulf and sheep from Berbera and Zeyla; the exports were millet (*jowarree*), copper and some coffee, but trade was trifling.[13]

Twenty-eight years earlier Henry Salt, the traveller in Abyssinia who later became Consul-General in Cairo, had reported less unfavourably; 'Aden as a place of trade is still of some consequence. It is the chief mart for the gums brought over by the Somali traders from the north-east district of Africa,' but the town was a 'wretched heap of ruins'.[14] Salt, however, was talking of a more prosperous time when the Abdali ruler of Lahej and Aden was Sultan Ahmed. Enterprising and much respected, he maintained order with a small regular army encouraging Indian merchants to come to trade, and had wanted the East India Company to have a representative in Aden in the same way as it had one in Mocha. The Sultan had shown notable hospitality to the three hundred British and Indian troops who were on their way back to Bombay under Lieutenant-Colonel Murray in March 1800 from the island of Perim, where they had been sent to help deny the Red Sea to the French armies in Egypt under Bonaparte, but had had to leave as there was no water on the island. Sultan Ahmed had, in 1802, also welcomed Commodore Sir Home Popham, commanding H.M.S. *Rodney*, who had been ordered by the British Government to try to revive trade in the Red Sea and to transport troops from India on their way to Egypt to drive out the French.

The Commodore had been treated with great indignity on his way to visit the Imam of Sana so that he was much relieved to find a friendly reception at Aden and Lahej and a treaty of commerce was made between him and the Sultan.[15] There was no mention in this treaty of handing over Aden to the British, though it has been stated that the Sultan offered to do so to Colonel Murray and that he had also made this proposal to Commander Haines in 1820 when Haines was on a mission to the Imam of Sana. This able Sultan of Lahej and Aden died in 1827 after a benevolent reign of thirty-five years.* His successor, sometimes referred to as his nephew, cousin or son, was Sultan Mahsin bin Fadhl, an interesting but not

---

* 'It is sad to relate,' commented Haines some years later, 'that after the return of the troops from Egypt to India, both Aden and this treaty were alike forgotten, and the once flourishing city had already sunk into an insignificant village.'

very attractive character whose battles with Haines were to become legends in South Arabia. He had inherited considerable wealth from Sultan Ahmed who encouraged trade, and Lahej was a good agricultural area lying north and west of Aden as far as the entrance to the Red Sea off Perim and was on the trade route between the rich towns of the Yemen and the sea at Aden. The capital lay about thirty miles in a north-westerly direction from Aden and was a refreshing place to visit with its palm groves and cultivation, through which ran a stream from the mountains.

Haines was in Aden in March 1835 on one of his visits aboard the *Palinurus* and a party from the ship went out to Lahej including Lieutenant Wellsted, who described the Sultan as a corpulent elderly man of 'a grave and saturnine disposition'. The Sultan, reclining lazily on a cushion, received the naval party in his palace. Chairs were brought with pipes and coffee and the room was lighted by lamps suspended from the ceiling while four slaves stood at either corner holding wax tapers. The Sultan produced the treaty made in 1802 by his predecessor, Sultan Ahmed, with Sir Home Popham and told stories until late in the evening about the English troops under Colonel Murray who had come from Perim. 'At this period', wrote Wellsted, 'there was an impression that our Government was likely to occupy that town [Aden], and I believe our host spoke the sentiments of his countrymen in general when he expressed a strong desire that this should take place. . . . A lively recollection is preserved there of the excesses of the Turks during their stay in the Yemen and that race is everywhere spoken of with abhorrence.'[16]

Sultan Mahsin was shrewd, cunning, obstinate, avaricious and of an unstable character. He was prepared to consider selling Aden but at the same time he had a pride in the port although he did nothing to improve it. Wellsted had been impressed by the enormous brass guns at Aden, some of them over seventeen feet long and thought he would appeal to the Sultan's avarice by pointing out that the brass could be sold for a considerable sum. But the Sultan reacted with feeling and retorted 'that he was unwilling to deprive Aden of the only remaining symbol of its former greatness'.

To Wellsted, on another occasion, the Sultan appeared as 'an intelligent old man'; to Haines he was 'indolent and almost imbecile', but this was largely because he was a bad ruler and by his oppression had harmed both himself and his people. Haines was more attracted by the Sultan of the Fadhli tribe, Hamed ben Abdulla, who received Haines and some of the other officers at his port of Shuqra; he was slight and not very attractive to look at 'but resolute and determined in character and much respected and feared by his neighbours'. The Fadhli tribe numbered about fifteen thousand of whom four thousand were said to bear arms of some kind and their country, which included Shuqra, the capital, and a few villages, lay to the east of Aden. The people were poor but a good deal more aggressive than the richer and more numerous Abdalis.

To Haines it was clear that Aden of all the places he had visited was the best site for a staging station and a depôt for coal and he considered that the shortage of labour would soon be made good. His enthusiastic report to the Bombay Government played an important part in the decision to have Aden. Haines wrote that it would become 'a place of the first mercantile importance and be a town of the first magnitude in Arabia' if it were under the British Government. Its geographical position halfway between Bombay and Suez was an advantage, and its harbour was safe, easy of access either by day or night and 'sufficiently capacious to enable an immense fleet to ride within it in perfect security'. The town of Sana was only seven or eight days journey from it for camels with merchandise and the districts where the coffee was grown were nearer to it than Mocha while the rich towns in the province of Hadhramaut were open for its trade. 'It is the best adapted port in existence for our overland communications via the Red Sea; it is in fact perfect as such, and if a pier were built steamers could at all times and seasons lay alongside of it and receive their coal.' While it was clear to Haines that Aden, in spite of the shortage of labour, was the best place for a coaling station, it was not everyone's choice.

In 1837 another House of Commons committee was taking evidence on establishing steam communication with India; some of the experts were still considering Socotra, or recommending Mocha, Perim and Kamaran Island. Colonel Campbell, the British Consul-General in Egypt, wrote to the Foreign Office in November 1837, to encourage the idea of possessing Aden. 'It would not only prevent the possibility of any attempt by Mohammed Ali [Viceroy of Egypt] and others to extend their conquests beyond the Red Sea, but, moreover, besides its advantageous position as a coal depôt for our communication between Bombay and Suez, it would most probably throw the whole trade of Mocha coffee into that port, and give to England the whole command of that article, a great quantity of which is at present bought by Americans.'[17]

At the beginning of the nineteenth century, American ships took nearly three quarters of the total Yemen coffee production of thirteen thousand bales and by 1809 their competition had pushed up the price per bale from 56 dollars (about £11) to 75 dollars (about £15). The New England merchants had developed the trade route to the Red Sea along the East Coast of Africa after rounding the Cape of Good Hope. This saved them the transhipment expenses which added to the costs of the trade carried on by the East India Company and by the French companies based on Mauritius and Réunion islands, with the result that at the beginning of the nineteenth century the Americans dominated the trade of the Yemen.[18] This was of concern to the East India Company who benefited from the trade of the Yemen through the large number of Indian merchants, or Banians, at Mocha, Jedda and Hodeida and the Company maintained a British Agent at Mocha to deal with this trade. When the Company's navy bombarded Mocha in 1820 it was not only to avenge the insults to their Agent but also to make the Imam of Sana, ruler of the Yemen, reduce the high export duties on goods from the coastal towns. Eventually, under a treaty between the Company and the Imam in 1821, these export duties were reduced to two and a quarter per cent.

The energetic maritime community of Massachusetts were sending their ships halfway round the world to East Africa, the Red Sea, Indian Ocean and the South Pacific. 'One of the most interesting results of the American Revolution was the intrusion of American enterprise into the honey-pot of oriental trade round which the sea-going people of Europe had been buzzing for two centuries, but which had been barred off from British colonists by the mercantile system and the East India Company's monopoly.'[19] American ships' captains were competing with India in the sale of cotton piece-goods; they were whale-hunting in the Indian Ocean, slave-trading, buying frankincense, gums, skins and ivory; and even collecting guano from the Kuria Muria Islands off South Arabia long before the British

Government made its ill-fated attempt to obtain it as fertiliser for the farmers of England. In 1833 the United States Government made the first important financial treaty with the powerful Sultan of Muscat and Zanzibar, whose ships traded to India and China and who saw the advantages of being connected with American traders.[20]

The East India Company found the Americans serious rivals in spite of the long distance they had to come, for there were many vigorous independent traders. Charles Millet, for instance, Captain of the brig *Ann*, sailed from Salem on March 26 1826 with cotton-goods, nails and tobacco and arrived on June 20 at Mocha where he took on a cargo of coffee and called on a number of Arab ports to sell his goods on his return journey; he made other such journeys. In eighteen months between 1832 and 1834 thirty-two American ships called at Zanzibar as compared with seven British, and many of these went to Mocha, for coffee was a commodity they particularly wanted.

The profits derived from the Yemen coffee trade was one of the reasons why Mohammed Ali, Viceroy of Egypt, sent troops to conquer the Yemen after dealing with the Wahabi revolt against the Ottoman Sultan. In 1833 the Egyptians, who had established them-selves on the coastal plain—they had difficulty, as they did in the 1960's, in advancing into the mountains—set up a monopoly in the coffee trade. They charged the East India Company traders the high duty of seven and a quarter per cent, while the Americans still obtained about half the trade, which was not ear-marked for the Viceroy of Egypt, and only paid half that amount in duty.

Lord Palmerston, the Foreign Secretary in the Melbourne Government, instructed the British Consul in Egypt in 1837 to 'demand peremptorily' of the Viceroy that restrictions on British trade were to be immediately removed as Britain would not permit Egyptians 'to continue this system of universal hostility to British commerce'; if the restrictions were not removed the British Government would take such measures 'as the interests and honour of Great Britain may appear to them in such case to require'.[21] The restrictions were removed, but there were other difficulties and Palmerston's battle with Mohammed Ali continued until 1841 when he ceased for some years to be Foreign Minister.

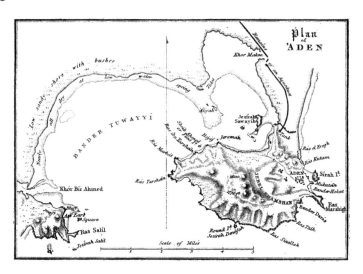

The Egyptians claim the Yemen and Aden

(1827 to 1838)

At the beginning of the nineteenth century Egypt, under Mohammed Ali Pasha, began to extend its control in areas which had been nominally under the government of the weakening Ottoman Empire, while the East India Company had for some time been taking over control from the Mogul Empire. Impressed by the achievements of the British trading company in India, Mohammed Ali developed trade and carried out reforms in Egypt, which he wished to protect from the dead hand of Turkish administration.

The Pasha would have liked to have worked with the British in some kind of an alliance and there might have been much to be said for it. British merchants in such commercial centres as Alexandria, Baghdad and Bombay did not consider that Palmerston's suspicions of Mohammed Ali Pasha were justified and were in favour of Mohammed Ali extending his empire because they thought it would increase security and help trade. It has been argued that although he pursued a system of monopolies there was order and justice and with him bargains could safely be made. 'He might, with English aid, have built up, under the shadow of the Turkish Caliphate, such a power as our own East India Company built under the shadow of the Delhi Empire.'[1]

Mohammed Ali Pasha wished not only to capture Aden but also Muscat, Bahrain, Basra and Baghdad. By 1837 the whole area of the Nejd in Arabia was overrun by the Egyptians and Lord Palmerston sent a despatch to Colonel Campbell on December 8 1837, that the movement of Egyptian troops in Syria and Arabia 'seems to indicate intentions on his part to extend his authority towards the Persian Gulf and the Pashalik of Baghdad. . . . You will state frankly to the Pasha that the British Government could not see with indifference the execution of such intentions.'[2] Campbell had also been told to warn Mohammed Ali against any attempt 'to invade or conquer the country lying at and beyond the mouth of the Red Sea'. This instruction was repeated the next year (May 24 1838) when it was stated that the British Government would be pleased to see the Egyptian troops leave Yemen, and that the Pasha should establish a good system of administration in the countries already under his rule 'instead of employing the energies of his mind and the resources of the countries he governs in aggressive expeditions against neighbouring districts'.[3]

It was to be expected that sooner or later there would be a rift between the ambitious Mohammed Ali who had built up a strong Egyptian army and navy, and his suzerain, Sultan Mahmud II, who wished to centralise authority of the Ottoman Empire at Constantinople under the Porte. In order to pay for his armies Mohammed Ali had instituted a system of monopolies and state trading which the Sultan disliked as it was for the benefit of Egypt and not for his Empire. The Sultan, however, found it necessary to call on Mohammed Ali to help him suppress the Greek revolt in their War of Independence and offered the Pashalik of Crete as recompense with the promise of the Pashaliks of Syria and Damascus if success were achieved. The intervention of the European Powers and the destruction of the Turkish and Egyptian fleets at Navarino in October 1827 ended that episode, but even so Mohammed Ali considered that he was entitled to Syria and Damascus and decided that he would attack before he was attacked. The Egyptian forces under Mohammed Ali's son, Ibrahim Pasha, captured Syria and Damascus having defeated the Ottoman armies in 1832 and 1833; they could have captured Constantinople and overthrown the Ottoman Government, if the European Powers had not intervened.

It was a typical Middle East crisis. British officials were convinced that Russia wished to advance to the Mediterranean and the Persian Gulf and intended to try to invade India. The British Ambassador in Constantinople, Lord Ponsonby, and Consul Campbell in Egypt thought that Mohammed Ali's armies would be a better barrier against the Russians than were the Turkish,[4] but Lord Palmerston did not like these views. He feared that a further weakening of the sprawling Ottoman Empire would lead to the danger of war in the scramble by the European Powers for the pieces in Europe and Asia; nor did he want the two main lines of communication between England and India—the Euphrates route through Baghdad and the Suez route through Egypt—both to be under the control of one ruler, Mohammed Ali. The Pasha's ambitions, Palmerston believed, were 'to establish an Arabian kingdom, including all the countries of which Arabic is the language. There might be no harm in such a thing in itself, but as it would necessarily imply the dismemberment of Turkey, we could not agree to it.'[5]

Palmerston and the Government of India did not object to Egyptian troops taking the Yemen if order were restored and trade developed, but were opposed to Mohammed Ali carrying out his ambition of having Aden and Bahrain. Mohammed Ali wished to keep on good terms with the British and asked Consul Campbell in June 1833 whether the British had any objection to his occupying the Yemen, but he annoyed Palmerston by sending troops without waiting for an answer.[6]

When Haines visited Mocha in the *Palinurus* in 1836 the Egyptians were established in the Tehama or coastal area of the Yemen, occupying all the main ports. Mohammed Ali had based his claim to the Yemen on a firman he stated he had received from the Ottoman Sultan but Haines pointed out in a long historical memorandum that the Turks had no legal claim over the territory which belonged to the Imams of Sana. They were descendants of the Prophet Mahommed's son-in-law, Ali, and the only interruption in their

34

Mukalla, a watercolour by Robert Moresby
Mocha, a watercolour by Charles Hamilton Smith

Palace of the Sultan of Lahej

hereditary rule had been after the Ottoman Sultan, Selim I, had conquered Egypt at the beginning of the sixteenth century and his successor Sultan Suleiman established control of all the Yemen in 1538 after the capture of Aden and an expedition to attack a Portuguese trading post in India. After the Turks left the Yemen about sixty years later the sovereignty of the country was again assumed by the descendants of Ali. 'For the last one hundred and eighty years', wrote Haines, 'the Imams of Sana, though shorn of their former greatness, have always been looked upon as the legitimate Lords of the country. Their seaport towns have been wrested from them and recovered again frequently.'

While the *Pahnurus* lay off Mocha Dr. Hulton, the ship's medical officer, and Midshipman Cruttenden set off in July 1836 in Arab dress with six mules for the journey of several weeks to Sana, the capital of the Yemen, a climb of over seven thousand feet in the heat of July. They crossed the coastal plain of the Tehama where the Arab farmers tilled the fields, despised by 'the bold mountain Arab who, accustomed from his infancy to plunder, and frequently murder, looks down with scorn on the being who can dirty his hands in cultivating the ground, and bear the yoke of their Egyptian governors without daring to resist their repeated acts of cruelty and oppression'.[7] The country people in the plains were suffering from the result of a four-year drought and the merchants of Sana were overstocked with coffee, grown in the surrounding districts, afraid to send large quantities to the coast because of the troubled state of the country. Cruttenden was delighted by the beauty and fertility of this mountainous country and was interested in its history and archaeology, having studied the works of Karsten Niebuhr who had visited Sana in 1763, the only survivor of the ill-fated Danish expedition. The Imam al-Mahdi had died in 1834 and his son Ali was Imam with the title of al-Mansur. He had two palaces surrounded by extensive gardens with fountains, one with twenty jets of water rising to about fourteen feet. The apartments on the ground floor of the palaces were large rooms very splendidly furnished. The Imam was friendly but his officials did all they could to prevent the travellers wandering about the city and in the countryside. 'Twice we were at the private apartment of the Imam, and each time we left perfectly disgusted. The Imam, with five or six dancing and singing girls, got shockingly drunk, and he seemed surprised at our refusing to join him in drinking raw spirits. The liquor is made in Sana and tastes like bad whiskey.' His Highness, when in his cups, was 'excessively liberal' and when the Englishmen asked to be allowed to walk freely round the town and the neighbourhood—'all was instantly granted, but unfortunately His Highness was too tipsy to recollect his promise'.

Cruttenden estimated that there were about seventy-five thousand people in the neighbourhood and, of them, thirty thousand lived in Sana. 'The houses are all tenanted and unlike other cities, such as Aden, Sana is still as populous as ever, though owing to the negligence and apathy of the governors it is fast verging to its fall and will be an easy prey to the enterprising Egyptian army now in the Yemen. . . . But I do not think that they [the Egyptians] will be able to remain there, for the walls of Sana are so extensive that it would require an army of at least fifteen hundred men to defend the place against the continued attacks of the Beduins.' This view was confirmed the next year by Captain James Mackenzie of the Bengal Light Cavalry in an excellent report he made while travelling back to India from England—the Egyptians would not remain long for they were much disliked and the Arabs wished to maintain their freedom.[8]

Sultan Mahsin of Lahej sells Aden to the British

(January 1837 to January 1838)

The importance of occupying Aden had been discussed at the end of the eighteenth century when Bonaparte's armies occupied Egypt and there were plans for launching a French conquest of India. The war between Britain and North America from 1812 to 1814 had also led some to think again of Aden. Henry Salt, British Consul-General in Egypt, had suggested to the Governor of Bombay that cannon should be sent to help the Sultan of Aden defend the port as the British were at war with the Americans 'who are intimately acquainted with these ports and whose ships are generally of a force superior to any of our merchant vessels likely to be employed in the service'. Nothing was done, however; peace was signed with America and the French threat diminished. Little interest was shown, therefore, in 1820 when Sultan Ahmed of Lahej told Haines that he would like the British to have a foothold in Aden or in 1822 when he told Hutchinson, the East India Company Agent at Mocha, that he would grant the Company the right to set up a British Agent in Aden in return for help against neighbouring tribes; Hutchinson had to reply that the Government of India did not wish to make any political arrangements but only to maintain commercial relations.[1]

The situation had changed again, however, by the late 1830's. Demands had become more insistent both from England and India for facilities to be arranged for a steam service between Bombay and Suez. Socotra had been found to be no good as a coal depôt and nothing else had been discovered to be as satisfactory as Aden, judging by Haines' reports; now there was the danger that if nothing were done about Aden, the Egyptians might take it.

In January 1837 the people of Aden plundered a large Indian sailing ship, the *Duria Dowlat*, which ran aground on the coast, and this set up a chain of events leading to the taking of Aden by the British. The ship, which was flying the British colours, belonged to the Nawab of the Carnatic. She had a valuable cargo and on board were a number of pilgrims going to Mecca via Jedda, fourteen of whom were drowned, while the survivors were stripped of their possessions and a number of Indian ladies of high rank were subjected to great indignities and would have been carried off into the interior if a prominent family in Aden had not rescued them. It was not until June that Commander Haines, who was continuing his survey of South Arabia, was in a position to send the first reports of this event to Bombay. In August the Governor-General of India received a request from the Nawab of the Carnatic for an investigation into the circumstances of the wreck and asking that the British authorities should protect any property saved. Bombay was informed and instructed the senior magistrate to take depositions from the agent and others who had arrived in Bombay from the wrecked ship. These depositions set out the cruelties suffered and accused the Sultan of Aden of seizing the cargo.

This case encouraged Sir Robert Grant, Governor of Bombay, to write a memorandum on September 23 1837: 'The establishment of a monthly communication by steamer with the Red Sea and the formation of a flotilla of armed steamers, renders it absolutely necessary that we should have a station of our own on the coast of Arabia, as we have in the Persian Gulf, and the insults which have been offered to the British flag by the Sultan of Aden have led me to make enquiries, which leave no doubt in my mind that we should take possession of the Port of Aden.'[2] The reaction of Lord Auckland, the Governor-General of India, was sensible: 'It would not be expedient or proper to take possession of the town and promontory of Aden, on account of the pillage of the ship', and besides that, it might lead to a collision with the Egyptian or Arabian powers. He considered that satisfaction should, in the first instance, be demanded of the Sultan of Aden for the outrage; 'if it be granted, some amicable arrangement may be made with him for the occupation of this port as a depôt for coals and harbour for shelter. If it be refused, then further measures may be considered.'[3]

Haines was ordered once more to interrupt his survey of the southern coast of Arabia and to return to Bombay, where he received instructions to deal with the plundering of the *Duria Dowlat* and to obtain Aden by purchase if possible. He left in the sloop-of-war *Coote* and on December 28 1837 reached Aden, where he met the Sultan who denied that he had any knowledge of the plundering of the ship. The property, however, was being sold from the Sultan's warehouse in the Crater bazaar, and there was some evidence that there had indeed been a conspiracy between the agent in charge of the ship and the Sultan's family to wreck the ship and seize the goods. Haines made it clear that he did not believe the Sultan's denials and an indemnity of 12,000 dollars was demanded or the return of the property. After a great deal of discussion and various attempts to intimidate Haines, goods valued at nearly 8,000 dollars were returned and a bill was signed by the Sultan to pay the remainder.

As to the cession of Aden, Haines was optimistic that he would reach an agreement, partly because of his conversation with the previous Sultan in 1820 and also because he knew that Sultan Mahsin feared that the Egyptian forces in the Yemen might take Aden without making any payment; besides the Sultan gained little profit from the customs dues in Aden of which he had to pay neighbouring tribes a share.

Having sent presents to Sultan Mahsin at Lahej, Haines received a friendly letter: 'if God pleases, my friendship will be the same as my father's and a treaty shall be witness. What you say I will listen to and have no fear in my heart. We and the English are one.' There then began a long correspondence[4] carried on in Arabic with the aid of Haines' interpreter, Mullah Jaffar, and it was on the basis of these exchanges that the Government of India and the Court of Directors in London decided that the British had a right to take Aden.

Haines, in a letter of February 11 1838, expressed satisfaction that the dispute over the *Duria Dowlat* had been settled and their friendship was as before. This made him believe that the Sultan wished to keep up the relations which had existed to their mutual benefit in his father's time. He was empowered by the Government to make a treaty 'for the purchase of Aden, the land and points surrounding it and the land connecting it as far north as Khormaksar with the harbours of Gabit Tenojee, Bunder Serah, Bunder Duras and smaller bays, with Serah [Sira] Island and all islands within the same.' The Sultan would see the advantages in trade and security in having 'such an intimate and connecting link with the British'. Aden was annually dwindling into greater insignificance, and would perhaps shortly be an object 'merely to excite the ambitions of some minor Power'. The area amounted to about fifteen square miles.

Haines explained that he had drawn up a draft treaty in Arabic to cover and explain points which he thought might worry the Abdali Sultan and his advisers and to make it clear that the British intended no oppression and wished to treat his family with respect. Under the treaty the Sultan and his family would be independent and allies of the British; he would be free to reside in Aden and retain possession of his two houses there and his trading vessels would have British protection and permission to fly the British flag. Haines asked for comments and also the amount the Sultan wished to ask for the sale of Aden.

The Sultan replied to his 'dearest friend' . . . 'The language you wrote was intelligent and true indeed. We and the British are friends of a very old day. What they wish I am happy for. You have given me this information, but let it be private between us. . . . As the British did for my father, so do for me.' The Sultan, with his son and advisers, came to Aden to discuss the matter; he had requested secrecy but, 'like a silly man he trusted the whole to six merchants who soon dispersed it through the town'. Sultan Hamed, the heir apparent, paid two visits to Haines and asked many questions about his future position if Aden were made over to the British, and seemed afraid that he would be forgotten and treated with contempt. On January 13 at 9 p.m. the Sultan visited Haines with his sons and Rashid ibn Abdullah, the principal merchant in Aden. They discussed the terms until past midnight. 'The subject of our conversation that evening was conclusive,' reported Haines to Bombay. 'They at first entertained the idea that indignity and abuse would follow them out of the town, if our flag was flying. This I soon erased.' Rather surprisingly Haines underestimated the importance of Aden, derelict as it was, to the family's sense of prestige and was a little too complaisant in his attitude. He was almost certainly right, however, in reporting that their calculation was as follows: 'if we do not part with Aden on advantageous terms to the British, the Egyptians will have it for nothing'. The Sultan admitted that he had received a letter from the Egyptian Commander but would not show the contents; said that they required his country and made promises. 'At last he announced that he would rather have the English, but would they receive him as an ally, and protect his country from being molested; in fact receive him and country on the same terms as the Nabob of Surat.' Haines said that he could state this wish to Government and that, as the Sultan had promised Aden to the British, he would write a few lines to the Egyptian Commander-in-Chief requesting him not to injure Aden or molest the Sultan's territory. Arrangements were then made to choose a place for a coal depôt.

As the Sultan was about to leave he said: 'Now I have promised everything you wish.' He would proceed inland and arrange matters with the chiefs so that all would be ready for March 15 when he expected Haines to return 'with troops, guns and everything necessary to take possession'. Haines replied that it was unlikely that a garrison would be sent until the final arrangements had been made. The Sultan asked to be given Haines' watch ('a silver hunter by McCabe'), and a new sword belonging to Dr. Arbuckle, surgeon of the *Coote*; both were handed over. Haines, with Lieutenant Swan and Mr. Hamilton, officers of the *Coote*, went on horseback to the northern gate to pay their respects to the Sultan and his family on their departure for his capital at Lahej. They were hurrying inland as there was war between the Fadhli and Yafa'i tribes. 'The day of peace is past,' the Sultan wrote from Lahej, 'and they come to me for powder and shot. I require some powder, shot and cannon from you, for our affairs are now arranged; the town and harbour are yours. We go; afterwards do as you like and go where you like.' The Sultan continued to think in terms of an alliance which would bring him help in return for his parting with Aden; indeed, Haines had used the word alliance in one of his letters to the Sultan.

Sultan Mahsin wrote from Lahej demanding secrecy from the chief men in Aden, 'their hearts are burning but do not let their falsehoods break our friendship'. But, of course, the chief people in the town knew what was in the wind, and Haines reported that from what he had learned he could confidently assert 'that the British flag in Aden would be received as a boon conferred upon its present oppressed inhabitants'. Another letter came from the Sultan saying that the Fadhli Sultan of Shuqra 'wishes to injure me: you must look to what he does'. Haines replied that a letter could be sent to the Sultan of Shuqra which would prevent his encroachment on the Abdalis, but he saw no reason to do so since he had not yet received any decisive answer on the question of transfer; 'I entertain a doubt as to your final answer. Promise me the transfer under your seal for any sum you may think requisite and I can then prevent the encroachment of others.'

This stirred the Abdali Sultan and he wrote an important letter on January 22 1838, with his signature and seal attached. It was not very clearly expressed but it did hand over Aden though the payment required was not stated: 'You wrote on the subject of Aden. My support and dependence is upon it. My neighbours from east, north and west obtain money from me and my dependents for the same is from Aden. Between us a conversation passed and we arranged the final answer for two months, or in March, and you in the meanwhile go to Bombay and inform your Government and I will have a council of my chiefs to explain to them. When we have both completed it and you return in March you can then make houses or forts or do what you like, the returns will be yours; but consider the money I have to give my neighbours from it, so that when the town is yours you must answer them all.

'If, when you are in the town, people come to fight you either by sea or land, I am not answerable. You must answer and please all. All this which I have written depends upon you. When the town is yours, give me half the customs duties for good; after you return in March we will meet and arrange. If you will not give me half the duties, give me pay either by the month or by the year as you please, but let my name be respected, and my orders extend over my own people and yours over yours. If the Turks* come and take the whole country by strength from me, or any other people [come], you must not blame me. In March I look only for you Commander Haines—for no other gentleman.'5 But the matter was not quite settled. Sultan Mahsin sent another letter, also dated January 22, explaining that he had meant that the Arabs and Jews of Aden should continue to obey him after the British had taken possession—'my orders to be over my own people, the Jews and Arabs, and whatever order I give them they must obey and my other subjects to be mine with [those of] Lahej but Aden to belong to the British'.

The matter seemed quite clear to Sultan Mahsin and he was annoyed that Mullah Jaffar, the interpreter, had to come to Lahej for an explanation. 'I have finished but you have not,' wrote the Sultan to Haines, 'and now wish for other subjects which is not correct. I have given my seal that Aden is yours and you must now give me yours as a security to me. You have both my letter and seal; if my letter with seal does not please you give it back.' Haines had no wish to give it back, but he was startled by the second letter for he considered that there would be complete confusion if the British in any way shared with the Sultan control of the people of Aden who were a mixed population of merchants, traders and fishermen, Arabs, Jews, Somalis and Indians—they were not bound to the Sultan in quite the same way as the Abdali tribesmen of the interior. He could not achieve his dream of a prosperous Aden if the Sultan had the right to interfere, but he was not as understanding as he usually was about Arab attitudes and his reply was abrupt and emphatic: 'You could not have given this consideration for it is ridiculous. Take these away (Arabs and Jews) and what remains but a heap of ruins and graves. All who choose will remain as British subjects, and all who wish to be yours can reside in your territory, otherwise they must, when residing on British ground, be subject to our laws; we oblige no-one under our flag to remain by compulsion; they are free.'

This was an important question and had not been properly dis-

* Egyptians; little distinction was made between Turks and Egyptians. They were both foreigners to the Arabs.

cussed by the Bombay Government which had taken it for granted that the treaty would be similar to agreements in India. There the Government took over the inhabitants with the territory conquered or ceded and the Indians became British subjects, but no Arab territory had been ruled directly by the Government of India, except in the case of the island of Karrak in the Persian Gulf which contained only a small population of Arabs, mostly seamen and pilots from Basra. The treaty with regard to Aden stated 'the Sultan of Aden agrees to cede in perpetuity in free sovereignty to the British Government the land of Aden . . . all persons who may choose to reside within the limits defined . . . shall be entitled to British protection according to the laws which may be established by the British Government'.

Sultan Mahsin, however, wanted a treaty such as his father had had. Under that treaty of 1802 the British Resident in Aden was to have no control over Arabs, but deal only with disputes of registered British subjects (mostly Indians); all disputes between the subjects of the Sultan and those of the British nation were to be settled by the established laws of the country. 'Let it be known to Your Excellency,' Sultan Mahsin wrote to the Governor of Bombay, 'there is an Arab proverb—let the body be burnt but do not let the *watan* [native country] be pierced; it is better to sell one's mother than do this. It will cut a man off from his resources and deprive him of his dignity.' It was a fair warning and if the Sultan had been allowed to retain his sovereignty over his people he would probably have been content, and would not have spent nearly nine years trying to retake Aden from the British, which interfered with trade and hampered the port's development. His retention of sovereignty might have worked if the Government of India had only wanted a depôt for coal, but it wanted a secure depôt and there had been indications that it would not be secure unless the British controlled the peninsula; besides, the Government also wished to develop trade so as to obtain some return for their expenditure and British ideas of free trade would not have fitted with the Sultan's ideas of high duties.

At the time, however, the Sultan seems to have accepted Haines' terms that the British should control the people of Aden, since he asked for the return of his second letter of January 22 which gave his views on that, but not for his first letter with his seal which established the transfer of Aden, although in rather vague terms. But there was still the question of the sum to be paid. Haines wrote that the Government would not agree to the Sultan having half the customs dues, which were trivial, though, after 'a great outlay' by the British, they would be increased; 'you cannot, therefore, imagine that the British Government would incur so great an expense without the place being for a certainty theirs'. He knew that the customs dues only amounted to 6,000 dollars annually and it was no good the Sultan thinking he could receive a sum such as 50,000 dollars which had been suggested.

If the Sultan would name a price which was acceptable, Haines could close the deal without further reference to the Government, but if no decision were taken he would probably return to Aden in March and then there might well be further delay, for during the south-west monsoon of June to September the passage from Bombay to Aden took two months. 'Consider this and give, while you have the opportunity, a decided answer: the sum is surely not a very tedious calculation, taking into consideration that your town is daily deteriorating in value, and your revenues from Aden for the last year are only 6,000 dollars. I am now on the point of quitting your country and leave it with the most friendly feeling for all, and hope the danger you apprehend from the Turks [Egyptians] may not fall on your country while I am absent.'

This letter of January 24 roused the Sultan and meetings were held with his advisers at Lahej. On January 26 at 8 p.m. Rashid ibn Abdullah came on board the *Coote* as envoy from Sultan Mahsin with a short letter from Sultan Hamed to say that he was coming to Aden; Rashid stated that all had been concluded and the amount asked was 8,700 dollars annually. They did not want a large sum at once for they feared that it would excite the avarice of their neighbours but that an annual stipend 'would ensure them always a home in Aden' under British protection and sufficient support. Rashid added that Sultan Hamed, Sayyed Hussain Weiss and Hajj Hussain, a rich merchant from the Hadhramaut who had long been resident at Lahej, were coming as witnesses to the agreement and horses were to be sent the next morning to take Haines and his party from the shore into Crater town.

Rashid left and Mullah Jaffar, the interpreter, was sent from the ship to find out the exact arrangements about the horses. Haines received a message that they would be ready at daylight on Sunday, and at 8-30 a.m. on that day he left the *Coote* in the ship's pinnace and made for Ras Tarshain, which became known later as Steamer Point. With him were Lieutenants Swan and Hamilton who had volunteered to come as witnesses to the agreement. Haines believed that he had at last reached the end of his mission and expected no treachery but, as always, he was prepared for the possibility of trouble and carried two loaded pistols in his belt.

As the pinnace rounded the promontory of Ras Hejuf they could see horses by the shore and Mullah Jaffar waving to them to draw in. When the party came ashore they found the interpreter in a very excited state. He told them that they were all in great danger, since there was a plot to seize Haines and force him to hand over all the letters about the agreement, which had been signed by Sultan Mahsin, and the bond to pay the balance of the money on the goods of the *Duria Dowlat*. Haines decided it was wiser to return to the ship.

5

Plot to kidnap Haines

(February 3 to June 1838)

The plot to seize Haines had been planned by Sultan Hamed and Sayyed Hussain Weiss and it is possible that Sultan Mahsin did not know of it. The story, as it was pieced together for Haines' report[1] to Bombay was as follows.

The Sultan, after long discussions at Lahej, had agreed to Haines' terms for the hand-over of Aden and to the sum of money of 8,700 dollars to be paid annually. The information that Rashid ibn Abdullah had given to Haines when he arrived on board the *Coote* had been correct. Rashid, however, did not then know that Hamed and Sayyed Hussain Weiss had left Lahej secretly for a village near, where they had planned to entice Haines to Aden and seize him. A hundred armed men were to accompany them into Aden and another one hundred and fifty were to be ready at Khormaksar in case men from the *Coote* should try to cut off their retreat from Aden to Lahej and to rescue Haines.

When Hamed and the Sayyed arrived at the Sultan's house in Crater the final details of the plot were completed. But Damjee, the

47

Indian merchant who had been appointed to look after the property of the *Duria Dowlat*, learned of what was being planned and also received an urgent message brought by a Beduin in great secrecy from Lahej which had been sent by the merchant Hajj Hussain (who was to have been one of the witnesses to the agreement). 'Beware', it read, 'and prevent the English gentlemen from meeting the Sayyed and Hamed, who have sworn on the Koran to take their chief [Haines] prisoner and to obtain all his papers; they may not be satisfied with detention, for he is firm and they are dogs. For our character, prevent it.' Rashid showed the message to Mullah Jaffar when he arrived from the *Coote* to find out about the horses, but it was not easy to send a warning as six armed Beduin had been assigned to watch Mullah Jaffar's movements. The interpreter set about making preparations as if for the arrival of the officers, ordering horses, arranging for carpets to be spread and water to be brought, pretending not to notice the Beduin watching him. In this way he managed to lull their suspicions and was allowed to leave Aden with the horses to meet the party when they came ashore from the *Coote*, while the plotters waited for Haines to come into Crater.

'What might have been the termination of their infamous intentions had they attempted to carry them into effect, it is impossible to say', wrote Haines, 'for if an attempt to capture us had been made by force, we might have used our weapons. Therefore the probability is that we should have fallen by their overpowering us. For our fortunate escape we have to feel grateful to the merchant Hajji Hussain, who was determined to save us, also to Rashid ibn Abdullah for his integrity and the interpreter, Mullah Jaffar, for his firmness, decision and good sense.'

When the plotters knew that their plan had been given away they heaped curses on Rashid ibn Abdullah whom they regarded as responsible for the betrayal. Sayyed Zain ibn Aidrus who had previously made an offer to hand over Aden to Haines if he, the Sayyed, were paid the money instead of the Sultan, had been a party to the plot and was enraged, calling Haines and his officers *kaffirs* and 'beasts'; he attacked Rashid for having allowed the *kaffirs* to gain an advantage over the sacred followers of the Prophet—a scene which was reported to Haines by Mullah Jaffar, who was present. Haines wrote an angry letter to Sultan Hamed: 'There is (as you so frequently say) but one God who sees not only the actions but inward feelings of man; He (though you must have forgotten the laws and tenets of your Koran) knew the intention of your coming from Lahej and frustrated them by warning those who have acted with upright feelings of honour and principle towards yourself and family. I have the minutest information of what passed at Lahej after Rashid left, which I shall report to my Government, who will act as they consider requisite. Aden and its harbours are ours by your father's seal and signature, and therefore after your bad intentions the British Government are fully justified in doing towards it as they may deem correct.

'What have you gained by intrigue and intended treachery? I have the bond for the transfer of the land and harbours we required under your father's signature and seal, and what bond have you now from me? Had you acted honourably you would have received papers from me equally binding as the seal of your father's for the transfer, and it is now not too late if you send me the sum you arranged for with Rashid, which I know.' Hamed had, he stated, done great harm to his family and tribe; 'you no doubt yesterday were confident that today I should have been your prisoner at Lahej when you could have intimidated me, but I trust that if ever I have the pleasure of visiting your town it will not be without that with me which will prevent intimidation'.

Haines was both distressed and puzzled. If Sultan Mahsin had been responsible for the plot, then there was no hope of negotiating the purchase of Aden and his mission had failed. But he believed that the responsibility lay with Sayyed Hussain Weiss, the Sultan's son-in-law, 'who would be delighted to see the Sultan's family ruined so long as it was advantageous to his own ambitious designs, which are to have supreme command over the whole territory. Unfortunately the Sultan is a weak, imbecile, avaricious man and Hamed, the elder son, a young ignorant Beduin and both are easily swayed by their intriguing relative.' Haines was probably right in arguing that the document they most wanted to retrieve was the promissory note for the balance of payment of four thousand dollars on the cargo of the *Duria Dowlat*, 'imagining that by the time the payment was due their father would be in the grave and they would be called upon to meet the demand'.

Haines wrote a long letter to Sultan Mahsin. If he had known about the plot, after all his expressions of regard and friendship, Haines could only regret the want of faith and principle in one whose age should have taught him to have thought only of preparing himself for the grave. 'What could have induced your family to have thought of such a disgraceful way of obtaining the papers which have passed between us. Why not have asked me for what you wished?' He would have returned the Sultan's letter of January 22 with his seal if he had changed his mind and decided not to hand over Aden after all. 'Had you in the first instance candidly said that you did not wish to part with the country, it would have been enough, whereas you gave the British the place by seal, and then by treachery your family endeavoured to obtain all the papers that had passed. Not a request have you made to me, but it has been attended to and listened to with the ears of friendship, and what return has been made for it? What will the British Government think and will not your neighbours even be ashamed? Your son Hamed and Sayyed Hussain Weiss have been badly advised and will repent of it.'

The Egyptians were behind much of the trouble which developed, for they foresaw that they would suffer much from the loss of Aden, which they had confidently expected to obtain; 'in every respect', wrote Haines to Bombay, 'the finest harbour in Arabia, and under the British flag would inevitably injure their already conquered possessions and totally ruin Mocha'. In either of the monsoons it was possible to enter and leave one or other of Aden's harbours, whereas in the Red Sea it was difficult to enter ports; Aden would attract trade from the African coast—vessels from Berbera with coffee, frankincense, gums, elephant tusks, hides and other goods could reach Aden in a day in the north-east monsoon and return again in another. It would afford an opening for Indian cottons, piece goods, silks, chintzes, cutlery and iron; many of these commodities were being manufactured in Egypt as a result of the initiative of Mohammed Ali Pasha, who wanted to open up Yemen and South Arabia for their sale. 'Under these circumstances it is not surprising that the Egyptians should have endeavoured all in their power by threats and promises to have thwarted me. I was informed that I was represented as a most designing snake and that the Arabs had better have nothing to do with me.'

Haines wrote this letter on February 3 1838 from Mocha Roads, where he was to leave the *Coote* and take passage for Bombay in the *Berenice*. He informed Ibrahim Pasha, commanding the Egyptian Army of the Yemen and nephew of the Viceroy, that the town of Aden and the peninsula now belonged to the British, and that he was returning to Bombay: 'I have in my possession the correspondence of the Sultan of Aden, written in his hand and with the imprint of his seal, in which he makes a gift of Aden to the Government of India.' Ibrahim Pasha passed on this letter to Mohammed Ali Pasha, adding that arms and munitions of war, the importation of which had been forbidden in Yemen for some time, now came into the Yemen from the Aden coast and that the Mocha customs dues would fall to nothing with Aden in British control.[2]

Colonel Campbell, the British Consul in Egypt informed Lord Palmerston that Haines' letter had caused considerable uneasiness to Mohammed Ali Pasha who did not like the idea of having the British as near neighbours to Mocha; the representatives in Egypt of the three Great Powers—France, Austria and Russia were envious of the position achieved by the British in the East, and worked on the mind of Mohammed Ali 'giving him false and erroneous impressions of our views in the possession of Aden'. Campbell stated that he considered the Pasha's claim to Aden was invalid and that the books of geography he had consulted mentioned Aden as independent.

Mohammed Ali Pasha reminded Campbell that the British Government had agreed to the Egyptian expedition to the Yemen and it was not fair that Aden, which was a part of the Yemen, should then have been seized, for he did not accept the argument that the Sultan of Aden had achieved independence at the end of the eighteenth century. His claim was based on the fact that Aden had formerly been part of the Turkish Empire and he hoped the Indian Government would be persuaded that Aden was part of the Yemen. 'If the aim of the British Government is only to have a convenient place to put coal' Mohammed Ali Pasha told the British Consul, 'I can affirm that, after gaining control of this country, everything would be done to procure the English what they need. An Arab Government, such as that of Aden, would never be in a position to render the English the services that an Egyptian Government could render.'[3] The Pasha repeated this offer in June 1838[4] after receiving a very friendly letter from Lord Auckland, the Governor-General of India, who thanked the Pasha for the help he had given in facilitating communication through his dominion of the overland mail service: '. . . it is only a potentate of Your Excellency's liberal and enlightened mind who can appreciate the advantage of a free and general intercourse.' [5]

George Eden, Earl of Auckland, who came to India as Governor-General in 1835 with his remarkable sister Emily and their younger sister Fanny, was famous for his politeness and charm and the family was much liked in Indian and English society in India. He was certainly right to encourage good relations with Mohammed Ali who was always ready to help the East India Company even in the most difficult times.

6

The rights and wrongs of
taking Aden

(February to October 1838)

When Haines returned to Bombay in February 1838 he reported to
the Government that he considered that the Peninsula of Aden
could be obtained for an annual grant of 8,700 dollars, but he considered that a force should be sent. If it were found that 'the wishes
and interests of the Sultan were thwarted by the children', then he
considered that Aden should be taken by force because of the insults
offered. It could be captured without great loss by the men who
would afterwards garrison it, assisted by the crews of two or three
Government vessels. He urged that everything possible should be
done to avoid injuring the inhabitants 'for they would be delighted
to see the British flag planted and have in no way thrown impedi-
ments to my obtaining the wishes of Government'.[1]

The Bombay Government was hesitant, for Haines' story made it
clear that force might have to be used; it was worried, too, about the
expense, and about the reaction of Egypt and of other Powers. The
Government was distressed to find that the authorities in England

had taken it for granted from Haines' letter to Ibrahim Pasha (which had been sent on by the British Consul in Egypt), that the matter was settled and Aden was already a British possession. The Secret Committee wrote from London to Bombay in that strain on May 30 (1838) and Bombay had to explain that nothing had been settled and that the matter had been referred to the Governor-General, since Bombay could not on its own responsibility 'embark on this or any other distant enterprise, at a time when all the resources of this Presidency may be put in requisition to secure interests of far greater importance than the occupation of Aden'.[2] Indeed, Lord Auckland had embarked on his ill-fated enterprise of placing Shah Suja on the throne of Afghanistan instead of Dost Mahommed and in March 1838 the 'Army of the Indus' amounting to over twenty thousand men had assembled to march on Kandahar and Kabul.

There was clearly no possibility of Haines being able to return to Aden in March as arranged since he fell seriously ill and, anyway, the acting Governor of Bombay, Mr. James Farish, who had succeeded Grant was still waiting for a reply from the Governor-General on what action should be taken. There was plenty of time, so it might have been thought, to work out whether there was some possible alternative arrangement in view of the attitude of the Abdalis of Lahej. The Government only wanted to obtain a depôt for coals which was secure, and the Sultan had made no difficulty about the depôt nor about having a British garrison. In return for a share of the customs or a stipend Sultan Mahsin and his son Hamed would probably have agreed to the same terms as Sultan Ahmed had agreed to in the Treaty of 1802—a two per cent duty on goods brought by British ships for ten years; after that never higher than three per cent. If the Bombay Government could have foreseen— and there had already been hints of it—the heavy expenses that were to be incurred as a result of tribal hostility, it might have allowed the Sultan to retain his sovereignty over his people. His capital was at Lahej and his powers in Aden would not have been very great considering that the energetic British would be there with a garrison, but his position of prestige need not have been affected. It would certainly have been more difficult and tedious to have governed Aden through the Sultan, and it was not an arrangement that

Haines, or anyone else at the time, recommended or even apparently considered.

It is interesting, however, that several years later, after the disastrous Afghan War when a section of public opinion in England was turning against occupations of foreign territory, an article on Aden in *Blackwood's Magazine* stated that it was evident the Arabs would gladly have yielded 'to any amicable arrangement short of absolute cession of the town which they regarded as disgraceful . . . and even if Aden had fallen into the hands of the Pasha of Egypt, there can be little doubt that the Viceroy would have shown himself equally ready to facilitate our intercourse with India in his Arabian as in his Egyptian harbours. The desired object of obtaining a station and coal depôt for the Indian steamers might easily have been secured in various ways without running even the risk of bringing on the British name the imputation of unnecessary violence and oppression.'[3]

In the 1830's there seemed nothing morally wrong in taking Aden, indeed, it was considered that the British were, at considerable expense, bestowing a benefit on unruly tribes. 'It seems to be a law of nature', wrote Captain Mackenzie in his report of 1837; 'that the civilised nations shall conquer and possess the countries in a state of barbarism and by such means, however unjustifiable it may appear at first sight, extend the blessings of knowledge, industry and commerce among people hitherto sunk in the most gloomy depths of superstitious ignorance'.

When Mr. James Farish, Acting Governor of Bombay, sat down to study all the papers on Aden he was concerned that steamers were being prepared for the service to Suez and they had not yet made final arrangements for a coaling depôt. He had no moral scruples about taking Aden by force though he was sensitive as to how Foreign Powers might react. He came to the conclusion that immediate action should be taken to gain possession of Aden, although no reply could be received for some time from the Governor-General of India as to the policy to be pursued as a result of Haines' reports.

In an interesting minute of September 5 1838, James Farish set out the arguments which drove him to that conclusion.[4] 'It is so evident from correspondence between Lord Palmerston and

Colonel Campbell, that H.M.G. attaches very great importance to the occupation of Aden by the British, and view the aggression of the Pasha of Egypt on Yemen with the utmost mistrust and suspicion that I cannot, on reconsidering the subject, feel satisfied that we are acting rightly in allowing time to escape without taking some measures to keep alive the claim we have established and to which the home authorities show themselves determined to adhere.

'Under existing circumstances the Pasha can have no cause to complain; it has been proved by former treaties that Aden is an independent chieftainship and Boghos Bey [The Viceroy's Minister] assured Colonel Campbell "that if it appeared that Aden did not depend on the Imam of Sana, the Pasha himself would be happy to contribute all in his power to facilitate the cession of Aden to the Bombay Government". It is true that as soon as the Pasha discovered that Aden really was independent of Sana, he attempted to evade this declaration; but it stands on record in answer to any other statements he can make. If, however, with his usual wily character he should possess himself of Aden, while we were deliberating, difficulties that might lead to the most serious consequences would arise, and the blame for having occasioned them might be cast on this Government.

'Another thing evident in the correspondence is the jealousy with which the great European Powers watch our proceedings, and they would gladly be able to represent our occupation of Aden as a forcible seizure, instead of a free cession. I am, therefore, clearly of opinion, under every point of view, that it will be better to send Captain Haines in the *Coote* without delay to conclude the treaty. This proceeding will have on the face of it an amicable character and as he should take about thirty Europeans as an escort, their presence, and the knowledge that a sufficient force is on its way to Aden to occupy it as a possession ceded to us, will, I have no doubt, prevent any shuffling on the part of the Sultan and any attempt at outrage on the part of disaffected individuals.'

Acting Governor Farish would have liked to have awaited the orders of the Governor-General before adopting this decisive step, but he believed the policy would be successful judging by the communications he had had with Haines since his recovery from a severe illness. He wished the *Coote* to sail as soon as possible. Haines should take with him the interpreter, Mullah Jaffar, who had witnessed the treaty, and Shaikh Tyeb Ibranjee, the former native agent at Mocha, who was a personal friend of the Sultan of Aden; Lieutenant Western of the Engineers would go to report on the fortifications and on the accommodation for the troops. Haines was authorised to give small presents where suitable and to increase the offer to the Sultan to 8,700 dollars a year 'rather than risk the free and willing cession of the place'; if it were all terminated satisfactorily the payment for the plunder of the *Duria Dowlat* might be remitted and the sum be defrayed by the Bombay Government. 'Captain Haines should be very cautious not to exhibit any excess of liberality, lest impressions and expectations of a very undesirable character should be engendered in the minds of those rude Arabs.'

Regarding communications with surrounding tribes there should be no discussion of commerce or other topics 'that will excite the jealous feelings of the Pasha of Egypt, or possibly lead to embarrassing connections and obligations . . . that so long as British rights and interests are respected we do not interfere in any quarrels between the tribes, unless our mediation is required by both parties'. No definite instructions would be given on how to conduct negotiations but Haines would go without appearing to doubt that the cession would be ratified.

If the Sultan held to his engagements the Bombay Government would be satisfied that the information that there had been a plan to kidnap the Government's envoy was unfounded, 'but that if the Sultan should draw back from his pledged word, he must be considered guilty of an intended insult which Captain Haines must report to his Government, and if a force be thereon immediately sent to take possession of the place, we should hold it without any acknowledgement to him or his family'.

The expectation that the Egyptians might advance to Aden from the Yemen was one of the main reasons for the sudden decision to take action. Lord Palmerston had warned Mohammed Ali Pasha not to occupy Aden; if he had occupied it already he must immediately withdraw his troops. Farish had seen a copy of this despatch of July 25 1838 and instructed Haines that if he should find Ibrahim Pasha (the nephew of Mohammed Ali Pasha) in possession of Aden he must tell him that he was 'violating British territory' and that his remaining there would be 'at his peril'; the Egyptian Commander was to be reminded that the British Government had informed the Pasha of Egypt that there were to be no Egyptian encroachments beyond the Straits of Bab-el-Mandeb.

Mr. G. W. Anderson, member of the Bombay Council, did not entirely endorse the Governor's long report and minuted that no attempt should be made for the present to obtain Aden except by peaceful means; he considered that an escort of thirty Europeans had the appearance of a threat. The other member of Council, Mr. J. A. Dunlop, accepted the Governor's minute, as it had been agreed that no attempt was to be made to get possession of Aden 'by any other than peaceful means' and he did not think that the escort would constitute a threat. Dunlop's agreement gave the Governor the right to take action on his minute.

It must have been clear to all three members of the Council that if entry were refused to Aden, it would then have to be taken by force unless they were to accept a humiliating withdrawal. Indeed, a letter had already been despatched to the Court of Directors on August 27 1838 signed by Farish, Anderson and Dunlop stating that judging from the manner in which Haines' mission had terminated 'we do not think that we can fairly calculate that no opposition will be encountered so that a force is necessary'.[5] Now they informed the Court that they were taking immediate measures 'to obtain peaceable possession of Aden', and Lord Auckland told Bombay he was glad that they were resorting 'to no other than peaceful means'.

When Haines arrived in Aden harbour on October 24 (1838), he sent a letter ashore to Damjee, the agent, asking him to come on board the *Coote* as soon as possible, but there was no answer. He learned that young Sultan Hamed had arrived in Aden with about one hundred and fifty well-armed Beduin and that the town was in alarm. Haines informed Sultan Mahsin, who was at Lahej, that he had been sent to complete the arrangements for the transfer of the land and the harbours 'as previously agreed between us in the month of January last', and enclosed a letter from the Bombay Government to this effect. He asked that the Sultan should meet him or that someone should be appointed to complete arrangements as to the amount of the annual sum to be given. A speedy conclusion of the affair would convince the British Government 'that no insult was intended them in January when a seizure of the person of their accredited agent was attempted and further that such disgraceful intention was not known to you, but was contemplated and attempted by others without your connivance or authority'. Haines also wrote a polite letter to Ali ibn Abdullah, the Amir of the town, asking him to forward the letter.

It soon became clear that the Sultan of Aden had come to regret the promises he had made, partly because he was by nature an intriguer and seldom kept his word, but mainly because his eldest son, Hamed, and a strong party of his Abdali Beduin objected to the transfer of Aden.* The messenger sent by Haines to get news was detained for some time at the entrance to the town in Crater and was then escorted to Hamed who asked him questions about the ship's armament and the number of troops on board. The messenger returned to Haines with nothing satisfactory to report—indeed his information was that the townspeople were prevented from going out to the vessel and supplies for the ship were forbidden. Haines then ordered a blockade of Aden and asked Bombay to send another ship.

---

* Bombay, however, had to wait several weeks for this unwelcome, but not unexpected news. At the same time some confusion was caused by a report to the Bombay Government given by Commander Lowe of the steamship *Berenice* 'that the Sultan of Aden is stated to have expressed his intention of peaceably giving up possession of Aden to the British Government'. This information, without waiting for a report from Haines, was passed on to the Court of Directors in London from Bombay on October 31 1838.

7

Arabs refuse entry to Aden

(November to December 1838)

When Haines first arrived in Aden he had considered living ashore
in tents, but the hostility of the Beduin, who had been reinforced,
made him decide to remain on board the *Coote*. A letter from one of
the officers with Haines was published in the Bombay press stating
that there were about one thousand Arabs 'all ready for battle'. The
British party had pitched five tents on shore under cover of the
ship's guns 'for the troops that may be expected from Bombay, but
we do not put up in them'.[1]

An insulting and threatening letter came to Haines from Sultan
Hamed: 'Your letter to Ali Abdullah has been received and I understand it. You had better take care. At this time Sultan Mahsin is not
over my head. I am above you and above my father. If you come to
the gate I will permit you to enter and then be upon your head
[attack you]. This the language of the Beduin, "Sultan Hamed is
our Sultan and we are his servants. If Hamed orders we will perform
and come suddenly upon you." ' 'My feet are bad and I cannot rise
off my bed', wrote Sultan Mahsin from Lahej. 'My agents in this

affair are Hamed, who is with you, and others I now send, and pray you settle this affair so that it will be advantageous to both countries.'[2]

Thereupon Haines wrote to Hamed that he would be happy to receive him and his delegation and they would be treated with honour and hospitality. He stated that he would not take any notice of Hamed's discourteous letter, knowing that he had seen but little of the world and was not well acquainted with the British character. Haines trusted that the meeting would terminate the business and unite Hamed's family and tribe in the closest ties of friendship with the British.

When Hamed made difficulties about sending a delegation Haines sent him a letter on October 31 which set out the situation: 'My orders are positive and decisive and your conduct since the arrival of the vessel has not been friendly. You should consider that the British, who are powerful both by sea and land, have the bond of your father for the land and harbour of Aden and that bond must be fulfilled, but remember that the British, though strong, are merciful and don't oppress. To convince you of the truth of what I assert, I send you a copy of the Treaty of Transfer to which I require your signature. You will observe you are not only to receive 8,000 dollars but other advantages, study it and delay not, partake of the fruit while ripe or it will become useless.

'Further let me call to your mind how deeply and repeatedly you have insulted us. Our injuries, unless immediate friendship is made, will demand satisfaction and chastisement will soon follow, most probably sufficient troops will soon arrive, when it will be too late for you to repent, and the transfer will then be settled our own way. I waited on your tribe when I first arrived as the British agent; it is now for you to repay the compliment to the British. I have no choice of agents; send one, two, three or four according to your pleasure, but let them have power to conclude for I am not come to play and be assured that whoever does come shall be honoured and respected.'

Haines at the beginning of November was still confident that he would win through without serious trouble, but he realised that a force would be needed. He had been told that the first reaction of the Beduin in Aden was: 'Are the English so poor they can only afford to send one vessel? And she came only to talk. Why did they not send her before? Had they sent their men and vessels we would have given up, but until they do, they never shall have the place.' He asked Bombay to send the military force which had been planned.

While nearly all the influential men in Aden considered that the agreement should be concluded, the Beduin were in no hurry to come to terms for they were quartered on the merchants and being fed at Hamed's expense. Sultan Mahsin had allowed his son to take control and the Beduin seemed to have control of Sultan Hamed. The fortifications had not been repaired but three of the better guns had been mounted on the northern pass and two others commanded the eastern bay and the passage between Sira Island and the southern gate; the Arabs had a few Egyptian artillerymen in their pay stationed at the northern gate.

The Arabs put forward one excuse after another. No proper delegation ever came and Hamed said that in any case no one had the right to discuss the transfer of Aden. They hoped to evade, wrote Haines, until the Government gave up their idea of taking the place as had occurred in the case of Socotra which they talked about as an example of what would happen with regard to Aden. The Arabs played the game of throwing doubt on everything, British intentions, Haines' credentials and on the promises made in the past by Sultan Mahsin.

Isolated aboard the *Coote* Haines was obliged to conduct negotiations by letter which he did not consider was the best method: 'correspondence with the Arab is disadvantageous, it prolongs disputes and in the end will prove of no avail. More will be done in a personal conference of a few hours than in a month's correspondence'. In conversation with Sultan Mahsin, for instance, Haines would have been able to shame him from making the statements he did in a letter he sent to Haines for the Government of Bombay.

In this the Sultan purported to report what had happened in January of the previous year when, he said, Haines had visited him and tried to force Aden from him. 'I told him that this could not be done, as a man would rather be burned than surrender his right. I also remarked that Government would not wish to deprive anyone of his possessions.'

To Haines he wrote denying that he had ever signed any agreement and treated the whole question as something new and rather surprising. 'You have written to say that you want Aden and the land as far north as Khormaksar. You told him [his son Hamed] that you possess my seal. Any man of sense would not talk that way. An Englishman would never talk so. You wrote to Hamed that we were playing; we are not men to play either with government or yourself, nor should you play with us.

'Your letters are not proper. Your language is not the government style of language but your own, but if you have other than such displeasing language send it to me. If you have a letter saying the Government authorised you to write in this way, we will receive it and bow to it, but if you come to enforce a thing we must have the government authority so that we may know it by seal, nor can we give the country without Government authority.'

Haines replied that he did not understand what the Sultan could require more than the seal of Government authorising him to conclude the transfer; 'the fact is you wish delay and are not prepared to treat either its agents or ships with civility. Nay, you have insulted the British tenfold. I have already informed your agent that if the place is not quietly transferred, agreeable to promise, and the Government send troops up to take possession you will not then receive anything. If you wish to be friends with the British, and to ensure a provision for your family, perform the bond immediately and past transgressions will, I daresay, be forgiven by Government. You write of the British Government as if you were speaking of some petty Shaikhdom. Undeceive yourself—they are powerful and will not be trifled with. Would you play with a lion, as with a cat?'

Sultan Mahsin made out in a letter sent to Shaikh Tyeb Ibranjee, who was on board the *Coote*, that Haines was an angry man and not to be trusted. He gave his own version of what had happened the previous year: 'In my heart I believe that Captain Haines has a face determined on fighting; to him I promised nothing, and he has told lies to government. When I saw his face so determined, I endeavoured to escape him and put it off for two months while each held council. He now says he has a bond in his possession with my seal for Aden, but I say it is a lie. If he has it I will act upon it, for I would not say a word if he shews me the seal.* I have a treaty with

* The Sultan's letter with his seal had been sent to the Governor-General of India and then to the Court of Directors in London.

his government. That man in his heart wishes to be Sultan of Aden, but he never shall until the sword is at our throats. Come to me. We will settle all with justice.' The Sultan had convinced himself that Shaikh Tyeb had been sent as an emissary of Government because Haines was being difficult.

Shaikh Tyeb knew the Sultan too well to be taken in by this letter and he was apprehensive about going to Lahej to see the old man; indeed there was very soon a message from the Sultan's son-in-law, Sayyed Hussain Weiss, that he wished to meet Shaikh Tyeb at the harbour. The meeting was arranged and Haines provided him with a strong escort of fifteen well-armed seamen and six European soldiers in a boat armed with a gun. Sayyed Hussain had fifteen armed Beduin with him and wanted Shaikh Tyeb to accompany him to Lahej, but the Shaikh declined. It had not been expected that Shaikh Tyeb would be so well protected; Sayyed Hussain had intended to take him to Lahej and to hold him there until Haines restored all the papers concerning the transfer of Aden, which the Sultan repeatedly asserted did not exist.

Quite a different attitude to the British was adopted by Sultan Hamed ben Abdallah Fadhli who sent a friendly letter to Haines offering help: 'We formerly met at Shuqra and were friends and you were very kind. I feel hurt you have forgot me and did not send to me. I have heard the Abdali are ready to fight. Let me know if it is in your heart to have the country and I will settle it.' In a letter sent at the same time to Mullah Jaffar he was more explicit: 'If the Captain wishes our men to be upon the head of Sultan Mahsin, you settle them by sea, I will by land. These Abdalis are liars and bad men; never believe them, they will promise but never perform. We are ready to assist you or do anything for you. Keep our friendship in your heart.'

He had certainly not forgotten the Sultan, wrote Haines, and would inform the Government of his kindnesses; he asked for wood and water which were sent. The Abdalis in Aden were angry that their enemy, the Fadhli Sultan, had let supplies go to the *Coote* and sent a delegation to offer wood and water, which previously they had refused, but Haines was now getting supplies also from the Somali coast, and in view of all the difficulties the Abdalis had created he declined their offer. The Beduin of the delegation said that they could not give up Aden without a fight otherwise they would not be considered as warriors, and that promises made by the Abdali Sultan about Aden were nonsense for he was an old man and in their power.

The Abdalis were in an aggressive mood and unwise enough to sink a sailing ship belonging to the Fadhli Sultan, who wrote to Haines that this insult, caused by the friendship he had shewn for the English, had increased his hatred for the Abdalis. 'When your letter reached me I informed my friends and tribe and showed them your presents. Write me everything you wish in your heart. If you require water, wood, provisions, on your order they shall be sent. I wish to send you a horse but cannot send it in a boat. Let me know the news from India.' Haines thanked him and said that he was receiving sufficient supplies from the Somali coast; '. . . pray do not send the horse, for there is no place to keep it on board and I seldom visit the shore. Believe me I receive the intention as a compliment equally with the gift.' He was sorry to hear about the loss of the boat and added: 'The reports you have heard about our suffering a loss is a falsehood—for not one man has fallen.'

This referred to an incident on November 20. The pinnace had left the *Coote* in the morning in charge of Lieutenant Hamilton, with Lieutenant Evans of the Bombay Regiment, on patrol to enforce the blockade. As they neared the point of the harbour Arabs beckoned them to come inshore but they kept about thirty yards away. Suddenly fire was opened on them from about fifty matchlocks; three balls struck the pinnace without injuring anyone. Haines was outraged and issued a number of strong orders. He informed Commander Denton of the *Coote* 'after so shameful and cowardly an attack' he wished him to take every favourable opportunity 'to resent the insult offered to the British by destroying the Beduin, or property, belonging to Aden'; and that he should prevent trade, or provisions being brought into the town from the bays of Aden or the northern gate; he should also capture any boat belonging to the Sultan, or the merchants of Aden and detain crews and property until the pleasure of Government was known.

Haines made the bold suggestion to Denton that they should set up a long nine-pounder on a small island called Jezret Feringee near the end of Swaya island. During the night of November 20–21

Lieutenants Hamilton and Western worked to have the gun ready to fire at daylight, when they were joined on shore by Denton, Haines and Evans with a small force of fifteen European soldiers, ten marines and some seamen with a five-inch howitzer. As a result of the fire maintained, parties of Arabs were prevented from entering the town and a number of laden camels driven back. Several shot struck the pass and displaced one of the guns, and two shells were sent by Lieutenant Western immediately over the gate. 'Every hill was occupied by Beduin,' wrote Haines, 'and they kept up a constant fire from great guns and musketry without effect. They were so exasperated that they came down in large bodies with the intention of storming our gun; the bank which connects Jezret Feringee to the mainland being dry they were enabled to come under cover of the rocks within eighty or ninety yards of our position. The firing then became brisk and lasted so for some minutes when the cross-fire from the pinnace and island compelled them to retreat with some loss.' After dark the British party and guns returned on board, well satisfied with their achievement and with no losses.

It was an effective but rather hazardous enterprise and the Bombay Government was a little startled to learn that Haines had been carrying on a one-ship battle against the town of Aden and risking the capture of the two senior officers, himself and Commander Denton.

Skirmishes continued. On December 5 the *Coote*, after a chase lasting six hours, caught up with a fast-sailing *ganjah*, the *Ateeh Allah*, a valuable ship belonging to a wealthy merchant of Lahej who resided at Aden. On board was Lieutenant Evans' Indian servant whose return Haines had repeatedly demanded after he had been captured; the man was being sent away from Aden on the ship to prevent his escaping from the town and giving information. A delegation with a flag of truce came down to the harbour to ask to have the ship returned, but Haines replied that it was a lawful prize in view of the attacks carried out by the tribesmen. He also refused to let them purchase dates from two heavily laden boats which had been prevented from landing their cargoes by the *Coote*'s boat.

Hamed was in trouble with his father for having allowed hostilities to start and a severe letter was sent to him when it was learned in Lahej that the *Ateeh Allah* had been captured by the British. 'The

Stafford Bettesworth Haines, 1802–1860

Ships of war manoeuvring for the attack on Aden, January 1839.
A watercolour by J. S. Rundle, mate of the Flagship H.M.S. *Volage*

poor in Aden suffer greatly,' Haines wrote 'owing to the Beduin making them almost their slaves, without the slightest remuneration either in goods or money; they are now employed all day grinding corn or millet, conveying water and provisions to the different guards on the hills and passes, and have had to carry stones for the loose breastworks thrown up in different places; in fact they perform all the labour while the Beduin recline at there ease.' The Arabs had a battery mounting three guns on Sira Island, one gun at the southern gate, two guns on the Turkish wall and one gun near Jebel Hadeed. They had about fourteen guns in all, most of which were manned by Egyptians. Haines was not sure whether the Egyptians were rene-gade troops who had deserted for want of pay or had been deputed to defend Aden by order of the Egyptian General commanding in Yemen in reply to a request for artillerymen sent by the Sultan of Aden to the Egyptians in Mocha.

The blockade and the firing on the town had its effect. The Beduin chieftains held a meeting with Hamed at their head and agreed to sue for a cessation of hostilities through Sayyed Zain ibn Aidrus. It was also decided that when the 8,700 German crowns were received in payment—and they took it for granted that this money would be received—it should not all go to the Sultan of Aden but that each subdivision of the tribe should receive a share. Haines was told that Hamed had to submit to the wishes of the Beduin—'they have led him into a labyrinth from which he cannot extricate himself, and they will ultimately plunder Aden and repay themselves and satisfy their avarice which alone brought them into it'.

A letter to Haines was brought under a flag of truce from Sayyed Zain ibn Aidrus, a descendant of the patron saint of Aden—'the false saint', as Haines called him. 'We are Sayyeds and reside in Aden', he wrote. 'It is our duty to come between two opposing parties and settle disputes. You and Sultan Mahsin have quarrelled and no one here wishes it. The people are frightened and the poor come crying to me daily. We are Sayyeds and both parties will listen to us; if you will permit me to come let me know. I wish to obtain information from both sides.'

'The Government sent me here with the kindest and best inten-tions', replied Haines; 'the Abdalis have declared war by firing on the Government's ship's boat. I am sorry that the poor suffer in Aden, but we have no remedy. I can only advise Sultan Hamed to permit them, as well as other harmless creatures, to quit the town before war on our part commences; otherwise in all probability many will fall by shot and shell. If you wish to see me be assured you shall be received with respect, for I know your office is to make peace and not war.' Haines did not, in fact, have a very high opinion of the Sayyeds of South Arabia, for he considered that many of them were intriguers who gained money from both sides in disputes which they had often themselves encouraged.

On the following day there was a letter from Sayyed Alawi, the son of Sayyed Zain, which made it clear that the Sayyeds did not want to come until they had everything in writing from the Sultan and from Haines. They wished for truth and then they would make peace. Haines was not going to allow the case to be investigated and judged by the Aidrus family which had been concerned with the plot to kidnap him, and answered briefly: 'I do not ask you to make peace, nor do I wish it. The Abdalis commenced hostilities by firing at us, and they will be heartily tired of it ere it terminates. As yet the fighting has been merely with boats. With salaams to your father and self.'

Haines realised that Aden would have to be taken by force since the Sultan and his son were unable to understand the situation: there was no meeting ground. Hamed kept on sending 'nonsensical' notes expecting to be paid the 8,700 German crowns and the ambushes continued. The Arabs believed that Haines would eventually leave and they would score a victory. The chieftains were fully aware that the Government of India was very occupied by troubles in India, Afghanistan, Persia and Burma as they received information through the Indian merchants in Aden. Arabs from Aden told Haines that the people there were convinced that the British could not spare men from Bombay owing to the wars being fought by the Government of India.

There were many stories being spread through the Red Sea ports to Egypt and elsewhere about Haines' difficulties and he was annoyed. Colonel Campbell received some rather exaggerated reports from British captains of ships who had communicated with Haines when passing by Aden on their way to Suez and the Consul had sent these reports on to Lord Palmerston: 'I learn that Captain Haines, who made the late convention for the occupation of Aden, was immediately forced to fly on board ship with all the English at Aden, by the fears of being massacred by the son of the Sultan, who had refused to consent to the convention made by his father.' Palmerston noted on the outside of Campbell's despatch: 'I trust that by this time the Bombay Government has received orders from the Government of India to re-occupy Aden. This commencement is exceedingly unsatisfactory.'[3]

8

The British take Aden
by storm

(January to February 1839)

The Government of India certainly had many problems of war and administration to deal with and, in spite of the fact that only a peaceful approach had been authorised with regard to Aden, the Government now had another little war on their hands.

The Bombay Government was worried and it seemed that immediate action was necessary especially 'after the threats held out by Commander Haines to the Arab authorities'. But it had been realised that there might be difficulties after the attempt to kidnap Haines and if the Government had wanted to express only a mild reaction to any other insults that might be offered it should not have sent a naval officer but a civilian official.

Had Haines retired from Aden to Bombay when he encountered the first difficulties, the Abdalis would have won a victory and the capture of Aden later would have been harder. By keeping up the correspondence with the Sultan of Aden and his son, Haines enabled the Government to maintain the argument that the Sultan had made a promise which he had broken. Had the Sultan said, as had the Mahra Chieftain, that he was not prepared to sell one span of his land, Haines would have reported quite differently to Bombay. This might have changed the Government's approach; the fact that it had proceeded with the Socotra expedition, although there was no agreement, is not necessarily a guide to its conduct, because it had been confident that Haines would succeed in buying Socotra.

In a further analysis of the situation [1] Mr. Farish noted that it had been made clear to the Sultan that the Government was prepared to ignore the earlier misdeeds of the Abdalis; 'the Chief was thus left free to maintain his faith and cede the promontory and town of Aden on the terms agreed upon, or to show reason for withdrawing from his pledge. He might then (had he been able to show any sufficient reason) have induced the British Government to allow what had passed to be cancelled and, foregoing any claim on his territory, to treat afresh on the question of redress for the plunder of the *Duria Dowlat* and of satisfaction for the insult offered to the flag on that occasion, and to their representative'.

The Governor was dealing with a hypothetical situation so that one cannot be by any means sure that that would have been the line of conduct followed. The fact remained, as the Governor noted, that the Sultan and his son had not adopted an attitude that would have allowed of 'temperate discussion'. The Chiefs of Aden had met the arrival of the British Mission 'with such a tone of arrogant superiority followed by such a series of uncalled for violence, as would lead to a suspicion that another and powerful influence had been exercised to excite opposition and afford assurance of support. . . . But it matters not who were the instigators of the extraordinary measures which the authorities of Aden so madly adopted and to which no Power could submit.'

Certainly the British Government had been insulted and it was a period when 'face' was most important for the maintenance of control by a comparatively few Europeans over a vast area, though there were a number of occasions a few years later when the British accepted insults from a bigoted Sherif of Mocha without taking any reprisals. The Government of Bombay may have felt, as the Sultan of Aden had argued, that Haines' communications with the Arab chieftains were not always 'the government style of language', but after studying Haines' reports it understood why he had reacted as he had. The Governor decided that Haines had to be supported and he trusted that Lord Auckland would approve the hurried measures that would have to be taken in order to have the advantage of sending ships during the favourable period of the north-east monsoon which blew strongly from December until the end of February.

It was certainly not the peaceful approach that the Governor-General had recommended and it is surprising that, in such an important matter of peace or war, the Government of Bombay was prepared to go forward without the approval of the Governor-General. It was harking back to the old days when the Bombay Presidency was in a position to take such decisions before the Act of 1833 centralised the administration of India in the hands of the Governor-General.

Rear-Admiral Sir Frederick Maitland, Commander-in-Chief East Indies, was asked for his co-operation in making available two ships of the Royal Navy, H.M.S. *Volage* and H.M.S. *Cruizer*, which were on an operation at the mouth of the Indus River. Major Bailie was appointed Senior Officer commanding the troops under the authority of Haines as Political Agent. Captain H. Smith R.N. of H.M.S. *Volage* was in command of the operation. It was a small force consisting of two hundred and eighty-six rank and file of the Bombay Regiment with full complement of N.C.O.'s and commissioned officers; twenty-two rank and file European artillery in addition to two eight-and-a-half inch howitzers with their complement of artillerymen to be sent in the *Anne Crichton*; three hundred and fifty rank and file of the 24th Regiment Bombay Native Infantry; sixty Golandauze and pioneers and ten garrison guns for defence.

The Accountant-General was instructed to prepare 40,000 German crowns (about £8,000) for shipment to Haines at Aden for the use of the force, sufficient, it was considered for at least three months; nine-pounder field-pieces were equipped for service with their carriages and wagons, flints and one hundred thousand musket-balled ammunition were got ready and one thousand nine hundred shrapnel and common shells were fitted ready for the twelve-pounder howitzers.

In spite of all this shot and shell the Governor thought it might be possible to capture Aden without loss of life; 'the importance of our obtaining a footing peaceably, or at all events without loss of life of anyone, is incalculably great, in regard to the feeling with which our afterwards occupying the place would be viewed, independently of all other weighty considerations and should never be lost sight of by Commander Haines.'

The main force left Bombay on December 29 but the schooner-of-war *Mahi* with the armed barque *Anne Crichton*, with her detachment of artillerymen, were sent ahead and arrived at Aden on December 18 to reinforce the blockade. When the expedition arrived off Aden on January 16 1839, Haines despatched a letter to the town addressed to all the chieftains. 'The answer', he informed Bombay, 'was frivolous and unsatisfactory, and with it I received a message saying they only wanted time to obtain Beduin reinforcements and they were preparing the great guns for service. In consequence of the above information, I considered it advisable to lose no time in capturing it, more particularly as we had but few days water for the troops, and I therefore wrote to Captain Smith and to Major Bailie to that effect.'

In his letter of January 16 to Captain Smith, Haines stated that all 'mild and conciliatory' measures having proved unavailing 'I am under the necessity (as the last and only resource left to obtain satisfaction for the repeated insults offered to the British) to solicit force may be used to compel them to evacuate the ground ceded to the British, under the Sultan's seal, in January 1838'. He pointed out that many of the poor inhabitants of Aden, mostly Jews and Banians, had been compelled by the chieftains to remain there and he asked that their lives should be preserved as also that of any chieftains and Sayyeds. As he knew the harbour well he offered his services.[2]

On January 17 Captain Smith and Major Bailie planned the landing from the Eastern, or Front Bay, anchorage; an attempt was made on the same day—unsuccessfully—to land some guns on a small island. On the morning of January 18 the expedition sailed round to the Eastern Bay; Captain Smith had accepted Haines' offer and he was piloting H.M.S. *Volage*; as she came in near Sira Island the Arabs fired with muskets and several large guns; Captain Smith decided to proceed to Front Bay and anchor for the night.

In order to land forces to capture the town of Aden, it was

necessary first to silence the guns on the well-fortified island of Sira. This had been from the time of the Ancient Egyptians and of the Romans the effective defence; even the redoubtable Alfonso d'Albuquerque, who had made Portugal mistress of the Indian Ocean at the beginning of the sixteenth century, regretted that he had failed in only one thing—to close the straits of the Red Sea to Muslim shipping by capturing Aden.

On the morning of January 19 the British expedition was ready for the attack. The troops were to land in two divisions round Sira Island which rose to three hundred feet with a battery of about twelve guns guarding the only landing place; from here a zig-zag path went up steeply to a gateway, flanked by bastions about one hundred and fifty to two hundred feet above the sea, and a wall ran round the whole island with bastions at intervals. On the sea face was a battery of five guns and higher up a strongly-built round tower with more batteries of guns.

At 9.30 a.m. *Volage* anchored about three hundred yards from the lower battery on the north side of the island and the schooner *Mahi* (Lieutenant Daniell) took up position on the southern side. 'Both ships opened fire on this formidable work', reported Captain Smith, 'and also on the Round Tower and batteries on the heights, to which the enemy replied with spirit from all their batteries, but, owing to the vessels being laid close to the shore, most of the shot passed over them'.

At 10 a.m. *Cruizer*, anchored near *Volage* and *Coote*, opened fire also from the southern side. 'In a short time two of the guns in the lower battery were dismounted, and most of the people were driven from the remainder; they, however, took shelter behind the ruins of the battery, and kept up an incessant fire of musketry upon the ships, and although the lower battery was almost knocked to pieces, still we had great difficulty in dislodging the men. At this period, I directed the fire to be opened on the Round Tower and batteries on the heights, which were filled with men armed with matchlocks, and in the course of an hour, I had the satisfaction to see this tower, though sixty feet high and strongly built, a mass of ruins.'

Firing continued from the lower battery on Sira Island and Lieutenant Daniell was directed to drive the enemy out. The *Mahi* was only a small ship of one hundred and fifty-seven tons with three guns; having ordered the soldiers below, Daniell took her right up to the battery ramparts. A couple of broadsides were fired and then Daniell with his two officers, Lieutenant Benjamin Hamilton and Mr. Midshipman Nisbett, jumped ashore and charged at the defences. The Arabs were taken by surprise and fled firing a few shots, one of which severely wounded Nisbett. Hamilton continued the attack through the battery and up the heights followed by a few seamen; round a corner of a cliff he came upon thirty Arabs who surrendered thinking him a member of a storming party. He forced them to descend to the shore where he handed them over to the soldiers who had in the meantime disembarked.*

By 11.30 Captain Smith considered that the fire had been sufficiently reduced from the Island of Sira and gave the order for the troops to land on the shore in front of the town. Lieutenant Dobree, I.N. led in the first division, and with Mr. Rundle and a quartermaster of the ship, were the first on shore. They made for a sixty-nine-pounder which had been fired several times, cut down an Arab who fired his matchlock from behind the gun, and Mr. Rundle was the first to plant the British flag. 'So completely were the enemy driven from all points (with the exception of the island) by the fire of the ships', reported Captain Smith, 'that the whole of the troops landed with the loss of only two men killed, and three wounded.'

Both divisions formed up in the most 'steady manner' and advanced from the eastern shore through the houses of Aden contained within the cup of an extinct volcano known as Crater. The Arabs retired before them and the British flag was hoisted on the Sultan's palace. 'On debouching from the town a flag of truce was hoisted at Aidrus, the principal Mahommedan Mosque, where all the inhabitants, both male and female, had sought protection', reported Major Bailie. 'The halt was immediately sounded and I advanced with a white flag, met the Mahommedan priest, and explained to him through my Arab interpreter, that none of the inhabitants would be touched;

---

* There is some uncertainty as to the details of what happened when Sira Island was stormed. Twenty-five years later there was an acrimonious exchange of letters between Captain Daniell and Captain Hamilton which are contained in a printed document sent to the Under-Secretary of State for India by Captain Hamilton, dated May 6 1864.

to keep all unarmed people and females with him at the Mosque and to collect any arms there might be.'

Major Bailie then proceeded with the flank companies of the European Regiment through the defile to the gateway at the Northern Pass which led out to the interior. The Arabs kept up a desultory fire from the heights on the right of the advancing column but the skirmishers were dislodged by a detachment of European troops. The Northern Gate with two guns was deserted and left in charge of an officer and fifty men, while the rest of the column returned to the town where Major Bailie found one hundred and thirty-nine Arab prisoners who had been sent to the mainland from Sira island. An Arab interpreter was told to explain to them that they had to give up their arms and then they would be escorted to the Northern Gate and allowed to go to Lahej or wherever they wished.

'In taking their creeses from the Arabs', wrote Bailie, 'they became alarmed, I suppose, for several of them jumped up, drew their creeses [daggers], stabbed the Sergeant-Major of Artillery in five places, and inflicted a fearful wound on the Arab interpreter. Some of the sentries immediately fired on them, when they broke away in a body, killing two men and wounding two, and a sergeant of artillery, since dead; the remaining sentries fired on them, and killed and mortally wounded twelve Arabs. . . . Had it not been for this unfortunate occurrence, so deeply to be regretted, the loss of life would have been very trifling.'

It was estimated that there were one thousand armed Arabs to meet the attack; the defence was courageous but rather disorganised and the size of the guns captured showed that serious damage might have been done to the invading force if they had been in a position to fire at the ships when they approached inshore.* Captain Haines reported to Government that he was proud to have piloted H.M.S.

---

* The captured guns included three brass guns on carriage and in battery—eighty-five, sixty-eight and thirty-two-pounders; six iron guns in battery ranging from eighteen- to three-pounder; not in battery were an eighty-nine-pounder brass gun and a six- and four-pounder iron gun. The total was thirty-three guns with three thousand pounds of powder, one thousand two hundred shots of different sizes and eighty-eight grape shot. Three of the fine brass guns were set aside for presentation to H.M. Queen Victoria and were later sent to the Tower of London.

Volage. 'I could not but admire the splendid fire from the shipping and mortar vessel; and the behaviour of the little *Mahi* drew the admiration of every person. Nothing could have been more regular than the landing; the men were steady to a degree, and they stormed the place gallantly. But what is still more to be admired and a greater proof of their discipline is, that after landing, neither male, female or property was molested. . . . The whole loss [British] in killed and wounded is fifteen, eight of which occurred after the place was in our possession. The loss of the enemy has been very severe. One hundred and thirty-nine are now said to be missing, besides many wounded inland, and we have twenty-five men, too severely wounded to return inland, among them one chieftain, Shaikh Ragib Hazzabi, and Ali Salaam, a nephew of the Sultan. I have supplied the unfortunate sufferers with food and everything to make them as comfortable as circumstances will admit of, and they receive kind medical attention from Dr. Malcolmson of the 24th Regiment; I have also given a few dollars for the support of their families.'

The *Bombay Government Gazette*, in an 'extraordinary issue' of February 20 1839, published a number of despatches describing the action, and concluded with a General Order by the Governor-in-Council congratulating Captain Smith, Commander Haines, Major Bailie and the troops and seamen on their high discipline 'and particularly in their abstaining from all violence to the inhabitants, and respecting the families of natives, conduct which reflects honour on themselves and on their country'. Subsequently it was decided by the Court of Directors to present Commander S. B. Haines with a Sword of Honour worth two hundred guineas and to Lieutenant E. W. S. Daniell a Sword of Honour to the value of one hundred guineas.[3]

The Government of Bombay informed the Court of Directors that everything possible had been done by Commander Haines to achieve a peaceable surrender of Aden and they referred to his 'constant and earnest endeavours to avoid hostilities and the highly judicious and humane exertions adopted by him for the relief of the wounded and for reassuring the chiefs of the friendly footing on which it is the wish of Government that they should be viewed'.

Sultan Mahsin sent two accredited representatives from Lahej to Haines to make his submission. One was his son-in-law, Sayyed

Hussain Weiss, who had been concerned with the attempt to kidnap Haines, and Abdulla Khatif, his steward. An agreement was signed by Haines with them in Aden on February 2, but there were no witnesses and the document was worded in such a way that the Sayyed made himself responsible for peace and trade without mentioning the Sultan. On reflection Haines decided that another agreement should be signed by them which referred to the responsibility of the Sultan and be attested by four witnesses. This was done on February 4 and read: 'On the word and promise of Sultan Mahsin, I promise that no insult or molestation shall take place on the road, or between the English and my people, and that all shall be peace and quietness; and I agree that between my people and your people there shall be no difference of oppression, and that the English agree that all shall be peace, and that all merchants shall be free to trade without oppression.' Eight other agreements were signed with neighbouring chieftains.[4]

By February Bombay had received an answer from the Governor-General to the letter asking for advice about sending an expedition to Aden. Lord Auckland's letter was written on January 21, two days after the capture of Aden and several weeks before he heard of the result: 'Upon a very careful perusal of all the papers which regard the question, the Governor-General is satisfied that the course pursued by the Government of Bombay in adopting measures to enforce our just rights at Aden is warranted and proper'—which must have been a relief for Bombay.

9

Haines the new Sultan

(January to March 1839)

Although the Bombay Government was entirely satisfied with the
way Haines had carried out the mission, he was informed that he
would only be temporarily in charge of the political and civil control
of Aden, as it had always been intended that both powers would be
vested in the same officer and 'a military officer will hereafter be
selected for this charge'.[1] But Haines was quick to show that he was
a decisive and able administrator with good judgement and, above
all, that he understood tribal life and Arab ways. It is doubtful if the
Government could have found anyone else in the East India Company service who could have filled the post so ably and it was finally
decided to leave Haines in charge to the annoyance of the Military
Department of Bombay.

Haines had to build up relations with the surrounding tribes and
deal with the Abdali Sultan of Lahej, who was one of the most tricky,
obstinate and unreliable chieftains that the British ever had to deal
with in South Arabia. It was essential for Haines' prestige and for the

safety of the garrison that he should have as good an intelligence service as possible and this he set about building up in a remarkable way by appointing Arab and Jewish agents in various parts of South Arabia. The Sultans were soon to find that their movements and intrigues to recapture Aden, and their plans of where and when they would attack, were known beforehand to Haines, who became respected and feared throughout South Arabia and the Yemen.

The Government of India learned to trust Haines' reports and were impressed enough to ask him some years later how he managed to obtain them. 'My only trustworthy informers are Jews', he replied. 'I secretly employ them through Menahain and Shumadiel, resident Jews of Aden in Government employ. Through these I receive letters in Hebrew containing simple truths from their different positions—Sana, Kattaba, Taez, Lahej and the neighbourhood and I now and then present them separately with a trifling sum of money.' Jews of Lahej and of the neighbouring tribes were employed by Haines from the first occupation of Aden; 'they are the accountants and cashiers of the Arab chieftains generally and therefore well enabled to give correct intelligence. Their interest is with us in Aden in consequence of their wives, families and property being in the town.' Jews were also employed by Arab Chiefs as treasurers because they were under their direct control, being outside Muslim law and the tribal organisation which maintained the principle of collective responsibility. Not only did they know the intentions of the chiefs from their position but as traders they had interests in many places. There were about eighteen thousand Jews in the Yemen in the principal towns and villages and, of course, they wrote to each other in Hebrew which the Arabs could not understand.*

Haines believed that a good intelligence service was the best way of dealing with Arabs. 'They must be defeated,' he wrote, 'with their own weapons, by quietly letting them know that you perceive their intentions before they are prepared to carry them out, and let them feel that you are their superior in tact, intellect, judgement and

---

* There are now scarcely any Jews left in the Yemen since, after the Arab-Israeli war of 1948, they left in a remarkable exodus. I saw hundreds of them in their camps in Little Aden waiting their turn for their airlift to Israel which was one of the most remarkable air operations ever carried out.

activity of purpose, that their secret thoughts are known to you, that your information is sure and that you are prepared to counteract their designs; goodwill, kindness and respect will do more than the bayonet.'[2]

Haines had had frequent contacts with Arabs for nearly twenty years and they were not such mysterious beings as they appeared to some of the officers writing from Aden to the Bombay Press. 'It is to us a totally new settlement,' wrote one of them, 'in a country as yet unknown to us, peopled by a race whose habits, manners and religion in no way assimilate with ours; and it will certainly require some time, more particularly after the way in which we have come among them, to wipe away their prejudices, or even to induce them to tolerate us, with comfort, as their neighbours.'

After describing the remarkable bravery with which the Arabs defended Sira Island this officer gave a good description of these men who seemed strange to him and whose language he could not understand. 'Their height is rather below the average height of Englishmen; they have remarkably small limbs—hands, feet and ears, peculiarly small; head well formed, with intelligent expression of countenance; an eye quick, sharp and full of animation; sight remarkably keen, correct and long; but the chest was, in all, best developed, large in every way, expansive and deep; the frame generally awry, every motion of the body exhibiting to the sight muscular movement. Such a frame cannot be formed for strength and much strength they have not, but for activity and endurance they cannot be surpassed.'[3]

The people of Aden were then concentrated in Crater where the troops were also encamped. This is the hottest part of the peninsula for it is within an extinct volcano and the surrounding jagged hills reflect back the heat of the sun, but against this there is the advantage that the cooling down of the great mountains of volcanic rock in the evening and the warming up process in the morning create regular local breezes.

'Arid stony hills surround an extensive cemetery,' wrote one officer to Bombay; 'the filthy and squalid residents . . . are quite in keeping with the foetid remains of dogs, cats and human bones. From the contemplation of these pleasing scenes there is no relaxation, as any attempt to move beyond the limits of our Golgotha, would be attended with the loss of life. The men are on duty two nights out of three and we have already lost five Europeans and have thirty in hospital out of three hundred.'⁴ *The Bombay Gazette* of March 25 1839 urged the Government to send reinforcements: 'The accounts given in the letters of our correspondents are truly deplorable; the Europeans were so overworked as to have scarcely a night in bed, and a great number of the sepoys were on the sick list through various distempers.'⁵

Although the Sultan of Lahej and his son Hamed had informed Haines of their submission and of their desire to be friends with the British, the troops had to do constant guard duties outside the Crater area along the Turkish wall watching for any attack from the interior. If the Arabs had rallied and attacked before the fortifications had been strengthened and reinforcements arrived, they might have succeeded in retaking the town considering the smallness of the British garrison. Lieutenant Western worked hard to make the fortifications more secure and he was joined by Captain Foster of the Engineers, sent from Bombay. They concentrated on defences against attack from the Arabs inland and were not concerned with fortifications on the seaward side against ships of a foreign Power.

Haines was able to report at the end of February that all the neighbouring tribes appeared to be anxious to be on friendly terms and permit free intercourse with their territories, even in some cases being prepared to put themselves under British protection. Sultan Mahsin had wished to come to Aden but Haines had put him off stating that it would serve no purpose until he had received instructions from the Government. Haines had secured the safety of the roads to the interior by negotiations with the tribes, and caravans, which had been plundered after the capture of Aden, had been quietly restored; the farmers of the Yemen and of Lahej were bringing in their produce and merchants had loaded several boats with coffee, wheat and millet from the interior. Haines thought that there would be fighting among the tribes owing to the 'enmity and jealousy that lurks in the bosom of one tribe against another', but he did not think that even revenge would prompt them to attack Aden and run the risk of reducing their strength by losses suffered in front of well-manned defences. He under-estimated, however, the eternal surge of Arab optimism, but he did emphasise in the same despatch

Preparing for the attack of Aden by J. S. Rundle

Warships off Sira Island after the attack on Aden, January 19, 1839, a drawing by Lieutenant E. W. S. Daniell commanding the *Mahi*

The storming of Aden by J. S. Rundle, who planted the first British flag on shore

the need for reinforcements and for rebuilding some of the fortifications.[6]

A good deal of work had to be done to put the defences of the Turkish wall into order and to try to ensure that the Arabs could not infiltrate round the ends of the wall, wading through the sea at low water. Plans were made for strengthening the Main Gate, an imposing cleft through the hills leading out of Crater towards the Western Harbour, or Back Bay, towards the Turkish wall and the isthmus to the interior. Everyone going out of Aden or coming into it by land had to pass through this gateway over which there was a strong battlement with two guns. 'To add to the strength of those powerful protectors', wrote a visitor, 'there are small forts, built on the pinnacle of each impending rock, which commands the pass to the height of five hundred feet, and from which an irresistible fire could at any time be kept up.' Having passed through this 'formidable gate', there was a steep pathway, with a high wall of solid rock on each side for about a quarter of a mile, 'when the sight of Aden opens up to view and then the scene is, certainly, enough to strike the mind with no ordinary feelings of admiration and surprise. You see the irregular plain before you with a few scattered towers or mosques which seem, in the distance, all that is left to grace the present miserable-looking huts that are built upon the ruins of former might and splendour. On looking from this plain the next object which attracts attention is the magnificent amphitheatre of rocky mountains towering up around you to the height of one thousand seven hundred and eighty feet.' Along the ridge at their summit were about forty sharp peaks each holding a strongly built watch-tower; the hills fell away on the eastern side of the town where the sea, from the Front or Eastern Bay, washed against the town walls. It was near this shore, looking out towards Sira Island, about three hundred yards away, that the British troops had made their cantonment.

The writer stated that the troops were in healthy condition and free of malaria or intermittent fever, arguing that as vegetation could not grow on the barren rocks there could not be any vegetable decomposition for the sun's rays 'to excite that malaria, which is generally so productive of intermittent fever within the tropics'; but in the interior, where there was vegetation, malaria existed.[7] The part played by the mosquito was not known in Europe until towards the end of the nineteenth century, though many of the Somalis on the coast of Africa knew of the connection, as Richard Burton reported but he discounted it as a superstition.[8]

Haines took over a house in Crater which was extremely hot and the rooms inconveniently small—but he was too busy to mind. He found Aden healthy and preferable to the climate of the Persian Gulf. He had left his wife, Mary, in Bombay, where their son, Stafford, was born in February 1839, a month after the capture of Aden. It was some years before Haines was able to build good enough quarters at Tarshain (Steamer Point) to have his wife and son to live with him.

Towards the end of February there was a visit from an envoy of the important Shaikh Sherzebee of the Hujariya territory in the Yemen to say that the chieftain wished to visit Haines. Shaikh Sherzebee had received several letters from the Egyptian commander-in-chief in the Yemen offering him the highest rewards and promises if he would hand over his country to the Egyptians, but he had refused and had said that he would defend it to the last. He wanted to arrange for the produce of his fertile country to find an outlet through Aden. The Egyptian commander warned the Shaikh that if he went to Aden he would be imprisoned by the English at the request of the Egyptians who were on excellent terms with them. 'It is not surprising,' reported Haines to Bombay, 'that the Egyptian authorities should be so anxious to obtain possession of Hujariya, its revenue from coffee alone when trading with Mocha was 60,000 dollars (£12,000) annually to the Chief, and the Egyptians are well aware that if Shaikh Sherzebee can find a channel for barter through Aden their town of Mocha will become of less value, and that it will be the first step towards that decline which must eventually occur if the British flag continues to fly in Aden.'[9] An agreement was signed between Haines and Aoun bin Yussuf al-Sherzebee which stated 'whatever the English please shall be done'.[10]

Haines was reminded by this visit that it was time he wrote another letter to Ibrahim Pasha, commanding the Egyptian forces in Yemen, to inform him of the capture of Aden; 'busy engagements and the want of a favourable opportunity have prevented my previously giving you this pleasing information'.[11] On February 28

Haines wrote to the British Consul-General in Egypt and included a report on the tribes and a map of the Yemen: 'On looking over the report you will perceive that the ambition of Mohammed Ali Pasha is to conquer the whole of the Yemen, monopolise the coffee and to supply the whole country with the manufactures of Egypt. The British name stands very high for good faith and justice among the interior States, so that I consider that if the advance of the Egyptian troops was put a stop to, the roads over Yemen would in the course of a few months, by friendly negotiation, be open for free intercourse and the exports of the country give a return for British import. On the contrary if the Pasha of Egypt is successful in conquering the whole country—which he obviously intends by increasing his force at Taez—the entire commerce will be monopolised by Egypt and even our Indian trade, which has existed for centuries, will be entirely ruined.'[12]

Campbell sent Haines' letter on to Palmerston because he thought the details were of great interest. The Pasha had assured Campbell that he would regard Aden as belonging to Britain, but 'the possession of Aden by us is far from pleasing to him'. French residents in Egypt were busy telling Mohammed Ali that the British object was to get the whole coffee trade of Yemen into their hands and to supply Arabia with British manufactures; also that the British wished to command the entrance to the Red Sea in order to take possession of Egypt.

The Government of Bombay still feared that the Egyptians might advance on Aden, and succeed in stirring up the tribes against the British. The take-over of Aden had not gone as smoothly as had originally been hoped, and Government was depressed at the expense of the undertaking merely to achieve a coal depôt.

Haines' answer to this was that trade should be developed by charging duties which were lower than those charged at other ports, such as Mocha and Jedda. Lord Auckland supported this and told Bombay that Haines' attention should be drawn to the 1838 Anglo-Turkish Convention according to which, goods carried on British ships were not to be charged more than five per cent, though the Governor-General recommended lower tariffs for Aden, recalling that a main object of holding Aden was that it should become an emporium for the import and export trade of that part of Arabia.

'His Lordship would have it like Sincapore [*sic*], a port free from national distinctions and as free from charges and from interference as is consistent with the maintenance of a good port police, and of lights, anchorage and other harbour conveniences. . . . And if Aden should in consequence become, as may be expected, a place of extensive resort to merchants, he would look to a fair revenue from moderate internal taxes and upon ground allotted for building.'[13]

It was realised, however, that there were bound to be heavy expenses to begin with. Haines decided not to demand the balance of payment which was due for the goods of the *Duria Dowlat* as it would have caused a great deal of excitement in the interior (eventually the demand for the balance was cancelled). Many of the tribes considered that the British had injured them by taking the port from Sultan Mahsin, since there were now no customs dues for him to pay the tribes the annual stipend they used to receive from him.

The Fadhli Sultan threatened to attack Lahej unless he received his usual payment and Sultan Mahsin referred him to the British saying that he now had nothing left but the flesh on his bones. As a result of a message from Haines, the Fadhli Sultan agreed not to molest the Abdalis until orders had been received from the Government of India. 'We are like the dependents of Government,' wrote the Sultan, 'whose advice whether for peace or otherwise we are ready to accede to.'

Although Aden had been taken by assault, Haines considered that the Sultan of Lahej should be paid for the transfer and that he should continue payments to certain of the Arab chieftains on the same basis as he used to do out of the customs receipts; also the stipends should be given to certain tribes directly and not through the Abdali Sultan. Haines sent forward a list of these to Bombay but as it had to be approved by the Governor-General in Calcutta many weeks elapsed before a reply was received.

In the meantime the Sultan of Lahej was determined to speak with Haines. At 9 p.m. on March 8 a message came that he had arrived at Shaikh Othman with two hundred followers and wished to visit Aden with seventy armed men. Haines informed him of his rule that everyone visiting Aden had to leave their arms outside the gates, only chiefs being allowed to keep their daggers and swords. That was accepted and the Sultan was received with a three-gun salute at the entrance to the fortifications and was accorded a similar salute on reaching his palace, which had been prepared with new mats, carpets and pillows 'after the manner of the country'. They were supplied with provisions at Government expense during the week they were in Aden. The Sultan came straight to Haines to pay his respects and then went to his palace with his retinue of twenty-nine chiefs and forty-four followers, which included his powerful son-in-law, Sayyed Hussain Weiss, and his steward Abdulla Khatif. Haines returned the complimentary visit and then there was a meeting with the Sultan, his son-in-law and the steward, after which the Sultan asked to see Haines alone on the following day.

It was an interesting interview for by now Haines knew that the Sultan was prepared to lie and make promises if it would keep him out of trouble and that he wished to obtain as much as he could from the Government. It was probably true that he had not approved of the arrogant way in which his son Hamed and the Beduin had received Haines when he had arrived in the *Coote*, but he was seldom as blameless as he liked to make out. 'He declared himself', reported Haines to Bombay, 'quite innocent of any participation in the past treacherous and insulting behaviour towards us, and that the whole was the act of Beduin whom he could not control. I replied that what has passed was entirely their own fault. The wish of Government was for a kind and friendly transfer to have been made which would have been highly beneficial to them, and they left us the only one alternative which was to use force. We had now, however, come to a friendly understanding with each other and each had pledged his faith that no molestation should take place, which on our part had been strictly adhered to, but on theirs not so. British sentry guards had been fired at and Private Dickson, an unarmed European, had been murdered by a Beduin called Mohammed Dhubee; the Sultan swore that the murderer would be given up to the British and signed and put his seal on a statement to that effect. He then wanted to know whether the British would treat him with respect? Asked whether he had been satisfied by the manner in which he had been received, he said: "Oh! certainly you have honoured me and I have given you great expense and trouble, but what I mean is, will you take my house (i.e. family) and country under your protection. Will you treat me and my children as you do many of your Indian rajahs?

And will you grant me an annual stipend to support my dignity?" '
Haines said that these matters were being referred to the Government but he could assure the Sultan that it was now disposed to treat him with kindness and consideration. It was important, however, that he should control his people and punish those 'who attempted to molest the poor on the roads, and that he should caution all not to enter British ground with any other intention than that of barter and friendship. . . . This was all faithfully promised on his part and twenty-nine Chieftains who came with him were called in to witness the agreement.'*

Before leaving Aden the Sultan gave Haines a letter for the Government of Bombay in which he expressed himself with some dignity but little humility.[14] 'There is', he wrote, 'a good friendship between me and your Government. The former Governors showed me marked attention and respect which will be perceived on a reference to the letters formerly addressed to me.' He then admitted what he had previously denied: 'Commander Haines made his appearance here in January 1838, and an agreement was concluded between him and me. He then returned to Bombay whence he came here again on October 24 1838, and demanded my territory. The Beduin were apprised of the engagement between him and me, and they deprived me of my authority. What is done is gone by and Your Honour has been informed of it. I was distinguished by the Port of Aden, and I depended upon it for my support—my interests have been injured by the Beduin. It is needless to dwell upon this subject, for all events must take place as ordained by the Ruler of the Universe. . . . The object of this address is to announce to Your Honour my friendly disposition. Let it be known to you that the *chowkees* [boats] which I had at sea and five houses and godowns which belonged to me on the land were destroyed with a great many guns. . . . It is necessary that attention and respect should be manifested towards me and a stipend assigned for my maintenance in the same manner as in the case of the different Nawabs and Rajahs of India.

'It is my intention to enter into a defensive and offensive treaty with you and to conclude an arrangement under which we shall live

* This was not made into a formal agreement until June 18 1839, by which time the payment of stipends had been agreed; see p. 95.

with Commander Haines as a force assisting him on every occasion. I shall take upon myself the responsiblity of minor details and all affairs of an important nature should be conducted and disposed of by you. The Commander is a good-tempered gentleman and is well disposed to the poor and indigent. Mullah Jaffar is also a good man.'

After an exchange of presents the Sultan and his retinue left on March 14, being given the same salutes on his departure as on his arrival. He had presented to the Government six horses, three camels and a creese. Haines was a little worried that he had no presents ready to give, but he had purchased in the town two shawls and two pieces of silk and with money managed to make a gratifying return.

When information about the visit was received by the Government of Bombay it was agreed that Haines should be informed that his proceedings 'at the interview with the Chief of Aden [*sic*] may be entirely approved'. 'The Sultan, indeed', minuted the Governor, 'now acknowledges the justice of our proceedings and repents that the conduct of his son and of other evil counsellors should have interrupted the former negotiation. He says in his letter to Captain Haines, "the English and ourselves will be ever one and there is nothing bad. It was so when we met last year. I had no faithful adviser to show me the right path. I tell you now your advice will guide me. In the first place I want to be under the English flag and a servant of the Government. It was my son's fault, it was God's will. Today Aden is under the British and whatever is their will I am agreeable." '

The Governor was quite sure, however, that it would be impossible to share the Government in any way with the Sultan, for his conduct and that of his tribe 'proved that Aden could not be used with any safety as a coal station unless brought under our rule'. But he apparently hoped it would be possible to administer Aden without the presence of troops. 'Before the period could elapse for our troops to be withdrawn, it will be seen whether the benefits which the British rule confers in all countries subject to it will reconcile the Arabs of Aden to the change and ensure us peaceable possession of that important station.' [15]

Haines becomes ill with overwork

(March to August 1839)

It was not always easy, even for the optimistic Haines, to retain his
vision of a prosperous Aden in barren, hot and claustrophobic
Crater, menaced from inland by Beduin. One of the first things to
be done after looking to the fortifications was the enlargement of the
coal depôt at Ras Shaikh Ahmed near the Morbut headland and
Shaikh Tyeb Ibranjee was put in charge of the coaling arrangements.
As the population increased it was a little easier to find labour for
the coaling of ships. But there was a serious lack of any skilled
labour and Haines asked Bombay to send carpenters, blacksmiths
and builders, also fifty convicts to work on the roads and clear the
water-tanks. The wells produced good water but could only supply
a limited population and more needed to be drilled.

Local Arabs were appointed to deal with the customs and the
chief men of Aden continued to carry on the administration of the
bazaar and of trade from the interior, while disputes were referred
to the Cadi as they had been in the past, for their own Islamic laws

were retained. Sayyed Zain Aidrus, head of the most influential family in Aden, helped to maintain order and Mullah Jaffar played an important part in passing on Haines' orders. The military under Major Bailie dealt with their own problems but the commissariat officer often had to refer to the Political Agent for help to obtain supplies as Haines was in charge of the naval vessels, which on occasions had to be sent to Berbera, Mukalla or Mocha to buy what was required. Any dispute between an Arab and a European or native member of the garrison was referred to Haines; the different customs of Hindu, Parsee and Muslim sometimes led to disputes—over such things as drawing water and animal sacrifices.

A great deal of time was taken up by daily visits from members of neighbouring tribes and their many subdivisions to solicit peace and to satisfy their curiosity as to what was going on. All had to be given hospitality and there were lengthy discussions, though nothing could be settled as to whether or not anyone was to be paid a stipend until a reply was received from the Government.

Haines had no responsible European under him, though for a time Lieutenant Benjamin Hamilton, who had distinguished himself at Sira Island, came from the *Mahi* to help, and a clerk, Mr. Dark, was lent from the *Coote* to copy despatches. There were one or two Indian clerks to deal with the accounting of the large sums of money which were sent from Bombay in rupee notes and coin for the military, navy and civil establishment for which Haines was responsible. The Bombay Government had not planned a proper establishment for Aden and Haines had far too much work.

The day after the Sultan of Lahej and his retinue left Aden Haines collapsed with a severe fever and on March 19 was carried on board the *Coote*. Once on board the ship he began to feel better and was most anxious to return to Crater for there was no one to take over except Major Bailie, who knew nothing of the organisation of the town or the problem of dealing with the Arabs from the interior. But Haines had a severe relapse and the two surgeons, Malcolmson and Mackenzie, advised that he must have a month's sick leave, so a passage was booked for him to Bombay on board the steamship *Berenice*.

Haines handed over to Major Bailie but was so unwell that he could not put any instructions on paper. He had wanted to comment in writing on a long report from Captain Foster because he considered that too much ground had been ear-marked for the military cantonment, whereas nearly all the Crater plain would be required for a large mercantile town. He informed Bailie that four boxes containing 16,000 dollars for the use of the various departments were on board the *Coote*, as there was as yet no proper building ashore to serve as a Government Treasury.

To leave at such a critical moment when the town was being organised and the tribal chiefs were waiting in uncertainty distressed Haines and he wrote a number of letters to Bombay during his voyage in the *Berenice*. He considered that the recent visit of the Sultan of Lahej had been highly beneficial in keeping the roads clear of marauders, for Aden had begun to receive supplies of all kinds from the interior; he hoped that his sudden departure would not alarm them and cause dissension, '. . . at a time when I feel assured that my presence and the power I possess over the minds of the different chieftains materially tended to keep the tribes quiet'.[1]

The sea voyage to Bombay benefited his health; he was reunited with his wife and had the pleasure of seeing his son for the first time, but he had to spend many hours reporting to officials. The Government regretted that it had been deprived of his services 'at a period when they were so valuable', and when he said that he was prepared to return on the next steamer it was very gratified. 'The highly creditable manner in which Commander Haines has thus intimated his alacrity to return to his arduous and anxious duties after a severe illness within four days of reaching the Presidency,' wrote Governor James Farish, 'is deserving of the approbation of Government.' It would have been better if Haines had been allowed to complete his sick leave considering that he had had no leave for several years. But the Government did not think in those terms and considered that dealings with the chiefs and commercial arrangements would be best conducted by Commander Haines, 'who seems to have acquired the confidence of the chiefs and of the people and who has discharged his duties with ability'.[2]

The Government agreed that he should be given staff to copy letters and deal with the accounts but they were all junior and ill-paid clerks who could not take responsibility. It was not until six months later that a Political Assistant was appointed. Even so the

Government was disturbed by the expense of a developing Aden and made even more gloomy by Captain Foster's report, which showed that there was a great deal to do even to make the defences moderately safe against attacks from inland, without considering the seaward defences against ships of a Foreign Power.[3] Foster pointed out that Aden was entirely dependent on supplies of food and building material from outside: 'Of itself, Aden produces nothing, not a blade of grass nor a stick of firewood, nor do I think its water could be depended on for any length of time. It must, therefore, like Gibraltar, have its magazines of every description.'

The labourers were quite ignorant of every kind of work and their wages were exorbitant. To work on the field defences outside the Crater main gate the Jews demanded 16 *munsuries* a day and the Arabs or Somalis wanted 20 and they had to have water brought to them which was another heavy expense; he considered that was extravagant considering that 3 to 5 *munsuries* was all that was required for a man's food each day. Foster estimated that the cost of making good the defences, including cleaning the tanks to hold the rainwater, would be about 130,000 dollars (£26,000), and it would cost 200,000 dollars (£40,000) to complete the defences against a small force from the sea and double that to hold Aden against a large force.

The Bombay Government considered such expenses to be much too extravagant and decided that no money should be spent on protecting Aden from the sea; the cantonment planned for the troops was far larger than necessary 'out of all proportion to that left for the town', and there would be the added expense of paying for the houses which Captain Foster proposed to pull down. Members of the Council averted their eyes from the expenses of the fortifications and concentrated on the proposal in the report for an irregular cavalry unit and recommended that to the Governor-General.* But Lord Auckland had a cheaper and, as he thought, a better idea—to bring the Arabs into service as a horse patrol 'and thereby identifying them with ourselves in the preservation of

---

* Captain Foster also pointed out that mounted orderlies would be useful, since from headquarters in Crater it was two miles and six furlongs to the field-works, one mile and three furlongs to the Main Gate or Northern Pass and four miles and five furlongs to Steamer Point.

order . . . making it in their interest to aid us in the good work.' The mountain air of Simla stimulated the Governor-General to write another letter three days later (April 22 1839) enclosing a report which explained his views 'as to the fittest mode of dealing with barbarous tribes of plunderers like the Baluchis of Upper Sinde', five hundred of whom had been enlisted as mounted guards and escorts in the hope that they would be converted into 'friends and allies'.[4] Haines was able to make some use of the idea but what he really wanted were rough-riders from Poona and it turned out to be very difficult to get them.

Haines' return to Aden on May 20 1839 caused a sensation since the story had been spread to the interior that he had died. Sayyed Hussain Weiss had begun an intrigue which had led to war between the Abdalis and the Haushabis with the death of thirteen tribesmen. 'He is,' commented Haines, 'the most powerful man in the interior and the most difficult man to deal with.' Major Bailie had got into a muddle over letters from Consul Campbell about the Company's Agent at Mocha who was mistakenly dismissed. The Sultan of Lahej had openly expressed delight at the report of Haines' death and had started to organise a confederation of tribes to attack Aden, and he hoped to get better terms out of the Government with Haines out of the way. Numerous envoys arrived in Aden from the tribes to make sure that Haines really was alive. His return restored tranquillity.

At last a despatch came from Bombay with the approved list of stipends for rulers and chiefs. Formal agreements were to be drawn up under which those receiving stipends would affirm 'their allegiance to Government' and they would bind themselves to use their utmost exertions to keep the roads and communications with the interior secure 'and to aid with all their means the British authorities in Aden'.[5] The total amount of the stipends was not to be more than the 8,700 dollars (£1,740) which had been stated originally as the annual payment for Aden. Haines was advised in Aden that the wording of the document was severe and that he might have difficulty with some of the chiefs. But he was encouraged when a delegation arrived from Sultan Ali Ghalib of the neighbouring Yafa'i tribe and signed the treaty on June 8 1839, receiving their first six months' stipend. The Yafa'i was a large and powerful tribe and it was hoped that this would set an example for the others. A week later, indeed, Sayyed Hussain Weiss, acting as agent for the Haushabis, with a number of chieftains from that tribe, arrived; the bond was signed and payment was made of 314 German crowns for the first six months; on the departure of the delegation a present was made of 60 dollars to be divided between them. Delegations from other tribes arrived and then the Sultan of Lahej came with thirty followers and honour was paid in the same manner as when he visited Aden in March; now he was even more infirm having fallen off a camel and injured his leg. For three and a half hours Haines was closeted with him without making any headway. It took another two days to convince him that for the Government to grant a stipend was a generous act considering all that had passed. The Sultan returned to his argument that there should be some form of alliance, but both the Government of India and the Court of Directors in London had been emphatic that the British must not be embroiled in tribal affairs. Yet, surprisingly, the treaty signed by Haines and the Sultan on June 18 and later ratified by the Governor-General of India contained the sentence 'in case of any attacks upon Lahej or the Abdali tribe, or upon Aden or the British troops we (the sultan) and the British shall make a common cause'. It was an important point gained but the Sultan later lost it by his intransigent behaviour and the clause was not repeated in subsequent treaties. He accepted that he could not have control over the people of Aden and agreed that 'any of our subjects entering Aden must be obedient to the British laws, and any of the British subjects, when in Lahej, must submit to our authority'.

One clause of the treaty stated that Sultan Mahsin and his four sons—Sultan Hamed, Ali, Abdulla and Fadhl—agreed 'with a view to the tranquillity of their territory, the protection of the poor and weak, the security of their tribe and the safety of the roads, that the Sultan shall be answerable for any outrages committed by his people on the roads, and that they shall not offer any opposition to the British Government; that the interests of both shall be identical'. It was stated that the claim for stipends from the Fadhli, Yafa'i, Haushabi and Amiri tribes would be the responsibility of the British Government. Sultan Mahsin and his children 'in perpetuity and from generation to generation, would receive from the British Government a stipend of 6,500 dollars annually to begin from January/February 1839'. British territory consisted of the Peninsula of Aden as far as Khormaksar (excluding Little Aden) and beyond that the Abdali country was under the authority of the Sultan.[6]

The bond was signed on June 18 1839 with Mullah Jaffar, Hassan Abdulla Khatif and three others as witnesses. When the Sultan returned to Lahej he assembled all the chieftains of the Abdali tribe and read them the bond, making them presents which he said would be repeated annually, but he required of them a strict performance of the promises he had made. Haines had also arranged to pay 150 dollars a month to maintain a camel patrol of twenty men under Sultan Hamed to be stationed at Shaikh Othman to ensure the delivery of merchandise from the interior to Aden. He believed that to employ the elder son of the Sultan and make him answerable for security by the authority of his father would identify the tribes with the British 'and convince the minor chieftains that the friendship of the British is not deceitful nor contrary to the wish of their own chief'.

As some of the tribes were not to be paid by the Sultan of Lahej, but by the British Government, Haines needed agents who would maintain liaison with tribes such as the Haushabi, Amiri and Alawi. He decided to appoint Sayyed Hussain Weiss as British Agent at 60 dollars a month, in spite of the part he had played in the kidnapping conspiracy, for though he was a crafty intriguer he was a man of 'superior ability'. There were various supplies, such as millet, which certain tribes had been accustomed to receive from the Sultan and these were to be dealt with by Abdulla Khatif as a British Agent at 40 dollars a month. These arrangements were known to and accepted by the Sultan of Lahej.

The agents of the Fadhli Sultan arrived in Aden on July 8 to sign the bond and receive the stipend. Bonds had now been signed by all the principal tribes near Aden, but Haines did not want the Government of India to be too optimistic and wrote on July 11: 'It cannot be expected that our turbulent neighbours, who have been accustomed to look on robbery and murder as no great crime, will at once be convinced of their errors, or the advantage of leading a quiet, contented and civilised life, nor can they estimate British generosity and kindness in its true light. Time will teach them to esteem us, or at any rate to regard us as a people who have been the means of improving their minds and adding to their comforts, and as the dread of our encroaching further decreases, I hope their respect will increase.' [7]

Considerable interest in developments in Aden was shown by the tribes of the Yemen. On July 2 a letter was received from the chiefs of the powerful Dhu Mohammed and Dhu Hussain tribes offering their territories and forts to Britain, which was either a manoeuvre to escape from possible Egyptian domination or to try to ascertain British intentions. Haines replied that the Government had no wish to extend their territory and only wanted to be friends with their neighbours who could make use of Aden for trade. There was also a letter from the Imam of Sana asking if the British intended to march inland.

Haines was more than fully occupied. Besides constant visits from chieftains and letters which had to be written to the interior, there was the whole problem of British administration. This had to be fitted in with the existing Islamic Laws, which were maintained and dealt with by the Cadi, and with the systems of the Jewish, Hindu and Parsee communities. He had to consult with Major Bailie and the engineers as to where the troops were to have their cantonments so as not to interfere with the bazaar, and how to improve the water supply and the hospital. He was distressed at the lack of labour and the slowness of building which meant that the troops were still living in tents which were insupportable during daytime in the summer. In all his reports, however, Haines emphasised that Aden was healthy and that the climate was a good deal better than that of the Persian Gulf. Apart from problems with the chieftains and the military, ships arriving had to receive coal and supplies; mail and passengers had to be dealt with, also customs dues, which at first amounted to about 770 dollars for the quarter of April to June 1839. The accounting for the money always took up a great deal of time. Lacs of rupees (a lac was 100,000 rupees) arrived in large wooden boxes, and their contents had to be taken on trust for there was never time to count and there were the large dollars or German crowns and consignments of small coin. The equivalent of several thousands of pounds sterling were spent each month on the Army, Navy, Arab chiefs and the administration. An official was needed to deal with the

97

customs and the finance in general and Haines asked for a reliable man from the Bombay customs but the Government considered that this was 'premature'.

The Bombay administration was not always itself very efficient with its accounts and Haines pointed out, in August 1839, that he had received no pay or allowances since September 1838; when he did get his salary part of it was deducted to pay Major Bailie 'extra responsibility pay' for acting while he went on sick leave and Haines had to pay his passage from Aden to Bombay and back, though, after much argument, some reimbursement was made.

One of the more tiresome jobs that remained was the copying of letters, each one having to be done by hand and then checked and signed by Haines as being a true copy, and he had a constant battle to try to obtain writers. Instructions to commanders of Company ships, and any correspondence with the military, with Sultans and Chiefs or with the British Consul in Egypt had to be copied to Bombay. Besides those he had to send further copies in duplicate to the Court of Directors in London adding any special intelligence which would interest them.

The object, of course, was to have a speedy service of news about South Arabia, the Yemen and the activities of the Egyptians and of the French which was of interest to Lord Palmerston as well as to the Board of Control and the Court of Directors of the East India Company; but it must have led at times to some confusion. An important despatch from Haines would be likely to reach London direct before it reached the Governor-General of India via the Government of Bombay. This had one advantage, in that it ensured that the Bombay Government could not suppress a report which it did not care for.

It is surprising how much material, such as reports from lieutenants and other junior officers, were despatched to the Governor-General and to London. Everyone wrote at great length and, indeed, officials were anxious for information, including small picturesque details, for Africa and Arabia were new fields and most of the exploring was done by young service officers. Even the Governor-General and his staff in their more colourful India whether at Simla, Calcutta or Ootacamund—followed Haines' accounts of Arab intrigues or negotiations with Somali and Dankali tribes with interest.

The foot of the Main Pass out of Crater looking towards Aden village and the
  Eastern Harbour

The Sultan's Palace in Aden

Drawings by J. S. Rundle

The Straits of Bab-el-Mandeb, by Robert Moresby

The landscape inland from Aden

Haines becomes ill with overwork

Since one job followed another in quick succession and Haines tried to get his reports finished before the day was over, it was not always easy for him to follow correct procedure. In the heat of August Bombay drew his attention to the extreme inconvenience which arose from his mixing up numerous subjects in one communication. 'It is a standing rule observed in all government offices that each distinct subject should be laid before Government in a separate letter and to this rule you are requested strictly to conform in future.'[8]

Aden was not pleasant in the summer with the *khamseen* wind blowing dust everywhere; the worst time was between 10 a.m. and 5 p.m. when the *khamseen* wind frequently blew from the westward with strong hot gusts accompanied with clouds of dust, 'rendering it almost an impossibility in a closed room to write, for the paper becomes immediately covered'. During the summer of 1839 gusts from the mountain of Shamshan were so violent that only a few tents remained standing and the men of the Bombay Regiment were obliged to crowd into the hospital before it was completed. Suitable quarters were needed for the Political Agent since he had to receive Arab chieftains, foreign travellers, ships' captains and distinguished passengers on their way to and from Suez, but the Government replied that it would be better to wait and see 'whether Aden is likely to become a place of commercial importance or not'. Eventually Haines himself had to pay for a house to be built at Steamer Point to live in as Political Agent and entertain visitors.

There were not only difficulties with the Arabs of the interior and with the Bombay Government, which could be exasperating in the heat of Aden, but there were difficulties with the military. Relations had not been very good between Haines and Major Bailie, in command of the garrison, since the latter had found himself in a position of greater power when he was acting as Political Agent; Haines on return from sick leave had to unravel at least one unfortunate decision taken by Bailie, but there had been no open breach until an incident at the beginning of August 1839.

At the end of July a letter had been received from Sultan Ali Ghalib of the Yafa'i tribe, who had been the first to sign the bond and had remained faithful to it, stating that he was anxious to send his sons to Aden to visit the Political Agent. The sons arrived at Shaikh Othman with two hundred armed and forty unarmed followers.

Haines was particularly anxious to do them honour and sent Mullah Jaffar to explain that although the rule was that all arms had to be left at the Main Gate they could in this case come in with ten men retaining their arms; but Haines had omitted to inform Bailie that ten were to be allowed to bring in their arms. There was difficulty at the gate when the party arrived, as there was no British officer available, only an Indian N.C.O. who eventually agreed that Mullah Jaffar should take responsibility for allowing the entry of arms. Haines apologised by letter to Bailie for his omission but pointed out that there should be a British officer available at the Main Gate into Crater especially when Sultans were expected with a large retinue. Bailie disliked this criticism and wrote on August 7 to the Military Department in Bombay that he had considered Haines' letter 'such an improper one that it does not become me to answer it'. When the Government of Bombay received the full report, it informed the Commander of the Armed Forces, who had written to the Government strongly supporting Bailie, that the letter of August 7 to Haines was 'highly objectionable' and that command of the garrison was to be taken over from Major Bailie by someone with higher rank, and Lieutenant-Colonel Capon was appointed.[9]

It might have been critical for Haines since there were influential officers who wanted a military government of Aden, and were working towards that end. But the Bombay Government realised that it had an exceptional man as Political Agent. Haines was officially confirmed in his post as Political Agent in Aden in October 1839. 'His Lordship is happy to have this opportunity,' wrote the Governor-General, 'of expressing the satisfaction which he has derived from the able and judicious manner in which that officer has acquitted himself in the important and interesting duties which he has had to discharge since our occupation of Aden.'[10]

The first Arab attack

(September 1839 to March 1840)

Throughout September 1839, three months after the Sultan of Lahej had signed the bond, there was growing unrest in the interior largely prompted by the Sultan. Haines knew that four of the lesser Abdali chiefs were plundering the caravans and he wrote to tell Sultan Mahsin who they were, enclosing a copy of the bond to remind him of his obligations. The Sultan protested in a series of letters: 'between us there is a treaty of friendship and peace, nor is there anything bad; somebody tells you falsehoods and you believe them and think I wish for mischief. I have no faults but you wish to offend me.'

Haines stopped the pay of Sultan Hamed's mounted guards whereupon the members of the tribe who had carried out the raids were seized and the property returned. The pay for August was then sent with a letter to Sultan Hamed stating that it had been kept back to remind the guard that they could not be remiss in their duty with impunity, and Haines hoped that Hamed would be able to visit Aden where he would be very welcome. If Hamed had been able to come to Aden he might have been given sufficient encouragement to stand up to his father and to persuade him from embarking on his long feud against Haines which slowed down the development of trade with the interior and led to great loss of life among the Arabs.

Hamed liked being in command of the camel patrol, for he was brave and energetic and enjoyed the adventure of chasing after plunderers; it also gave him a position of which he was proud. It was this that roused the jealousy of his father, who disliked his son's independence, since Hamed was financed by the British and the old Sultan was fearful that he, the eldest son, might push him aside and rule the tribe.

This was revealed in two interesting letters written by Sultan Hamed which Haines managed to see and copy. The first one was to Abdulla Khatif, the steward, stating that Hamed had taken Haines' letter and the money for the guard to his father who had said: 'Very well but I am displeased about it. Today your father is Abdulla Khatif and Sayyed Hussain Weiss; they will be serviceable to you.' Hamed had replied that he commanded the guard by his father's orders and that he had been told to arrange everything as he liked. 'Why did you not show me the letter?' asked the Sultan. 'You and Haines Sahib are one, and wish to take the country from me.' Hamed's request to go to Aden was refused and he repeated that Hamed obeyed Sayyed Hussain Weiss and Abdulla Khatif. 'You are not mine nor am I yours. What is it to you if I am inclined to do anyone an injury or if fire is brought on my head?' 'Your language is unkind,' said Hamed. 'You were first willing I should go to Aden and now you are not . . . and I wish to preserve my character, while you are endeavouring to destroy it and by constantly playing we shall be lost. I have ordered the guards to Shaikh Othman and your will is your own.'

To Sayyed Hussain Weiss, Hamed related that the Sultan had sent a man to disperse the guards. 'I then went up to my father and told him my mind on his conduct. He called on God for me not to injure him. . . . He does not respect his character and injury will befall him. I again endeavoured to get the guard for the road and told him I wrote for the money and it was sent: what did he want? Did he want to fight and quarrel with the English, who have their eyes open and are watching? I told him I would have nothing to do with it, and whatever injury happened would fall on his head. It is now published to all that my father wishes to break his faith and injure the English. What can I do? What will happen? It depends on God for wc have no strength nor have we men. God is bringing all this on my father. I have no more to say.'[1] It was difficult for a son to disobey a father especially when he was Sultan of the tribe and besides had a remarkable capacity for making emotional appeals and an amazing persistence. Hamed's resistance was worn down and, when he was promised the leadership of the central division which was to attack Aden, he capitulated. He worked hard to bring in the tribes and his father was prepared to spend considerable sums of money to win over chiefs and to pay mercenaries.

It was agreed at a meeting at Lahej, on October 8, between the Abdali and Fadhli Sultans (the first time they had ever met) that 3,000 dollars (£600) were to be paid for the help of the Fadhli Sultan against the British and he received an advance payment of fifteen hundred dollars. For the plunder of Aden there would be a free for all but the guns and ammunition were to be kept for the Abdali Sultan, who told extravagant stories to the tribesmen about the wealth of the British and that all the buttons worn by the soldiers were of solid gold.

The Yafa'i Sultan kept to his bond and refused to have anything to do with the plan, while Sayyed Hussain Weiss and Abdulla Khatif negotiated to keep a number of tribes from the confederation planning to attack Aden. 'Thus', wrote Haines, 'by the exertion of a little secret influence many powerful tribes were prevented from rendering the Sultan any assistance and, on the contrary, evinced opposition to his treacherous designs by annoying him instead of those he wished to annoy.' He estimated that a gathering of all the tribes, fifteen to twenty thousand men, could have outnumbered the garrison by more than twenty to one.

From October 9 to 17 the Sultan and his son tried by every means to persuade Sayyed Hussain Weiss to join them. The Sultan with all his sons even made a pilgrimage to the Sayyed's house at Saffran and decapitated a bullock at his door in token of peace. The conference

The Rise of Captain Haines

lasted all night, Abdulla Khatif being the only other influential person present. To the credit of the British Agents they refused to agree to the plan and pointed out that the Sultan's family would be ruined. The Sultan was so overcome by the arguments that he determined to save himself, as he termed it, by forfeiting the 1,500 dollars or crowns advanced to the Fadhlis and redeeming his character by endeavouring to act in the future with good faith.

Following these new resolutions the Sultan wrote to Haines: 'we are, Sir, inclined to preserve our lives; we do not wish to injure you by fighting or treachery, nor will I listen to falsehoods for they create ill-will between us and I wait for you'. Haines replied that all was known about what had occurred at the various meetings: 'I have remained quiet for I have determined time and consequences should show you who were your friends.'

The Sultan was so easily influenced that it was not expected that he would keep to his good resolutions, and Haines was worried because the effectiveness of the garrison had been much reduced by deaths and sickness. Little had been done to improve the fortifications and the Turkish wall was not sufficient protection against a large body of men who could outflank it at low water. He again recommended that a body of thirty cavalry should be sent from Bombay; the horses obtainable in South Arabia were 'too small for large men heavily accoutred in a charge'. Before concluding this despatch of October 20 1839 Haines was in a position to report that the Fadhlis were uniting with the Abdalis to attack Aden at night when the moon was low at the beginning of November, and he urged that reinforcements be sent by the next transport; 'their early arrival may save serious loss of life, the Beduin of this part never having seen the facility with which the British musket and bayonet can be handled or the execution it can inflict'.

The Arabs advanced on November 11, about four thousand strong, attacking the British outposts at half-past four in the morning. They succeeded in forcing a passage over the Turkish wall and round the flanks but were then caught by fire from two sides and other groups of tribesmen who tried to reach them were repeatedly repulsed. When daylight came the Arabs were in full retreat in a dense mass filling the whole breadth of the isthmus, many of their camels loaded with dead and wounded.[2]

The first Arab attack

Haines referred in his report to 'the steady and determined resistance of a small force against superior numbers who came on most intrepidly'. Colonel Capon expressed astonishment that the Arabs were able to gain the most craggy heights unperceived and pass the defences. He congratulated the troops on their gallantry and in the promptness with which they manned the field-works, defeating an attempt 'which for secrecy and suddenness in the outset bears testimony to the hardihood and skill of the enemy.' He thanked Haines for the warnings of the impending attack, which some of the officers had not believed would take place, and he praised the valuable service of Lieutenant Benjamin Hamilton who brought the armed launch of the *Euphrates* close inshore in the Western or Back Bay, enfilading the Arabs from the flank. Both Haines and Capon regretted that they had not had a detachment of cavalry to follow up the Arabs in retreat. Over two hundred of the Arabs had been killed, eighty-eight were wounded and eight out of nine prisoners died of their wounds; one sultan and twenty-three shaikhs were among the killed.[3]

Haines was distressed at the injury done to the rising prosperity of Aden and angry with the Sultan of Lahej who had sent three thousand Abdalis to the attack and supplied both commissariat and money to hold the coalition together. The Sultan was not contrite at having broken his bond but wrote accusingly to Haines: 'You have thrown dust in our eyes. By kind words and gifts you have blinded us, the while you were throwing up forts to destroy us! Ah, Commander, pity me for it is the fault of my tribe. Forgive me and give me my pension'. It was not only the forts that gave the Company's troops an advantage, but also their discipline; their fire-power was not greatly superior at that time though it became so some years later.*

Sultan Mahsin wrote another letter on November 27 accusing

* The Arabs had mostly matchlocks which required a fuse to ignite the powder, but some had flint-locks; these could fire about five rounds a minute but were not always reliable. Some of the Company's troops had flint-locks but mostly they had percussion locks, which were reliable but had less fire-power as a cap had to be fitted which was not always easy in the heat of battle and the rounds fired per minute were about three. All were smooth-bore rifles. It was only at the time of the Crimean War when the Minié rifle had been introduced that the Company's fire-power in relation to the Arab's was much more effective.

the Fadhli Sultan of being responsible: 'There is no fault in me—
if people tell you falsehoods they will not affect me. If you are friends
and wish me to join you, we will march upon the Fadhli and either
the Fadhlis or myself shall die. I have no treachery and I remain
quiet because of my weakness. The fault is yours, you have not given
me strength. If you cannot stand upon what I advise, I will inform
all you have no strength.' 4 Haines replied very briefly that his letter
would be forwarded to the Governor of Bombay 'for after what has
happened I must wait for his direction'. The stipends for the Abdali
and Fadhli Sultans were stopped.

Haines had hoped that the severe losses suffered by the Arabs
would have intimidated them, but they believed that the British
were 'afraid to advance upon them, or to fight at all, except we have
the benefit of a stone wall before us'. The Sultan of Lahej arranged
a meeting with the Fadhli Sultan to plan to collect a greater force
and take their revenge at the beginning of December. The field-
works were strengthened with guns taken from the vessels of war
and Haines sent thirteen Arab boats to various ports to obtain
supplies.

The Bombay Government was seriously worried by these reports
and immediately ordered that reinforcements—the 10th Regiment
of Native Infantry—were to be sent to Aden with the least possible
delay. It was prepared to sanction 'any deviation from their instructions', which the Commander of the Forces, the Military
Board, the Commissary General and the Superintendent of the
Navy might consider desirable in sending 'the greatest relief at
the shortest period'. But the Government had changed its mind
about the need for a detachment of horse, fearing that it might
encourage Haines to advance—'the less you have to do with the
interior the better'. A tribute was paid to the high courage
and firmness displayed and to the judicious arrangements adopted
by Haines and Capon. It was also announced that an assistant
to the Political Agent, Lieutenant Griffith Jenkins, had been
appointed to take charge of the harbour, coal stores, depot ship,
customs, police and post office and any other duties considered
necessary. 5

Another council of war was held between the Fadhli and Abdali
tribes on December 1 at a place five miles distant from the field-

works, when it was decided that the second attack should be deferred until after the Ramadan fast in a week's time, on the advice of the Fadhli Sultan. He had suffered from a fall when his favourite horse had been shot from under him while leading one of the divisions in the attack on Aden. The Fadhli Sultan's first friendliness to Haines had vanished and he sent a proclamation to each of the principal Arabs in Aden: 'That man, that *kaffir*, the enemy of Mahommed and of all Mahommedans, I will, if it please God, fight with him, until I see to whom God gives strength, for it depends on Him. I have stopped all the roads to Aden, nothing can enter. If you wish to come out, God's land is large.'[6]

Letters had been sent by the Sultan of Lahej to a number of tribes urging them to join in a second attack but they had all refused. Meanwhile, Haines despatched letters to the chieftains on the coast asking them to bring in supplies, so that Aden was well provisioned although only a few caravans were getting through as a result of the orders given by the two Sultans. He also sent the Company's brig *Euphrates* to blockade Shuqra, which was the main port of supply for the Fadhli tribe, in the hope that this would divert the tribe from maintaining their control of the roads to Aden. The Sultan of Lahej hoped to make it so difficult for the British that they would quit Aden in disgust 'and leave it to his quiet possession in its improved and increased state,' wrote Haines. In the meantime the Sultan had been sending his valuables inland as he feared the British would attack Lahej.

The arrival of reinforcements from Bombay on December 12 and signs of a quarrel developing between the Abdali and Fahdli tribes reassured Haines who believed that a second attack would be delayed, 'but they will plunder, fight and slay each other'.

On December 27 Sayyed Hussain Weiss and Abdulla Khatif came to Aden with messages from the Sultan of Lahej to try to convince Haines that he was innocent of any attack or plunder, but when letters were produced proving the Sultan's complicity they acknowledged the Sultan to be guilty and said that he threw himself on the mercy of the British Government and wished the previous treaty to be agreed upon and that he would never offend again. Haines replied that the Sultan with his children must come to Aden to ask forgiveness and leave two of his sons as hostages for his future conduct; until that were done no stipend would be paid.[7]

Sultan Mahsin was furious at the conditions imposed and determined not to send any of his sons as hostages. 'Why', he told Sayyed Hussain Weiss, 'if my sons are in Aden I can never do as I like again.' When he found that Haines would not modify his demands, he decided that Abdulla Khatif had been treacherous and was taking the side of the British. He ordered that he should be waylaid and murdered on the way home, but Haines learned of the plot and kept Abdulla Khatif in Aden until he could arrange for his safe return to Lahej. When the Sultan found that he could not bargain with Haines he tried to get out of his difficulty in another way. After several councils were held in Lahej with his sons and relatives, in January 1840, it was announced that Sultan Mahsin was abdicating because of his age and that his eldest son, Hamed, was elected to succeed him.

It seemed at first that Sultan Hamed had decided to change tribal policy. He assembled the chiefs of the various subdivisions of the Abdali tribe and announced that all those who committed murders and thefts would be punished and that the roads were to be kept open; he denounced his father's policy and declared that he would pursue an opposite course and solicit pardon from the British and propose an alliance with them. However genuine may have been Sultan Hamed's intention to pursue this new policy, it was not easy for him since he had the Fadhlis to reckon with and their Sultan had no intention of letting the Abdalis break away from the confederation.

On January 16 Haines received a letter from Sultan Hamed: 'I understand that there are none like the English and I do not wish to be at enmity with them. All that my father did before me was bad. I wish only for good. I have been on the throne only eight days. The Fadhlis plunder, murder and commit all kinds of injury to my subjects. . . . Nothing can be arranged between us until the Fadhlis are put down. How can I come to you while the Fadhlis are flying about? I am a sepoy, an English sepoy and you will find nothing bad in me. I have now a little sense. . . . The Government can if they wish march inland. I should be delighted to attack the Fadhli on one side, while you do on the other. Let me know the day and how you march.'[8]

Haines was not entirely satisfied by the letter, since it amounted to little more than a repeat of the demand made by the old Sultan that they should combine to attack the Fadhlis. He replied that he had already laid down the only way that peace could be obtained and was not prepared to modify it. Whatever Hamed might say, Haines knew that the old Sultan intended to direct proceedings and, indeed, it was not long before he again officially took control.

Messengers had passed between Sultan Mahsin of Lahej and Ibrahim Pasha the Egyptian General in Yemen, and the neighbouring tribes were 'buoyed up by hopes of assistance from Mohammed Ali Pasha of Egypt'. Haines knew that the Sultan had sent a request for guns, money and soldiers and that Ibrahim Pasha had replied that he could not give them without orders from Mohammed Ali Pasha, but he would write to him and suggested that Sultan Mahsin should do so too; in the meantime 'behave yourself as a man and protect your territory'. While Mohammed Ali Pasha did not want to clash with the British by sending Egyptian troops to attack Aden, he was doing what he could to persuade others to do the work for him.

In November, 1839, Haines had received a letter from the British Agent in Mocha, Hajji Abdulla Roussoul, a merchant of high standing whose reports had always proved reliable. The Imam of Sana was nervous that the Egyptians would take his whole country from him and had sent an envoy to Mohammed Ali Pasha, to try to come to a satisfactory arrangement. Mohammed Ali replied that he was willing secretly to assist the Imam of Sana with money, men and supplies, and would return his conquered territory if the Imam would drive the English from Aden. 'I am not strong enough to fight against the English, nor is it my wish to do so,' replied the Imam, but he would hand over his country if he were granted enough money, retained his private property and the Zaidee tribes remained under his control.[9]

Haines considered that these intrigues accounted for 'the disturbed state of the interior and the insults lately offered to the British' and he therefore passed on the information to the new British Consul-General in Egypt,[10] Colonel Hodges, who asked for an appointment with Mohammed Ali Pasha as soon as he received the letter to demand an explanation. According to Hodges' account, which he sent to Lord Palmerston the same day, February 22 1840, he spoke a good deal more brusquely to the Pasha than Campbell had been accustomed to do and was prepared to give less credence to the Pasha's statements.

It was a period of great tension between Britain and Egypt and also between Britain and France, who was supporting the Egyptian Viceroy in his bid to throw off his allegiance to the Ottoman Sultan. Ever since the Ottoman army had been routed by the Egyptians at Nezib in Syria in June 1839, and the Turkish admiral had sailed to Alexandria to hand over the Turkish fleet, the Pasha had considered himself to be in a strong position.

Colonel Hodges was convinced that the Pasha's intentions were 'to cause us as much annoyance and do as much injury as he can; it remains with H.M.G. to check him in his daring career or to crush him before he has time to carry his schemes of ambition into execution'. That had not been Campbell's opinion, but as Hodges' views more nearly resembled those of Lord Palmerston, Campbell had been removed. The Consul used the information he had received from Haines to force the Pasha to admit, after some denials, that he had sent an envoy to the Imam of Sana with a proposal that he should cede the Yemen to Egypt in return for a yearly allowance, but Mohammed Ali Pasha denied making any proposals regarding Aden.[11].

Messages were also being sent to London from British representatives about Mohammed Ali's ambitions elsewhere. The Sultan of Muscat, Sayyed Said, was apprehensive that the Egyptians would advance into his territory and argued that to check them the British Government should take possession of the island of Bahrain and place a garrison in the fort of Boraimi. Captain Hennell, the East India Company representative in the Persian Gulf, visited Boraimi where the chiefs stated that they were determined to maintain their independence against the Egyptians; 'as long as Boraimi can be kept out of the possession of Khurshid Pasha's agents', he reported to London, 'the Egyptian influence will never be established in Oman.'[12]

'There is no doubt,' wrote Haines to Bombay (February 1 1840) referring to encouragement given to the neighbouring tribes by the Egyptians, 'that we have secret and powerful enemies who are assisting in the attempt to dislodge us from our position here, but who are sufficiently guarded in their conduct to suggest their advice verbally, so that no written proof may hereafter appear in testimony against them.

'The apparent submission with which we endure the almost daily insults of the two tribes [Fadhli and Abdali], whom we could annihilate in a week, is likely to have a bad effect upon the people of the whole line of the Arabian and African coast, who are inclined to think that our peacefulness evinces a want of courage or weakness, and they are not yet sufficiently well acquainted with the British character to ascribe any other motive to our conduct; it is next to impossible to make a Beduin enter into our views unless self-aggrandisement is the consequence.'

Haines was of the opinion that peace could only be restored if the British sent an expedition against Lahej. He set out a plan as to how many troops would be required, the route they would take and when the troops should leave Aden for inland; a march on Lahej would be 'the only method by which the British name will be respected and Aden can recover the celebrity from which it has fallen as an important and invaluable trading port'.

Haines knew very well that this would not be a popular suggestion but he had come to the conclusion that argument had no effect on the Arab and he feared that disorders would prevent the growth of Aden, or that the Government would decide it was too expensive to keep a garrison there in such circumstances. He was being kept 'perpetually employed and disappointed', he wrote to the Secret Committee in London on February 7 1840, as a result of the difficulties experienced with the Beduin tribes and the intrigues of the Egyptians; 'the Beduin appear to entertain too large a notion of Mohammed Ali's power to act, imagining him to be an all victorious conqueror'. There was a report that two thousand more Egyptian troops were being sent into Yemen from the northern provinces of Arabia and the Beduin were expecting help from them. They were deceived not only by the idea of an Egyptian alliance but by the propaganda that 'as Christians we have neither influence or credit with Mahommedans and they are thus deluded people borne on from one extravagance to another. Since 1835 I have been fully aware that Mohammed Ali looked forward to the conquest of Aden as a certain and desirable event, for in reply to my official report that the British had been successful on this point he wrote: "I have been striving years for the possession of Yemen, but in one day you have taken its eye and rendered it useless to me".'[13]

At the beginning of March 1840, Haines received a message from the Imam of Sana which confirmed the earlier stories about Egyptian intrigues. Mohammed Ali Pasha had, indeed, sent an envoy with a treaty in which it was stated that the Commander was to be removed from Aden, that Sana and the adjacent country was to be made available to the Egyptians and all the coffee was to be sent to Hodeida for Mohammed Ali Pasha. If the Imam did not remove the British from Aden then the Egyptians would. No agreement had been reached and the Imam would prefer, he said, to make an agreement with the British rather than with the Egyptians. Haines' orders from Government were that he must be non-committal.

The Government of India, during these years that the Imam of Sana sent repeated envoys to Aden, lost a great opportunity to get on to friendly terms with the lawful ruler of the Yemen. Haines was very disappointed at the Government's attitude, for Aden was the 'Eye of the Yemen', its natural port, and, he wrote, 'if once a safe communication for commerce be opened with Sana, Aden would flourish'. When the Imam asked for a British officer from Aden to remain at Sana as a Political Resident, this valuable opportunity was refused by the Government of India. 'Although French and German travellers', wrote Haines, 'are annually found in the interior of the Yemen with Jews from Vienna and Poland travelling avowedly for information, still of the British nation which holds one of their most important sea-ports, the people are all ignorant.'[14]

12

Civil or military government?

(September 1839 to March 1840)

At a time when there were constant threats of attack from Arab tribesmen it was essential that there should be a single authority and that this should be vested in the Political Agent. Haines by his ability, determination and tact had shown himself to be completely in command of the situation in Aden and everyone deferred to him. He made use of the Arab leaders in Aden for the administration of the town, allowing them to follow their own system, and for security he employed a force of Mahommedan policemen trained in Bombay. The Commander of the garrison had responsibility only for his troops and when Haines advised him that an attack was impending he made his dispositions. If the civilian population in Aden, which was nearly five thousand by the beginning of 1840, became discontented with the way that Aden was administered the garrison would have been endangered, for the Sultan of Lahej was always trying to stir up the Arab population against the English. 'If there should be a rising among the inhabitants,' Captain Foster had reported, 'or traitors could by any means get admission, the consequences must inevitably be most disastrous and fatal.'

The Military Department in Bombay and the Government were alarmed at this possibility. There had also been a great deal of correspondence with Haines over the control of the manufacture in Aden of alcohol and of its import from India. 'Perhaps there is no way in which treachery and cunning could combine,' wrote the Governor, 'than by providing the means of gratuitously intoxicating our soldiers when an attack is to be made.' Soldiers had come back to barracks drunk from the fieldworks where they had taken alcohol to while away the time of guard duty. The garrison commander had naturally been worried about this and wanted tighter control over the sale of alcohol in Aden; he also objected to tribesmen from the interior—many of whom could be spies—having free access to the town especially during periods of alert; but Haines considered that the best way of controlling the sale of alcohol and the entry of spies was through his civil police force and by encouraging the Arabs themselves to report. He was not prepared to have free access stopped for it would have destroyed the whole conception of Aden as a prosperous trading port. It was often from the visiting tribesmen that he learned, through his agents in the town, what was being said and planned in the interior; also when spies were sent in to the town Haines was usually informed and he was able to find out who in Aden was giving them information.

The military never fully understood the extent of Haines' intelligence service both outside and inside Aden, and they tended to underestimate the Arab love of, and capacity for, intrigue. Ever since he had been temporarily in charge as Acting Political Agent, Major Bailie had been attracted by the idea of doing a little intelligence work on his own, and there were a few young officers such as Lieutenant Rigby,* who knew Arabic and liked to have meetings with the leading Arab merchants and religious leaders of Aden.

---

* Lieutenant C. P. Rigby of the 16th Regiment of Native Infantry, was a remarkable linguist, and spoke Arabic well; he also wrote an 'Outline of the Somali Language, with Vocabulary', which was issued in the *Transactions of the Geographical Society of Bombay*, the first study that was published. He was later British Consul-General in Zanzibar, and played a part, on the side of John Hanning Speke, in the controversy with Richard Burton over the source of the White Nile.

Captain Hobson, the Staff Officer, and a number of others were opposed to Haines because they considered that he had too much power for a naval officer—the Army looked down on the Navy—and that he was too dictatorial. A clique of officers round Bailie liked to feel that they had their fingers on the pulse of Arab affairs. Arabs who had grievances or stories to tell against Haines or Mullah Jaffar were not turned away, as they should have been.

None of this would have mattered had it not been for a serious quarrel which developed between Haines and Colonel Capon which was entirely the fault of the Military Department of Bombay, and could have endangered the safety of the garrison. The Military Department had never been interested in the idea of Aden as a trading port and regarded it merely as a military post which should be commanded by the Army; after the Arab attack, it was taken for granted by the Army that the Aden Peninsula was under martial law. The Bombay Government had resisted these pressures from the military and had caused considerable annoyance when it proclaimed its trust in Haines by refusing to accept the military arguments in support of Major Bailie in the recent quarrel.

On the appointment of Colonel Capon to Aden in September 1839, the Military Department stole a march on the Government; either by design or by mistake he was appointed to the command of Aden, and not, as he should have been, to the command of the garrison. Haines was not informed of the order issued by the Commander of the Forces at the Presidency of Bombay, and the Government of Bombay was not apparently aware that it had been issued; nor did they know that the Military had issued an order that Aden was under martial law.

It took six months for the Government of Bombay to realise what had happened and to end the confusion; during that time the inevitable quarrel developed in Aden on the important question as to who was in control. Colonel Capon, as a result of the instructions he had received, considered that he was responsible for security throughout the area. When a Somali was discovered in Aden with some spear-heads Capon decided that everyone in Aden must be disarmed, and he instructed Haines, as Political Agent, to issue a proclamation that any civilian found hiding arms would be tried by court-martial. Haines was startled that Colonel Capon should believe that he had the right to assume powers which belonged to the Political Agent and refused to publish any such proclamation. The Colonel then issued an ultimatum that he would publish it himself if Haines did not comply, but finding Haines angry and adamant he left the matter in abeyance, and took up the question of controlling liquor supplies by having the shops searched. No liquor was found but the Colonel maintained a military guard in the bazaar to keep a watch.[1]

The townspeople protested angrily to Haines that their rights were being invaded. 'It has already proved most injurious to the welfare of Aden and to the feelings of the people', wrote Haines. 'The Arabs in making their complaints to me exclaim: "If sir, we are to be treated this way today, God only knows what will be the next step." . . . Rash or severe military measures are in my opinion highly objectionable to well conducted people of the town whom the Civil Police find no difficulty in controlling.' The quarrel weakened the British position and the Sultans at Lahej, delighted by the news, exclaimed: 'Now for Aden!'

Colonel Capon saw the matter from a different angle. Security was, he considered, a military affair and the army lines were so close to the bazaar that he found it impossible to preserve proper discipline while Haines' authority was reckoned 'paramount'; a Commanding Officer's duty was not merely to dispose of his men when the signal of alarm was sounded but also to superintend their conduct when off duty. He considered that the Political Agent and all the townspeople were 'residents of a garrisoned fort' and that it was under siege; 'the enemy is only at a few miles distance, eager to take advantage of the least laxity of vigilance to slaughter everyone connected with the British'. The safety of the fortress, which included the whole area, was his business; 'your knowledge of naval discipline', the Colonel wrote to Haines, 'will lead you to admit that two persons cannot exercise the authority, and in no fort or cantonment in India will it be found that civil and military authority have been attempted to be combined as at Aden'. He hoped that by avoiding any insistence on 'rights' they might be able to act in unison, '. . . notwithstanding the difficult situation in which Government has placed both of us'.

Haines was not prepared to make any such compromise. He

considered that most governments were conducted in much the same manner as at Aden and saw no difficulty in carrying out the system under his control which had worked satisfactorily. The correspondence with Capon had revealed other matters which shocked Haines; Major Bailie, for instance, had received letters from Arab Chiefs in the interior without informing Haines; nor had he been told that a committee of officers had listened to complaints against him as Political Agent from Sayyed Alawi Aidrus who had been advised to appeal to the Government of Bombay, in spite of the fact that Haines had warned Capon that the young Sayyed had been acting treacherously in intriguing with the Sultan of Lahej. Haines was also told for the first time that Capon had received a number of criticisms from Arabs, as had his officers, of Mullah Jaffar. 'From what I hear daily,' wrote Colonel Capon, 'I much doubt whether your native assistant can always be trusted, when his prejudices may be concerned, as a safe organ of communication of your intentions and wishes to the people'; he had heard from almost every officer that the inhabitants of the town were under the control of Mullah Jaffar more than was consistent with the interests of government, that he was in the habit of speaking in the bazaar and coffee-shops in a derogatory way of the Sultan of Lahej from whom he had purchased a boat of which five or six thousand rupees were unpaid and that in consequence it was in Mullah Jaffar's interest that an open rupture should exist between the Sultan and the British. These were very serious charges and Haines held a meeting of townspeople to discuss them and all said, as might have been expected, that they held a high opinion of Mullah Jaffar.

When all this correspondence reached the Government of Bombay it was completely taken by surprise. Haines was informed in a letter of March 23 1840 that the order imposing military law had been cancelled and that new instructions had been issued making it clear that Colonel Capon was only in command of the garrison. The Government regretted the interference by the military in the civil and political authority vested in him by Government; it confirmed 'the assurance given to the inhabitants that they would be governed according to their own laws and usages' under Haines' authority, and there was no intention of reversing the system 'which has hitherto so beneficially prevailed for the government of the inhabitants of

Aden'. In some of the correspondence, however, Haines had deviated 'from the usual official courtesy' and it was considered that Colonel Capon's attitude had arisen from the incorrect wording of the original order announcing his appointment. All the same a severe letter was written to the unfortunate Colonel, who was told that 'serious detriment' was likely to arise if the military authority at Aden were to be vested with sole power of control; 'you are required not to interfere in any way with the inhabitants of the town and bazaar of Aden, except through representations to the Political Agent and to confine for the future your authority to the troops and followers comprising the garrison of Aden'. He was told that the tone of his letters to the Political Agent was 'unwarrantable', especially in assuming the right to interfere with the Native Assistant Mullah Jaffar, and attending to accusations against that individual from parties not under his authority: it was also objectionable that either he or the officers under his command should hold correspondence with the chiefs of the interior or with influential residents of Aden.

The Military had lost that round in the battle to control Aden. Haines had been confirmed in his post and was to be promoted Captain in October 1841.

13

Two more Arab attacks

(March to December 1840)

At the beginning of March 1840 Haines learned that there was a carefully laid plot by the Abdalis and Fadhli Sultans to have himself and Mullah Jaffar murdered. Haines was to be invited by a Sayyed to an important meeting outside the fieldworks on the pretence of concluding an unconditional treaty of peace and both were to be struck down while the conditions were being argued. On March 6, two days after this information had been received, the Sayyed appeared and 'with the kindest professions of friendship' requested Haines to meet a distinguished gathering to conclude peace. Haines declined stating that the only terms of peace were a demand for pardon and the delivering up of the two hostages as a surety.

As that plan had failed another attempt was to be made a few days later. Haines learned that the Fadhlis intended to send in a delegation with an escort and there would be an attempt to murder him in his office; they expected at least half the escort to be killed. A Fadhli Sultan arrived to ask Haines if he were prepared to receive a delegation and he agreed very readily provided the proposed terms of peace were brought. The delegation, however, never came as it was learned that Haines was prepared.

At the same time Sultan Mahsin was trying to form another

confederation of tribes to attack Aden and Haines had some difficulty in countering this, but the Yafa'i remained true to their bond as did the Haushabi Chief who refused to permit any of the tribes, who were joining the confederation, to pass through his territory. That put an end to the scheme and, as generally happened when the Abdali plans were overthrown, the Sultan wrote a series of friendly letters, full of hypocrisy; but they were clever, rather endearing letters aimed at undermining Haines' position with the Government of Bombay and did eventually persuade it that Haines was being over-suspicious of the Sultan. The Sultan addressed Haines as 'his friend, his great friend', and that had as much significance as 'your most loving friends' which was the way that the Court of Directors always concluded their letters.

'Come Commander,' he wrote at the beginning of March 1840, 'you know I have plenty of enemies and that all play with me, my own tribe abuse me. I have endeavoured to discover any faults on my side but cannot; whatever you hear you believe, you never endeavour to find out whether their words are truth. I have no deceit; do you wish to remove me by force without fault. You are for nothing and no one. I have plenty to say, the paper would not hold it. Now bring your heart to friendship for Government would not wish to injure me.'

Haines replied that the Government did not wish to injure him nor to extend its territory by one inch and if he wanted friendship he must do as had been demanded.

'Why should I write so that all should know I have committed error,' replied the Sultan, 'that both Arab and English should think I have done wrong and that it should reach Government? I am innocent with the Government. You do not wish me to come and want my children; you like to bring falsehoods upon me and to keep me at war. I have your letters and you have mine, which will show I wish to come and you are not willing. If the Government hear the lies that are brought upon me and that you do not listen to me, it will see who tells falsehoods, they will know.'

Hamed, in contrast wrote to Haines: 'I am well aware that you never wish to injure anybody. My father is superannuated and has lost his right senses.'

Haines remained convinced that a short military action against

Lahej was the only way to achieve peace. After further discussion
with Capon, he again informed Bombay of the number of troops
and guns required. His account of the route from Aden to Lahej
shows little change today except that the 'jungle' has disappeared,
and Shaikh Othman has developed into a large suburb.[1] But before
he had finished his plans for sending cavalry, artillery and infantry
rattling along the road to Lahej, Bombay had already written tartly
to stop any such adventure.

'If Aden cannot be made a valuable acquisition without entering
into aggressive warfare with the Arab chiefs in the interior, the sooner
the place is abandoned, or surrendered for a consideration, the
better.' The concluding sentence must have made Haines at least
raise his eyebrows; 'the Governor-in-Council requests that you will
be careful to signally punish any attack on Aden'.[2] 'One would on no
account authorise any forward movement of a military nature against
Lahej,' confirmed the Governor-General.[3]

As the troops were not allowed to advance they had to wait
patiently for the next attack which Haines knew would not be long
delayed. He had obtained copies of three 'secret' letters written by
the Fadhli Sultan to his father-in-law, Ali Ghalib, Sultan of the
Yafa'i, who passed them to Haines, for he had remained loyal to his
agreement. The Fadhli Sultan was trying to stir up a *jehad*, or holy
war, for, he argued, Haines intended to bring the Arab tribes under
his subjection and reduce the power of Islam; therefore they had to
fight the *kaffirs*, and those who lost their lives in the battle 'shall be
rewarded by our Prophet Mahommed in the next world'. The
Abdalis had agreed not to allow anyone to go to Aden, and those
that acted contrary to this order would be liable to lose their property
and their life; 'for all this Sultan Mahsin is to be blamed,' wrote the
Fadhli Sultan, 'for if he had not consented to the proposals made
to him by that foreigner, we Arabs should not have been under
any necessity to think of this and moreover no tribes opposed
them in entering and taking possession of Aden. Come let us join
together and fight with the foreigner and regain our country from
them.'[4]

Information continued to come in about Arab plans for the attack
from Abdulla Khatif and others. A meeting was held near Lahej on
May 19 between the Fadhli and Abdali chiefs who decided that the

attack should be on May 21 with the Abdalis leading. Haines at once informed Capon of the plan. Owing to the shortage of naval officers Haines took command of the gunboats in the Western Bay while his Political Assistant, Lieutenant Jenkins, was in command of the boats in the Eastern Bay to protect both flanks of the Turkish wall. Although the small military and naval force was waiting for the attack on the night of May 20–21 there was no indication of the Arabs' approach until the men in one of the gunboats saw them at the extreme left flank of the Turkish wall, 'crossing over in immense parties towards the north end of Swaya Island making directly for the mountain of Haddeed,' wrote Haines, who had a close view of the battle from his gunboat as he commanded the operation there.

The alarm had been given immediately when the Arabs were seen just before dawn and it was estimated that there were over four thousand of them 'continuing on through the midst of a heavy fire from the left field-work and gunboat'. Haines added: 'I distinctly heard their orders, and the cry "Come on for Aden", merging with the horrible yell of the war whoop, appeared to have an animating effect upon the Beduin who certainly behaved with great boldness and perseverance.'[5]

The Arabs succeeded in occupying Jebel Hadeed from which they fired into the fort and boats below, while others plundered the officers' tents near the left field-work. 'An incessant fire was kept up by the European and Native troops in the field-work,' reported Haines, 'and returned in pretty good order by the Beduin until about 3-45 a.m. when the Beduin were driven from their position and recalled by those on the outside and the combat suddenly terminated.' He praised the admirable manner in which the officers in the field-work had carried out the operation and the steady conduct of the men. At the same time the officer commanding at the Turkish wall regretted 'the facility with which the enemy can get possession of the heights in our rear by passing at a short distance round the left field-works at low tide and the impossibility of our seeing them on a dark night'.

There was some difference of opinion as to who had first sounded the alarm. Lieutenant Jenkins stated that the first alarm had been given from the gunboats on the left flank and they had at once opened fire. Colonel Capon, however, reported that the navy had been slow in giving a warning stating, incorrectly, that Captain Haines had left the gunboat on the western flank before the operation and that probably on his departure 'the usual vigilance on board was relaxed'.

The old rivalry between army and navy was revived as a result of a not very successful defence. Someone in Aden wrote an anonymous and malicious letter which was published in the *Bombay Courier* stating that Captain Haines did not, as he made out, command one of the gunboats, but was 'snugly on board the *Charger* three miles off' and came to the scene of action when all was over. It was answered in the newspaper by Captain McQueen, who was present on the merchant ship *Mary Mitcheson*. He stated that Haines was present directing the gunboats which played a very effective part in the battle.[6]

The loss among the Arabs was heavy; eighteen were known to have been killed, including one of the sultans, and sixteen wounded had been carried away under fire during the action. 'The successful foray of our enemies,' reported Haines to Bombay 'so far as their securing the baggage of the officers and men and other articles belonging to the left field-work, has caused great rejoicing inland; they consider it a victory, appearing perfectly indifferent to their own loss. The articles, which seem quite new to them, are exhibited as trophies and tales of extraordinary exaggeration are related (of course favourable to themselves) in order to augment the universal excitement; a few dollars which they had found in the boxes are magnified into many thousands to feed the disappointment and credulity of those who refused to join in the last attack and incite them to co-operate in the one now projecting.'

The Arabs may have rejoiced over the baggage captured but there was great distress at the heavy losses in men and the Fadhli Sultan was especially bitter at his losses. He considered they were largely due to a failure of the Abdali to support his attack and that there had been treachery. There was great emotion and a terrible murder was committed.

The Fadhli Sultan had called a meeting near Lahej with members of the Abdali ruling family and displayed captured letters, written to Haines by Abdulla Khatif and Sayyed Hussain Weiss, warning of the attack of May 21. It was decided that both British Agents should be killed. The Sayyed saved his life by calling on the Haushabi tribe to send a guard to protect him in his castle at Saffran; Abdulla Khatif was twice stabbed in Lahej as he was leaving the mosque but escaped and was hidden by a relative while the Sultan's family and their slaves plundered his sixteen houses, stripped the women of their ornaments and imprisoned his sons and wives.

On an oath of protection and safe conduct to Haushabi territory, Abdulla Khatif eventually came out of hiding but fell into an ambush laid by Sultan Hamed who struck the first blow, accusing him of being responsible for the deaths of many chiefs and Mahommedans and the slaves then stabbed him to death. Haines received a terrible account of his end. The mangled body was dragged by the head to the door of the Sultan's palace, where it was cut up and the pieces, by Sultan Hamed's order, were about to be cast to the dogs, when some Sayyeds intervened 'and this last horrible deed was prevented and the parts then collected and buried in a cloth'. 'He was firm and noble to a degree,' wrote Haines, 'and after accepting service from me, could not be prevailed upon, even by the fear of death, to divulge my secrets.'[7] There was a ruthlessness and brutality reminiscent of mediaeval England and Haines was convinced that the inhabitants of Aden would have been 'cut to pieces if either of the Arab attacks had succeeded'. In spite of the earlier rebuff given by the Bombay Government, he again recommended military action against Lahej: 'no other course of proceeding that can be adopted will tranquillise the country or remove the impression that our strength or cowardice will not permit us to march beyond our own stone walls'.

Colonel Capon had written again to Bombay for more troops and for two hundred cavalry to keep open communications. Confined as they were to Aden, he considered that no native troops could be kept there beyond six months under canvas, manning field-works with a quarter of the number intended to be placed there. Haines added his support for reinforcements, especially for Europeans; 'the Arabs dread the Europeans while they consider themselves equal, if not superior, to the Native troops, the advantage of discipline being beyond their comprehension'.[8]

The Government of Bombay was distressed at the news received from Aden but did not send reinforcements; instead, in June 1840, it discussed at length the reports on the fortifications and considered 'a moderate expense in strengthening the Turkish wall'. Lord Auckland was not satisfied by this reaction and urged the need for reinforcements and a real strengthening of the defences. The Governor-General supported Haines' argument that there should be an expedition to Lahej, since to adhere strictly to a mere defence of entrenchments would only encourage 'acts of aggression and defiance'. The barbarous murder of the British Agent at Lahej proved how this spirit of defiance and hostility was growing. The Governor-General quite understood the Bombay Government's wish to save money and to insist on defence, but he also thought that a body of cavalry with light guns might form a permanent part of the garrison to prevent surprise attack. He gave the Bombay Government full discretion to act upon these views.[9]

While the Bombay Government was trying to make up its mind what to do without incurring too much expense, there was considerable activity in the neighbourhood of Aden. The Abdali and Fadhli tribes combined to attack the Aqrabi Sultan Hyder ben Mehdi in his fortress of Bir Ahmed because he had remained faithful to his bond with the British and because his small tribe held a strategic position between Aden and Lahej, but two hundred Aqrabi and three hundred matchlockmen called in from the Subeihi tribe beat off the attacks. On July 1 the Abdalis and Fadhlis advanced to within a few miles of the British frontier to wait for reinforcements and decide on their plan of attack on Aden.

Since the murder of Abdulla Khatif, Haines had had to be extra careful about obtaining information from Lahej, but the relatives of the murdered man were determined to take their revenge on the Abdali Sultans and succeeded in keeping Haines informed of the plan of attack. On July 4 he learned that the Arab force, which numbered several thousand, would attack the next morning as the tide receded so that he was able to give good warning to the military and naval forces. Captain Hallam, who was in command of the garrison as Colonel Capon had gone to Bombay on leave, ordered the field-works to be manned, also three towers, which had been built on Jebel Hadeed to prevent the Arabs gaining the hill and firing on the left field-works from the rear. During high water an old boat was brought ashore between Swaya Island and Jebel Hadeed as an outpost to cover the gap between the end of the Turkish wall and the sea; it was a large enough old hulk to take thirty infantry and a four-pounder gun. Four other armed boats and cutters were stationed near the shore of the Western Bay and two on the Eastern Bay.

It was known that the Abdalis would be attacking on the British left flank between Swaya Island and Jebel Hadeed, while the Fadhlis with their Sultan, Hamed ben Abdulla, was to lead his tribesmen round the British right flank to the eastern side, taking advantage of the low tide. Sultan Hamed's brother, Sallah, was to take his men over the Turkish wall and join forces. The Fadhli Sultans must have realised that they would then have been under heavy fire from the heights above Crater where there were ten guns, and it seems a strange plan if they really had had any intention of carrying it out; the sequel suggests that they did not.

At 2.45 a.m. on July 5, the Abdali forces were seen crossing the flats between Swaya Island and Jebel Hadeed. The thirty infantrymen in the old boat on the shore opened fire with their muskets and with the four-pounder gun, but it went out of action on the first shot and at first it seemed as if the large force of Arabs had overwhelmed this little outpost as the boat was completely surrounded; but musketry fire kept the Arabs from boarding her and the *Charger*'s launch fired its twelve-pounder cannonade into the advancing mass of men. The Arabs passed boldly on towards Jebel Hadeed which they seemed confident they would capture, but were surprised by a heavy fire of musketry from the towers on the hill, by an enfilade from the launch and from an Arab boat which had been brought into service with a twelve-pounder howitzer manned by seamen, while musketry fire continued from the infantry in the boat on shore. 'Thus,' reported Haines, 'these head-strong men were between four cross-fires; still they persevered and reached as far as the pass between Jebel Haddeed and Ras Ali ben Mahommed, when they were driven back by the Arab gun-boat and fire from the southern tower on Haddeed. This occurred in the space of half-an-hour, not so their taking away their dead and wounded, which they courageously persevered in doing and thereby lost twice the number they otherwise would have done.' [10]

In the meantime the troops along the Turkish wall were directing their fire at the Fadhli forces who did not advance but kept well beyond grape-shot fire, at the same time shouting to the Abdalis to go on to Aden. Even in such an emergency tribal jealousies played their part. Sultan Hamed Abdulla considered that his tribe had suffered too heavily in the first attack on Aden because the Abdalis had held back and he was determined that that should not happen again. When he heard of the heavy losses suffered by the Abdalis he left the battlefield and returned straight to his country, delighted that he had discomfited his old rival, received large sums of money from him and had had his tribe fed at Sultan Mahsin's expense for a fortnight.

The Abdalis suffered heavily with three hundred dead and about fifty wounded. The defeat was a terrible disappointment to the Sultan of Lahej who had been confident of success and of obtaining a great deal of plunder. The tribe had been told to kill all the British in Aden but to bring Haines and Mullah Jaffar back alive as there were questions the Sultan wished to ask before having them killed.

The Bombay Government was still considering what plan to pursue with regard to Aden when news of the third attack reached them. Having received the Governor-General's letter supporting Haines' plan for an advance on Lahej and for a horse patrol, it decided to ask for more details, although Haines had already sent a fairly full dossier, and Captain Foster was asked for another report on the defences. This was not encouraging. The different regiments had spread their lines all over the valleys in Crater so that the limits of the garrison and of the inhabitants were 'all intermingled and confused', which Foster considered to be dangerous and there was insufficient room for the development of the civilian and trading population; it was difficult to keep the lines clean and it was not, as he had intended it should be, 'a neat, compact and well arranged little garrison town', so that a bad impression was given abroad 'visited as Aden is so constantly by inquisitive foreigners of all nations'. He wanted to construct fives' courts and introduce boating, cricket, quoits and other games 'to counteract that depression which the present harassing duties and dull monotony must lead to and which has such a baneful influence on all constitutions'.[11]

Many of the troops sought shelter in the caves of the Crater hills away from their scorching tents and those who knew the legend that

Cain had been buried by the Main Pass into Crater believed that the place was, indeed, under a curse. Several British soldiers escaped by ship and two took service with the Arabs in Mocha as gunners; but the majority of the troops were busy, in view of the continued threats of attack, and remained fairly cheerful. 'They are by far the greater favourites with the population than are the sepoys,' wrote Haines. 'They command more respect, and not a dispute of any kind has occurred between them and the people; whereas, with the Hindi sepoys, continued differences arise, particularly on the subject of water.' Haines did what he could for the welfare of the troops, growing vegetables to try to vary the diet but there proved to be insufficient water; he recommended that a sanatorium should be built on Steamer Point but the Government regarded this as an unnecessary expense.

The European troops stood up to the heat better than the Indians many of whom spent a great deal of time in hospital where Haines used to visit them to try to cheer them up. When asked if they were improving in health, most of them would say: 'No Sir, I have no strength. I shall die if I am not sent to Bombay. I have not seen my family for six months and know not whether they are alive or dead.' 'With these feelings,' wrote Haines, 'their minds give way, they lose their appetite and strength, break out in ulcers or become almost skeletons.' He recommended that their families should be sent from India, 'they will then lose their present anxieties and become contented, particularly if they are housed comfortably'.

Sir James Rivett Carnac, the new Governor of Bombay, agreed that many of the proposals were necessary 'if it be the intention of the Home authorities to retain Aden as a permanent possession', but as the expenses were so heavy the whole question would have to be referred to London. By September 1840 it was realised that Aden was likely to be a permanent possession, and that some of the proposals would have to be carried out, for there was nearly war in the Middle East and Aden was an important strategic post.

14

'The Egyptian Question'

(March to November 1840)

Throughout 1840 tension mounted over what was known as 'The Egyptian Question'. Exaggerated rumours were spread among the tribes of the Yemen and of South Arabia that the English and Egyptians were already at war. This encouraged the Abdalis to think that they would receive help, and as the monsoon winds, which favoured ships sailing from Bombay to Aden, were ending they believed that there was no fear of any British reinforcements. On March 19 1840, Consul Hodges wrote under 'flying seal' from Alexandria to Sir James Rivett Carnac that Egypt was 'the scene of great military movement' because it was rumoured that the great Powers had decided to settle the Egyptian Question in the interests of the Ottoman Empire and against the interests of Egypt.[1]

Mohammed Ali Pasha saw the threat from Europe as serious enough to make him withdraw his troops from the Yemen. 'This place will be entirely evacuated by the Egyptians in the course of four or five days and plundered by the Beduin and every British subject will lose all he possesses, if he escapes indeed with his life', reported Hajji Abdulla Roussoul to Haines from Mocha on March 23 1840.[2] 'I beg therefore that you will, not delay to send a vessel of war.' Haines at once despatched the *Elphinstone* (Lieutenant F. J. Powell), followed later by the *Euphrates* (Lieutenant Ethersay) and the *Mahi* (Lieutenant Daniell). He instructed Lieutenant Powell to be very careful to avoid incidents and reminded him of the serious consequences of a rupture with the Egyptian authorities, 'for all our communications through Egypt would be immediately closed, a circumstance of the utmost importance to our political and mercantile interests'.

With a possible French threat from East Africa and a war declared against China the Government of India was especially anxious to maintain speedy communications with England. The Governor-General expressed regret to Bombay that no more naval reinforcements could be sent 'since after the sailing of the expedition to China there would be no man-of-war in the Bay of Bengal'.[3] One of the ships which took part in the operations to capture some of the southern ports of China, which led the next year to the cession of Hongkong, was H.M.S. *Cruizer* commanded by Captain Smith who had been in charge of the operations for the capture of Aden.

Thanks to the friendliness shown by Mohammed Ali Pasha the mails to and from England were not, however, delayed through Egypt. Captain Lyons, R.N., the East India Company's representative in Egypt, had several amiable interviews with Mohammed Ali Pasha through the critical spring of 1840. Indeed, the Pasha was on much more friendly terms with Captain Lyons than with Colonel Hodges, for whom the Pasha had no liking and to whom he was not prepared to make any promises about the mails. Hodges complained to Palmerston that the Pasha was using Lyons as 'a stalking-horse' to reduce the Consul 'to a political nullity',[4] but the Colonel had only himself to blame.

Whereas the interviews between Mohammed Ali Pasha and the previous Consul, Patrick Campbell, had nearly always been friendly those with the irascible Hodges were often stormy. Hodges informed Lord Auckland on April 27 (1840) that he had told the Pasha he had documents to show that there had been Egyptian intrigues concerning Aden and Muscat and that the British Government 'would admit no interference or attempts of aggression'. The Colonel had

Steamer boilers from England being carried across the Isthmus of Suez
The steamship *Bentinck* at Aden

Mohammed Ali Pasha, Viceroy of Egypt, receiving British naval officers at his palace in Alexandria on May 12, 1840, three weeks after Mahmud, Sultan of the Ottoman Empire, had ordered his armies to enter Syria to attack the Egyptians under Ibrahim Pasha then asked what the Pasha intended to do with the Turkish fleet which was still in Alexandria harbour. The reply was: 'I shall keep it as a weapon taken from the hands of my enemy, until my differences are settled with the Porte and then I shall send it back to the Sultan.' Hodges had then said, according to his despatch to the Governor-General, that if the officers of the Turkish Navy knew their duty they would return the ships to Constantinople immediately, 'and I do not conceal from Your Highness that I am instructed by my Government to advise their adoption of such a course'. The Pasha, in a state of the greatest excitement, jumped up from his divan, and cried: 'Now you place me in a state of war. I warn you that the first defection I perceive, I will shoot the offender.' The Colonel seems to have been surprised at what was a very natural reaction and pompously concluded his despatch: 'the demeanour and tone of Mohammed Ali Pasha during the whole of the political portion of this interview manifested defiance and insolence. I observed towards him a calm, respectful but firm deportment.'[5]

Although this haughty and overbearing manner was characteristic of Hodges it was, to a certain extent, representative of a change in the attitude of the Great Powers to the rulers of the Middle East owing to the increasing power of Europe. Palmerston, for instance, expected the young Ottoman Sultan, Abdul Mejjid, and Mohammed Ali Pasha to do what he wanted them to do. In France, however, Mohammed Ali was a popular hero because it was thought that he was introducing French civilisation into Egypt and might be the means of increasing France's influence in the Mediterranean and the Red Sea leading to Abyssinia and perhaps India. 'The mistress of India,' stated Lord Palmerston, 'cannot permit France to be mistress directly or indirectly of the road to her Indian dominions.'[6] Besides that Palmerston continued to be apprehensive lest Mohammed Ali should become so powerful that the Ottoman Empire would be weakened and Russia's influence increased. The five Powers—Britain, France, Russia, Austria and Prussia—had at first acted together to try to deal with the Porte over the Egyptian Question, but France had broken away to support Mohammed Ali, and war seemed likely.

Haines was in a strategic position in Aden to follow events through despatches from Suez and from reports of the commanders of ships he sent to gain intelligence at various ports in the Red Sea area. He was fortifying, as best he could, the cliffs looking out over the Western Bay from which an attack might come by Egyptian or French warships, and guns were placed at Ras Morbut; also on Sira Island to protect the Eastern Harbour. Haines was in a better position to watch the Western Bay as he had moved from Crater to Tarshain, or Steamer Point, where he was having a house built for himself; he was soon settled enough to have his wife and son brought from Bombay. All the steamer and sailing traffic between Suez and Bombay came to the Western Bay and the steamers took on coal from the depôt at Ras Shaikh Ahmed west of the Morbut headland. From his new house he was able to receive ships' captains, to have early information of any French ships in the area and to know quickly when despatches arrived from Suez or Bombay.

If British residents had to be evacuated from Egypt it was for Haines to make arrangements. In June 1840 he informed Hodges that he had sent the *Elphinstone* to Jedda and that she was ready to proceed to Suez to help deal with any emergency. But the crisis seemed for a short time to have been resolved. The Consul-General informed Lieutenant Ethersay, who was in command as Lieutenant Powell was ill, that the *Elphinstone* would not be required at Suez since the differences with Egypt were 'in a state of amicable adjustment'. Ethersay reported to Haines on July 23 from Jedda that Mohammed Ali Pasha had sent envoys to Constantinople with 'modest and reasonable demands': firstly that Egypt should be declared independent, secondly that he should hold Syria as a vassal of the Ottoman Sultan and thirdly that he would restore the Turkish fleet. The Pasha had shown his new friendliness towards Turkey by celebrating the birth of a daughter to the young Ottoman Sultan, Mejjid, ordering seven days of feasting and illumination; Jedda, too, was celebrating and the guns were 'roaring'. Ethersay also reported that Ibrahim Pasha, the 'Little', had sailed to Egypt on July 8 with all the Egyptian troops from the Yemen. There was a story that Mohammed Ali Pasha, in view of the fact that he expected peace, had counter-ordered the evacuation of Yemen but that his instructions had come too late.[7]

If the Concert of Powers had been concerned only to help achieve a settlement between Egypt and Turkey, they could have encouraged the young Sultan of Turkey to accept the Pasha's conciliatory gesture; but Britain, Russia, Prussia and Austria were more concerned with teaching France a lesson. On July 15 1840 without consulting France, they signed a Convention in London which laid down that if the Pasha submitted to the Porte within ten days he should receive the hereditary Pashalik of Egypt and the administration of southern Syria during his lifetime with the title of Pasha of Acre. France's feelings were deeply hurt at this rebuff and the French Press clamoured for war against England which made Mohammed Ali feel even more confident of French support. A special envoy arrived in Alexandria from the Sublime Porte with the terms proposed by the Concert of Powers and Hodges wrote to Haines for the Governor of Bombay, on August 17: 'These terms were rejected yesterday, and it is probable that ere long coercive measures may be adopted against the rebellious Pasha. Indeed, in a preliminary step, all communication between Egypt, Syria and Candia is already cut off by our fleet.' He was of the firm opinion that the Pasha, backed by the moral and perhaps physical support of France, 'would resist force by force'.* [8]

Events moved rapidly in the Eastern Mediterranean. A combined British, Austrian and Russian fleet under the command of Admiral Sir Charles Napier sailed for Beirut at the beginning of August. This led to a rising of the Syrian people against the Egyptians; Sultan Abdul Mejjid took this as an excuse, on the advice of the British Ambassador, to depose the Pasha as Viceroy of Egypt on the argument that the time limit of the ultimatum had expired. On September 11, as the Egyptian commander in Beirut had refused to surrender, the Allied bombardment of the town began and Turkish troops were landed to co-operate with the Syrians against Ibrahim Pasha, son of Mohammed Ali Pasha and commander of the Egyptian

---

* Haines' Political Assistant, Lieutenant Griffith Jenkins, left Aden at the beginning of September 1840, on sick leave for England. When he arrived in Alexandria he was asked to accompany a deputation of Consuls to deliver what amounted to an ultimatum to Mohammed Ali Pasha. He then took the British Consul's despatches for Lord Palmerston to London.

Griffith Jenkins had only been in Aden for ten months and his departure was a loss to Haines. He was a very able Lieutenant who had participated in the Socotra landing and had distinguished himself at the capture of Karachi which was effected a few days after the capture of Aden.

troops. Colonel Hodges, who had had to leave his post of Consul-General in Egypt on September 23, went straight to Syria where he took command of an irregular unit of four hundred mountaineers fighting against the Egyptians![9]

Captain Lyons, the East India Company representative in Egypt who had been the link with Haines and Bombay, had also left Egypt but his deputy, Captain Johnson, took over and continued to pass on information. British Consular affairs in Egypt were entrusted to Mr. Schutz, the Dutch Consul-General, and, in spite of the crisis, Mohammed Ali Pasha stated that the mails between England and India would be allowed to pass through Egypt and he would ensure their protection. Following the defeats suffered by Ibrahim Pasha in Egypt, Captain Johnson also decided to leave Egypt 'not knowing what effect repeated acts of aggression may have on the Pasha,' but he informed Aden and Bombay that the Egyptian agent of the East India Company at Suez would continue to supply coal to British ships and that ships' commanders should communicate with Briggs, the British bankers at Alexandria.

The indefatigable Thomas Waghorn had remained in Egypt eager to carry on his mission to establish the Red Sea route more securely, and to show that, even in times of war, it could be maintained. In a letter to Lord Auckland, headed 'On Secret Service', Waghorn outlined a complicated cloak and dagger arrangement to get the mails through Egypt from Kosseir, south of Suez and East of Luxor. 'I wish in this emergency,' he wrote, 'to save India and England at the risk of all else to me.'[10] The Government of Bombay replied that it saw no reason to change the usual arrangements through Suez.

Yet some kind of plan such as that suggested by Waghorn might have been necessary, for the Bombay Government had instructed Captain Haines that if he received reliable intelligence of war having been declared by England against Egypt or France, or of Alexandria having been blockaded, he was 'to adopt similar measures as may be within his power against the Egyptian ports in the Red Sea and to detain all vessels belonging to nations against whom war may have been declared'.[11]

Instructions were also given that copies of all despatches to London were to be sent via the Cape and by the Baghdad-Euphrates route as well as by Suez. The Secretary of the Bombay Chamber of Commerce urged the Government to make secure plans as communications with England were so important to the mercantile community. The fortifications of Bombay were strengthened and arrangements made to seize the thirty-gun French ship *Dordogne*, then in Bombay harbour, in the event of a declaration of war. It was considered that Haines would have the first news from Egypt and that he should send a fast sailing vessel with despatches to be delivered directly to the Chief Secretary of the Government.

On October 8 the French Ambassador in London, Monsieur Guizot, saw Lord Palmerston and issued what amounted almost to a declaration of war, but Palmerston had been directed to receive Guizot in a friendly manner and to say that there was no reason why the Pasha should not be left in control of Egypt. Lord Auckland also was anxious not to exacerbate the situation and informed Bombay on October 26 that, in the absence of any offensive measures against British interests 'on this side of the isthmus of Suez', Haines was not after all to declare a blockade of any Egyptian ports in the Red Sea or to take any hostile action.[12]

This proved wise policy for Mohammed Ali Pasha was beginning to realise that France might not give him the support he expected. He had accepted another British Consul in Alexandria, Mr. John N. Larking, who wrote an important letter to the Governor-General of India under 'flying seal'. The Pasha wanted now, he wrote, to come to an arrangement with the Sultan through the mediation of the Four Powers and not through that of France and he announced this on November 8 1840. 'In public Divan he indignantly complained of the unmerited abandonment of his interests by France after solemn pledges to the contrary.'

The following day the Pasha learned of the fall of the important fortress of St. Jean d'Acre 'and for a time was thrown into deeper dejection by this than by any of his previous reverses'. But he immediately despatched a courier instructing Ibrahim Pasha to evacuate the whole of Syria. He told those in his confidence that he was prepared to give up the Turkish fleet and comply with all the Sultan's demands provided that he could be assured of 'the quiet possession of Egypt'.[13] It was the end of any idea of an Arab empire but the Pasha was content to concentrate on reforms in Egypt. 'To possess a land like ours which has no equal,' he wrote, 'is our greatest happiness.' [14]

When peace was restored the East India Company and various groups of merchants sent gifts to Mohammed Ali Pasha expressing their appreciation of the protection given to British residents in Egypt and for enabling the East India Company and the British Government to maintain their lines of communication even at the worst period of Anglo-Egyptian relations. 'It is difficult to understand,' wrote an intelligent French observer, 'what great interest England had in obstructing the Pasha of Egypt.' [15]

15

French rivalry in the Red Sea and in Abyssinia

(1840 to 1843)

The crisis of 1840 had not only encouraged French ambitions in the Mediterranean but also in the Red Sea and Indian Ocean, where the French had had such great influence in the eighteenth century. There was little left of their former possessions, 'mere flotsam and jetsam saved from the lamentable shipwreck of 1815', wrote Captain Guillain, for some time in command of the French naval vessel *Dordogne*.[1] The Red Sea had two trade routes, one to India and beyond but the English controlled all the stages from Aden to Japan and New Zealand; regarding the other route on the East Coast of Africa, Guillain considered that the French could dominate this 'African branch of the great seaway', for they possessed Bourbon (Réunion), Sainte Marie, Mayotta and Nossi-be; they had long traded at Zanzibar and expected to obtain possession of Madagascar.

Captain Guillain understood the importance of Aden—'the Red Sea also has its Gibraltar'—and he was far-sighted enough to realise that it would become still more important when the isthmus of Suez was cut, and he was confident that it would be. The British at Aden would be able to control the shipping using the Red Sea so that it was necessary that their position should in some way be 'neutralised'. In 1840 Admiral de Hill, Governor of Bourbon, commanded the French Squadron in the Indian Ocean and sent warships to the Red Sea and the ports of India to gain intelligence of British activities and to help the French Government of King Louis Philippe to find a coaling station in the Gulf of Aden.

A number of French warships visited Aden; the French officers were charming and inquisitive and Haines sent a number of reports about their activities in the area to the British Consul in Egypt. These were sent on to Lord Palmerston, who had also received intelligence from other sources of French activities and he asked the Board of Control to instruct the East India Company to do its best to counter French influence.

On July 2 1840 a letter was despatched direct to Haines in Aden by the Secret Committee of the East India Company asking him to send immediately a reliable officer to negotiate with the local chiefs for a foothold in the area of Zeyla and Tajjura (on the bay where forty years later the French built the port of Djibouti). 'We have so much confidence in your zeal and ability,' wrote the Secret Committee to Haines, 'that we willingly give to you entire discretion as to the measures which it may be advisable to adopt'; it did not want any compulsion used but pointed out that 'the settlement of any other European commercial agency, or military station, on that coast would be highly detrimental to British interests'.[2]

This letter reached Haines at the beginning of August 1840 and he immediately went into action, planning everything very carefully. He made out a draft treaty, collected twelve thousand dollars and gave detailed instructions to Captain Moresby, Senior Naval Officer Aden and commander of the steam-frigate *Sesostris*. He chose four good men to accompany him, Lieutenant W. C. Barker, commanding the *Euphrates*, Lieutenant Cruttenden, Hajj Abdulla Roussoul, the Agent for the East India Company at Mocha, who would be helpful in negotiating treaties, and Hajj Ali Sharmakay, an influential Somali who knew the Danakil people of Tajjura. Moresby had to go to Mocha to fetch Hajj Abdulla Roussoul and Haines warned him against the possibility of his being received with insults 'for the authorities there are arrogant and impertinent in the extreme'.

When the Egyptians left the Yemen in July 1840 they had handed over the sea-coast towns to the highest bidder, Hussain Ibn Ali Hyder, a Sherif of Abu Arish, who promised to pay an annual tribute with the help of a wealthy merchant of Hodeida. The Sherifs of Abu Arish from the northern part of the Yemen were respected for their holiness and had been at various times independent of the Imams of Sana since the end of the eighteenth century, controlling much of the Tehama coastal area until the invasion of the Wahabi puritans at the beginning of the nineteenth century. Sherif Hussain had been Secretary to the Egyptian Governor of Mocha in 1836 where Haines had met him and had learned to distrust him because of his bigotry and hatred of Christians. He considered that the religious excitement which then prevailed among the tribes near Aden was the result of the Sherif's 'indefatigable machinations' and would not be quelled 'until some decisive measure on the side of the British convinces them we are either formidable enemies or friends of sufficient power to be worth retaining'.

When Moresby arrived at Mocha he was fortunate enough to find the Somali Chief, Hajj Ali Sharmakay who had gone there to trade. There was at first some difficulty, however, in persuading Hajj Abdulla Roussoul to come on board the *Sesostris*, as he was nervous about leaving his family and property, as they might be seized in his absence by Sherif Hussain ibn Ali Hyder, with whom he was having trouble. In the circumstances it might have been better to leave Hajj Abdulla at Mocha, but Moresby gave a written undertaking that the Government would make itself responsible for any losses Hajj Abdulla might suffer as a result of leaving Mocha at that time.

The *Sesostris* then sailed for Tajjura with the two men and within forty-eight hours Moresby came to a settlement with the Danakil Sultan of Tajjura entering into a treaty with him for the purchase of 'an island or islands—for they are two joined together—called Mussaha for which I gave him 1,100 German crowns and thirty-two bags of rice'. In the treaty—which was signed on August 19 on board the *Sesostris*—there was no mention of the money payment as the Sultan did not wish his tribesmen to know he had received anything. It read: 'I, Sultan Mohammed bin Mohammed, ruler of

Tajjura, for myself and posterity bargained and granted the Island called Mussaha to the British Government for ten bags of rice.' There was also a commercial treaty of eight Articles.[3]

Formal possession was taken of Mussaha Island by hoisting the Union Jack and firing a salute of twenty-one guns. The same ceremony was carried out following the sale of the small island at the entrance of the inner lake of Goobul Karabh, for which the Sultan received 200 dollars and a barrel of cannon powder. It was a barren rock of about two hundred yards in diameter, forty feet above sea-level, and controlled a narrow passage to the great inner lake; boats had to take care at the ebb-tide when the water rushed out violently past the little rock.

'The Bay of Tajjura of which so little is known to Europeans', wrote Cruttenden in his report, 'forms a deep bight something in the shape of an hour-glass.' The hills inland were thickly clothed with acacia, tamarisk and the nebek tree—further inland were the dragon-blood and lubahn or frankincense trees. Tajjura consisted of about 100 to 120 houses and 400 people; the women had few pretensions to beauty, 'their eyes were good but they appeared decidedly inferior to the plump and jolly looking dames from Berbera and Bunder Kassim'. Its main source of wealth was slavery and both the Somali and Danakil tribes made excursions into the interior to steal children from the Abyssinians who were then sold as slaves in the Mocha market; female slaves were being offered in Tajjura at that time at 15 to 35 dollars each.

All the tribes assembled every year about the middle of October at Tajjura bringing with them slaves, gums, skins, ivory, senna, myrrh, frankincense, musk, gold dust, madder, ostrich feathers, honey and an immense supply of cattle of all kinds. In the course of a month the village was increased to ten times its normal size and suddenly became a place of importance: 'the beach is piled with merchandise and the suburbs of the town crowded with camels, mules and donkeys belonging to the huge moving mass of wandering merchants. Tribes from a distance of twenty days' journey come to this great fair and for two months the place is one continuous bustle and uproar, feuds arise, blood is spilt, lives are lost and all are reconciled again in a remarkably short space of time.'[4]

Moresby and all the members of the expedition commented on the great help given by Ali Sharmakay, an able Somali of a fine presence, six foot two in height, who had been famous as a swordsman and used to carry four spears to battle; at the age of fifty, he liked to carry a silver-hilted sword. When he had been *nakodah* of a boat he had come to the notice of the Bombay Government by his prowess in saving the lives of the Captain and some of the crew (the rest were murdered) of the brig *Mary Ann* which went aground near Berbera in April 1825. The next month Hajj Ali received an official testimonial and an award from the Bombay Government presented by Captain Bagnold, the British Agent in Mocha. Haines had a high opinion of him as did Richard Burton who knew him when he was Governor of Zeyla twelve years later; 'despite his years he is a strong, active and energetic man, ever looking to the "main chance".' Even when over sixty he meditated on the conquest of Harar and Berbera which would have made him master of the seaboard and 'would soon extend his power as in the days of old even to Abyssinia'.[5]

Hajj Ali Sharmakay explained to Moresby that it was useless to go direct to Zeyla to try to make a treaty, since the town was under the Sherif of Mocha who would first of all have to be consulted. Robert Moresby therefore returned to Aden to report and then proceeded to Mocha, but Haines kept Hajj Abdulla Roussoul in Aden until it was known what his reception would be. From Mocha Moresby reported that the Sherif was still angry and had seized much of Hajj Abdulla's property, arguing that he had traitorously gone with the English to help them buy land at Tajjura which belonged to Muslims. Strong feeling had been aroused when Moresby unwisely, as he admitted, ordered Midshipman Clarke of the *Sesostris* to hoist the Union Jack over the British Agency which was Hajj Abdulla's house. The Sherif sent his soldiers to haul it down and as often as Midshipman Clarke hoisted the flag the soldiers pulled it down, finally cutting the mast.

Haines would have considered that a gross insult to the British flag, but the Sherif gave an assurance that no insult was intended to the British but that he could not have a flag flying over his enemy's house and Moresby made no protest. He found the Sherif affable, raising no objection to a treaty being made by the British with the Governor of Zeyla and stating that he himself was prepared to sign a treaty of friendship with the English. Moresby drew it up and on the occasion of its signature there was rejoicing in Mocha: 'salutes of guns were fired from the forts and the Arab boats, which were returned by the *Sesostris* and *Elphinstone*'; Moresby added 'I think that our Government will be pleased with what has been done.'[6] But Haines was not pleased. He had not been consulted, it was a bad treaty and it should not have been made with a man who was so hostile to the British.

Indeed, a letter from the Sherif of Mocha to the Governor of Bombay was written at the same time as he had made the treaty with Moresby stating that any agreement depended on the British leaving Aden, which belonged to Muslims, and that it was a disgrace to the Mohammedan nation that it should have come under English control. The Sherif said that he and others had been asked for help from the tribes near Aden, and 'all of us have promised aid accordingly, but we have thought it proper to write this letter, for our object is not to resort to any forceful proceedings previous to giving Your Honour a warning and we demand the restoration of the Port of Aden'.[7] Sultan Mahsin of Lahej had been instructed by the Sherif not to enter into any peace agreement unless he gave permission.

The Sherif was at the same time intriguing with the French and a squadron was due to rendezvous at Mocha. Haines had received letters addressed to the captains of the French ships which he had sent on to Mocha but as there was no one there to receive them they had been returned. There were so many French warships due to arrive that Haines recommended an increase in the British naval forces.

In the meantime Captain Moresby, having received Sherif Hussain's permission to make a treaty with Zeyla, sailed for that port where he negotiated successfully with the commander of the Sherif's army, Sayyed Mohammed Bar, for the Island of Aubad near Zeyla, and signed a commercial treaty.[8] When the Government of Bombay received the treaties for Tajjura, Mocha and Zeyla everyone was congratulated for having acted with great judgement and discretion, but after Haines' comments on the Mocha treaty and Sherif Hussain's insulting letter had arrived it was decided that Moresby had been precipitate and that the treaty should not be ratified.

French rivalry in the Red Sea and in Abyssinia

The aggressiveness of the Sherif of Mocha encouraged Sultan Mahsin of Lahej to think that he would be given support for a further attack on Aden but he found that the Sherif was busy with his own affairs. There was little enthusiasm for an attack among the Abdali tribesmen, many of whom were farmers or concerned with the caravan trade and were finding commerce with Aden profitable.

In November 1840, however, a fanatic called Shaikh Faki Said appeared in the Yemen proclaiming that he had a divine mission to purify Islam, abolish taxation and to turn the infidels out of Aden. He promised invulnerability in battle and followers flocked to his headquarters established at Denwah near Oudain, about five days' journey from Aden. The Shaikh assumed the trappings of royalty, issuing his own coins with 'Sultan of the Land and the Sea' on one side and on the other 'The Expected Guided One'. When he demanded that Mocha should be handed over to him the Sherif put him off by saying that his first mission should be to turn the English out of Aden. Sultan Mahsin was in contact with Shaikh Faki Said and when he heard that the Imam of Sana was mustering twenty thousand men he was delighted, convinced that the forces of the Shaikh and of the Imam were joining to attack Aden and he prepared to take part with them. The information that Haines received, however, was more reliable. The Imam, who was the legitimate ruler and a Zaidi of the Shia faith, would not acknowledge a usurper of the Sunni faith, and his intention was to attack the Shaikh's army. Haines was not worried that Aden was endangered but noted the part being played by Sultan Mahsin. In December the Imam's forces defeated the Shaikh and his followers in a terrible slaughter at Denwah.

The neighbourhood remained quiet for several months which was fortunate for Haines had other work to do, such as reporting on French activities. An armed merchant ship called the *Ankobar*, after the chief town of Shoa, was loaded with small arms and was visiting various ports near the entrance to the Red Sea. Officers from the ship were trying to buy land at Edd near Massawa, which had a good harbour and was the nearest port to northern Abyssinia being seven days' journey from Axum and fifteen from Gondar. A number of French scientists and officers had been exploring Tigre and Shoa, such as Ferret and Galinier, Combes, Tamisier, Lefebvre, Rochet d'Hericourt and the two brothers Thomson and Arnaud d'Abbadie;[9] rival Protestant and Roman Catholic missions were also trying to gain an influence in Abyssinia. Several of these French travellers came to Aden to collect stores and to acquire information.

In December 1840 there arrived in Aden Thomson Antoine d'Abbadie who had left his younger brother Arnaud in Abyssinia. He was intelligent and good company but Haines was puzzled as to his activities. The brothers had been born in Dublin of a French father and an Irish mother passing themselves off as Irish or French, as it suited them, for they held passports of both countries. On his first visit to Abyssinia Thomson d'Abbadie had left England with a letter of recommendation from Lord Palmerston requesting that he should be helped on his way. But after the elder d'Abbadie's departure from Aden Haines became suspicious, as there arrived a number of letters addressed to him from the French Ministry of Foreign Affairs. D'Abbadie returned to Aden to pick up the letters and proceeded with Combes, who had been designated French Commissioner for Africa, to Zeyla and Tajjura on their way to Shoa. Haines sent a message to Ali Sharmakay in Somaliland to watch their activities, and at Tajjura they met opposition which prevented them continuing their journey inland.

One of the visitors to Aden, who was to give Haines valuable information about Abyssinia, was John Ludwig Krapf.[10] He was eight years younger than Haines having been born in Germany in 1810 and, after joining the Church Missionary Society in London, had been sent out on the Abyssinian Mission. Throughout the summer and winter of 1840 Haines received a number of informative and delightful letters from Krapf from Ankobar, where he had established himself as a close confidant of Sahela Selassie, King of Shoa. These letters were sent on to the Bombay Government and aroused considerable interest, especially the account of the intrigues of Monsieur d'Hericourt Rochet who had arrived in Shoa in October 1839. The Frenchman had won the admiration of the King by constructing a powder-mill and manufacturing sugar; he also dealt in necromancy which was most effective with the gullible Abyssinians. But what attracted the King most were plans to extend his rule over Gondar and the whole of Abyssinia. Rochet had pointed out the need for a regular and disciplined army equipped with modern weapons, which could be obtained from France if the King would enter into a treaty of perpetual friendship. Sahela Selassie embraced these plans with enthusiasm and in March 1840 Rochet left Ankobar with letters and presents for King Louis Philippe of France.

The Frenchman had spoken freely to Krapf, and Haines noted, as did the Bombay Government, that his real designs were very different from those he professed. 'In the course of the years,' reported Krapf, 'Rochet thought he could organise an army of two hundred thousand men whom he would take from the numberless and courageous Galla nation. Thus, in course of time, a French Abyssinia might be established in opposition to British India. This French Abyssinia might, Rochet thinks, be brought into connection with the French possessions in Senegal in Western Africa, particularly by the river Niger in the centre of this continent.'

Krapf referred, also, to the rising power of Mohammed Ali Pasha especially in upper Nubia and considered that if either he or his successors were to take Abyssinia the Egyptians, with the help of the French, could recruit a formidable army from the Galla horsemen, and that it would be difficult to retake the country owing to its mountainous character. The French, joined by Mohammed Ali Pasha, might then be able to carry out their object of undermining English influence on the Red Sea and Indian Ocean 'and become dangerous even to India'.

The King, Krapf believed, had a real desire to carry out reforms but did not know how to set about them. He wanted to concentrate first on military reforms as Abyssinia had for many years been in a state of civil war between the various Abyssinian Rases, and there had been no development of a country which was as beautiful and fertile as any country in the world; 'if the British Government would strengthen the Kingdom of Shoa it might save the Abyssinian people from total ruin . . . and the revolutionary plans of Monsieur Rochet and the French influence in Eastern Africa could be destroyed in its root'.

Krapf recommended that the Government of India should make its influence felt by protesting at the manner in which the King had treated the property of John Airston, an English traveller who had been a friend of Haines in Aden and was on a visit to the King of

Shoa when he died at Ferri near the Danakil-Shoan frontier—a protest 'which would keep the King in fear and cause him to act lawfully in a similar case'. The King had consulted Krapf as to what he should do with the dead man's luggage and had been told that according to English law all property must go to the relations of the deceased, but that advice did not appeal to the King. He had the luggage brought to him and took whatever pleased him—there were several valuable astronomical instruments 'on which the Abyssinians gazed like oxen without understanding anything'. Besides travellers who had some scientific knowledge or geographical interest in visiting Abyssinia, there were a number of young adventurers. One of these was a German Lieutenant called Kilmaier, who had tried in vain to buy arms from Haines in Aden; he had died on the way to Shoa and his property, too, was brought to the King by Kilmaier's servant, Samuel Georgis. 'The King,' wrote Krapf, 'acted in conformity with his principle. The Abyssinians in general are like children, whatever they have seen they wish to possess.' Krapf pointed out, however, that the King 'looks after living strangers very generously and therefore considered himself the heir of the dead'.

The return of Monsieur Rochet to Ankobar was eagerly awaited, but in the meantime Krapf prompted the King of Shoa to write to the English in Aden and Bombay with a present of horses. 'As to the Governor of Aden,' said the King, 'I shall send to him likewise a horse and a cloth which I am wearing myself.' Krapf suggested that he should also send a mule for Mrs. Haines as he thought she would like this. 'I shall do so,' the King replied, 'and send her the skin of a *gasselat* [black leopard].' The horses were in bad condition when they arrived in Aden and had to be destroyed, but Haines thought the letters, which were written in Amharic with translations by Krapf, were human and entertaining. 'This letter which is sent to you by Sahela Selassie, the King of Shoa, Efat, the Galla nation and Gurague is sent to the Commander Haines at Aden. Are you well? I am well. I have written all my desires in a letter, which I send to you to forward it as quickly as possible to the great company in India and to send me the reply as soon as it has arrived with you. I conjure you by Our Lord Jesus Christ, fare well, fare well. . . . In sign of friendship I have sent you a horse and a cloth of my country and a mule and a *gasselat* skin to your wife. If you want anything let me know it. God give you health and wealth.'

In the second letter the King wrote that he wanted to make friendship with the Company: 'As to myself, if my person is bad or good, you will have been informed about it by your countrymen who have been here. Well then, I wish very much that you may please to make friendship with me. God has given me a good and large kingdom, but arts and sciences are not yet come into my country as they are in yours, therefore you may please to assist me in this respect in sending guns, cannons and other things which are not made in my country. I am ready to send you things which perhaps are not in your country. . . . Fare well.' The list of presents included carpets, nice pictures, razors, 'glasses of gallantry', a hand organ, Arabic clothes, nicely bound writing books. Haines remarked that oddly enough they were the same articles the French Commissioner, Monsieur Combes, had brought from France on board the *Ankobar*.

Krapf's picture of Mohammed Ali Pasha and the French controlling Abyssinia by recruiting Galla tribesmen was not by any means an impossibility and caused concern in India. There was also the wish to develop trade with Abyssinia and the Bombay Government decided to recommend that a mission should be formed and a list of questions sent to Haines, such as the route to be followed, whether there would be a friendly reception on the way, the composition and number of the mission, what presents were required and how transport could be secured. By January 1841 the Governor-General had sanctioned a properly equipped mission and East India House had agreed, but did not wish it to be on such a scale as to attract attention 'and excite alarm or jealousy in other chiefs'.

The Bombay Government discovered eighteen packing cases in a Bombay warehouse which had been sent out in 1832 by King William IV for the Ras of Tigre and for some reason had not been sent on. They contained brass hanging lamps, dentists' instruments, pliers, hammers, saws, swords, guns and a three-quarter length oil painting of the Virgin Mary and Child in a large gilt frame.[11] These were taken over without any reference to London or any query as to whether they might be needed for the original recipient, the King of Shoa's main enemy, the Ras of Tigre.

In spite of their find and the instructions they had received to be economical, the officials of Bombay could not resist buying a great many more things: a field officer's tent, lined with scarlet cloth and furnished with a portrait of the Queen, two large pier glasses and two mirrors, two small chandeliers with wax candles and a handsome carpet; two brass three-pounders on carriages, five hundred stand of arms with spare flints and ammunition, one hundred pistols, a spy glass and telescope, three pairs of handsome pictures in gilt frames representing naval and military actions, a clock, a model steam engine, a hand-organ, two large musical boxes and six small, a chest of artificers' tools, guns, rifles, air canes, cutlery, twelve blank books handsomely bound, shawls, flowered silks, artificial flowers, a magic-lantern, coloured glass, snuff, bags of rice, tobacco, barrels of beads and a good many other things totalling five thousand articles.

Considering that the Government of India was continually pleading poverty as the reason for not sending Haines the staff he required for administering a growing town (and indeed, refused another request in April 1841 when the Shoa mission left Bombay) it was inconsistent that it should have been eager to launch such a large and expensive mission. Ever since the legends of Prester John had drawn Portuguese explorers to the mountains of this ancient Christian kingdom surrounded by hostile Muslims, there had been romantic ideas about Abyssinia and a belief, too, that it was a wealthy country, so that the Government was carried away by high hopes of future trade. The Mission, commanded by Captain Cornwallis Harris, consisted of Captain Douglas Graham, Dr. Kirke, Lieutenant Horton, a surveyor and two German scientists.

The Mission had received a seventeen-page memorandum of instructions stating that Harris was to report direct to Bombay but under 'flying seal' so that Haines would be able to read his letters and give any help required. The object was to enter into a convention with the King of Shoa and with the chiefs of the countries on the way to Shoa—'to explore the country, to report on its agriculture and to ascertain in what manner and to what extent commercial intercourse may be established with the interior'; to give an account of the slave trade and 'to endeavour to strike at the root of the detestable traffic in human flesh'; to find out whether it was true that gold lay in the rivers and that the coffee was superior to that of Mocha.[12] 'Knowledge of the still "mysterious Continent of Africa" might be increased', wrote Sir James Rivett Carnac, 'and the blessings of civilisation' be extended leading to the improvement of nations and tribes 'now sunk in barbarism and moral debasement'.[13] The hope was also expressed that steam communication between India and England would be facilitated by the discovery of coal, the existence of which had been reported from Tajjura.

Captain Harris in his book on the expedition[14] praised the outstanding hospitality of Captain Haines at Aden while preparations were made for the expedition, which helped them to pass their time in the 'repulsive and forbidding' sterility of Aden without trees or birds or wild animals; at the same time it was 'blessed by a mild but firm government' and the town had progressed to twenty thousand people with substantial buildings springing up. Lieutenant Horton, too, wrote in his journal[15] how fortunate they were to have such men to deal with as Haines and Cruttenden 'whose kindness we shall not readily forget'. But there was still opposition to Haines, and Horton commented that it was a great pity 'that British officers should disgrace themselves by writing anonymous libels in dirty journals to aid the secret enemies of English interests in these countries'. He took a dislike to two bigoted German missionaries, Mulheisen and Müller, who wanted to join the Mission in order to reach Krapf in Shoa. Krapf had sent to Aden the young Christian, Samuel Georgis, who had been Kilmaier's servant, and had asked Haines to arrange for the boy to go to the Christian Mission in Cairo. In order to make a difficult journey safer for himself young Samuel had announced that he was a Muslim, and this so infuriated the German missionaries that they endangered the boy's life by denouncing his pretence in public. 'For this cruel imprudence', wrote Horton, 'they were severely lectured by Lieutenant Cruttenden.' He had been appointed Political Assistant to Haines after Lieutenant Griffiths Jenkins had left on sick leave in England.

Sidney Horton, who was on leave from his regiment in China, had been given permission to join the Mission by the Bombay Government but the Supreme Government cancelled this and he was later recalled from Tajjura; his short journal is the best account of the Mission's delays and difficulties with the Danakils after it left Aden in May 1841. He was young, and enthusiastic about the objects of the Mission, 'it is something to be one, though among the least, of the instruments chosen', and from the brig-of-war *Euphrates* he looked longingly at the hills of Abyssinia, noting that a residence in the tropics made people appreciate the great advantage of mountains. 'A few thousand feet of elevation are equivalent (in climate) to many degrees of latitude, and we poor soldiers of the colonies soon learn to love the mountains which give us this great advantage without robbing us of the bright sky and vivid colouring of the tropics or of noble and exciting wild sports.'

On their arrival at Tajjura the *Euphrates* fired a salute of seventeen guns; the baggage was laid in heaps on the shore—not touched surprisingly enough, by the population—and the field officer's tent lined with scarlet was set up. The party was received by the Danakil Sultan who, as a welcoming honour, placed on Harris' arm a piece of dungaree such as he wore himself 'and which did not appear entirely new or clean'. Crowds surrounded the Sultan's house and Horton found it rather unnerving to see that the walls of the reception room, which were full of holes, were 'studded with eyes'. Mr. Hatchatoor, who had been appointed British Agent at Tajjura, had hired a hundred and twenty camels and twenty-five mules and he had had difficulty in achieving that number. The d'Abbadie brothers and other Frenchmen who had been at Tajjura for four months had spread the story that the English wanted to conquer the country and abolish the slave trade, while, if the people allowed the French to protect them, slavery would be encouraged. This had led to the growth of a large pro-French party in the area but Hatchatoor had won many of them over by pointing out that Mohammed Ali Pasha had put himself into an unhappy position by trusting the French; 'they are doing everything in their power to hurt our interests in this place', wrote Harris to Bombay, 'but the truth has its right path'.[16]

On the Mission's arrival the whole population of Tajjura had passed in review before them, wrote Sidney Horton, 'and according to the most approved plan of writing travels these days, I am fully qualified to give with confidence my opinion of the national religion, morals, literature, manners, politics, commerce and costume!' He was intrigued by the wigs worn by the Somalis and Danakils, 'highly admired by the Ancients as they now are by the Italians and Spaniards'; instead of using real hair they cut up a sheepskin and stitched it into the requisite shape, 'kept in neat friz by repeated titivation with a wooden skewer which is generally worn through the hinder part of this curious head-dress'. He found it amusingly *à la mode*, too, that they should have a great fondness for snuff; 'they inhale their dust with gentleman-like gravity and deliberation, but generally hold the pinch a little too long between the finger and thumb which must in some degree impair its flavour'. Danakils were generally tall, slight, active and very dark, rather like the natives of the Carnatic but with more good humour and a ready laugh; 'they are terribly dirty and any mode of conciliation would be preferable to that of shaking hands with them but it must be done. The absolute necessity of conciliating the scoundrels makes us submit to their taking possession of our carpets and beds, crowding our tents almost to suffocation and spitting copiously everywhere except in our faces. Their mere neighbourhood is sufficiently disagreeable as their skins and heads are profusely anointed with sheep's tail fat. Their politics, like those of all men in and out of the British Parliament, change with their interests; from the age of about twelve they wear the carved dagger at the waist which means a man of respectability, like a gig in England.'

It was estimated that the Danakils made about 30,000 dollars a year through the slave trade, 'and when their wives misbehave they convert them into dollars immediately'. The Sultan had just sold one of his young wives, which had roused the zealous missionaries Mulheisen and Müller to protest openly in the Sultan's house and express 'their disgust at his trading in human beings, and their earnest hope that the present mission would soon succeed in putting an end to this abomination'. Captain Harris was angry at this outburst and ordered their return to Aden telling them that such remarks might frustrate Government plans in sending an expensive mission to Shoa; but when they pleaded that they would be ruined if sent back, he relented.

Young Horton did not entirely approve this leniency for Mullheisen and Müller were clearly going to be dangerous companions on such a journey—but they returned to Aden when they realised how dangerous the journey would be.

Horton considered, very rightly, that the Harris Mission was far too large. It would have been better 'to send three or four persons well provided with cash and domestics and bearing a few light and valuable presents'. Harris had insisted on adding two more members to the Commission from Aden, another surgeon and Lieutenant Barker. Haines had agreed but was reprimanded from Bombay for doing so and the surgeon had to return from Tajjura but Lieutenant Barker had already reached Shoa by the time the order to report back caught up with him. There was the addition, too, of the military escort from the Aden garrison. Haines must have known that that was unwise, for it was an insult to the tribal chiefs who had given safe conducts through their territories, and in any case it was not large enough to meet any serious danger. It was well known that Sir Home Popham had got into trouble on his way to Sana in 1802 because of his escort of sepoys, but it is probable that Harris made his arrangements to get volunteers from the garrison direct with the military commander and Haines may well not have been consulted.

The military escort of the Harris Mission was, indeed, singled out for attack. At the beginning of June half of the Mission had left Tajjura while the other half remained there under Lieutenant Horton with the heavier presents because there were insufficient camels to take the entire party. When the Mission reached Goongoonta near Lake Assal two of the escort were murdered. 'An hour before midnight,' wrote Harris to Bombay, 'a sudden and violent sirocco scoured the wadi. The moon rose shortly afterwards and about two o'clock there was a cry from the quarter in which the escort slept. Hurrying to the spot, Sergeant Walpole and Corporal Wilson of H.M.'s 6th Regiment were discovered weltering in their blood and in the agonies of death, the one having been struck by a creese in the carotid artery, the other stabbed in the stomach, whilst beside them a Portuguese follower had received a frightful gash in the abdomen.' [17]

May was already late for the start of an expedition from Aden because of the mounting heat in the Danakil desert and there had been further delays in Tajjura because of the need for so many camels to carry the multitude of presents. When they had dispensed with the camels after reaching the wooded hills of Abyssinia six hundred Abyssinian porters were needed for the baggage and the journey of four hundred miles to Ankobar was finally completed in forty-seven days.

There was no doubt, however, that the presentation to the King of Shoa of these gifts was a brilliant success. 'On the introduction of each new curiosity,' wrote Harris in a despatch, 'the surprise of the King became more and more unfeigned, and when the European escort in full uniform with the sergeant at their head marched into the centre of the hall, faced in front of the throne, and performed the manual and platoon exercise amidst the ornamental clocks, musical boxes, jewellery, gay shawls and silver cloths which strewed the floor, His Majesty appeared quite entranced, and declared that he had no words to express his pleasure. The escort then marched out and 150 muskets with fixed bayonets having been piled in front of the throne, completed to overflowing the measure of his entire satisfaction. "God will reward you", he exclaimed, "for I cannot".' [18]

All the same this did not satisfy the King, for later on he laid such covetous eyes on the officers' private property that Harris and Graham had to give up their new double-barrelled rifles, which as game-hunters they treasured, also a saddle and bridle and an embossed silver hunting knife, while Barker had to hand over his patent air-bed—articles which were highly prized by their owners and which cost the Government 2,419 rupees to replace. [19] When Krapf, who had been very helpful to the King as well as to the Harris Mission, decided to leave for Europe through Gondar, the King took all his property including his gun with which he intended to defend himself on a perilous journey.

The King was, of course, also eager to have the rest of the presents which had been left behind with the second half of the Mission. Lieutenant Horton had been recalled to service in China and Haines sent Cruttenden to Tajjura to arrange for the presents to be sent to Shoa. One hundred and thirty-five camels were engaged, but even so, the near life-size painting of the Virgin Mary had to be left behind. Cruttenden tried to sling the picture between two camels but these haughty creatures shied away from so strange a burden. The presents when they arrived in Shoa were received with pleasure by the King and shut away with the others in the King's treasure-house in a mountainside.

After some difficulty a Treaty of Amity and Commerce was concluded but it achieved nothing and was forgotten after the death of the King in 1848. The presents, however, were remembered by the King's son who succeeded to the throne and when Lord Palmerston sent him a box of three hundred gold sovereigns the young King considered it an insult. 'Why!' he wrote, 'Commander Haines sent my father presents that required one hundred and fifty camels to carry them, while to me they send a small box of brass coins!'

Harris knew too little about Abyssinia to justify his long optimistic reports, which compare unfavourably with the later and more realistic accounts given by the British Consul, Walter Plowden, who did not consider that there was much opportunity of trade with Abyssinia. Harris did give an interesting account on slavery, two hundred pages in length, stating—very sensibly—that, considering how much money was spent in shipping African slaves to America and how much money was spent by the British Government in stopping the shipment of slaves, it would be very much better to use European capital and industry to encourage Africans to cultivate their own lands. He then made the rather startling remark: 'Africa is, and always was, more productive than America has ever been found to be', taking no account of manpower, for, as Haines stated, Abyssinians made poor labourers because they considered it beneath their dignity to dig and till the soil. Harris was not good at evaluating the many stories he was told by Abyssinians. He asserted, for instance, that he had discovered 'a vast navigable river termed the Gochol rising in the great central ridge styled spine of the world which is known to divide the waters flowing west into the Atlantic from those which discharge themselves east into the Indian Ocean'. The river flowed eastwards into the Indian Ocean and he emphasised what an important channel of communication it could be from the coast to populous, healthy and fertile portions of the interior.[20]

Great interest was aroused in Government circles in Bombay and Haines instructed Lieutenant Christopher, commanding the *Tigris*, on a voyage in 1843 to Zanzibar, to see if he could find any other rivers which flowed into the Indian Ocean besides the Juba and the Shebelli rivers, which might be Harris's river Gochol. Christopher explored the Shebelli river for one hundred and twenty nautical miles and thought that that might possibly be the river and christened it the Haines river. So it is called on a number of nineteenth-century maps but then it reverted to its former name. Both rivers rise in the eastern lowlands of Abyssinia and are not there navigable. Richard Burton tried in vain to find traces of Harris's river on his adventurous journey from Zeyla to Harar in 1853, but it did not in fact exist.

Harris remained with the Mission some months after concluding the treaty in order to go elephant hunting and explore the country. He was repeatedly short of funds and Haines had to make arrangements to obtain the special Maria Theresa dollars which became scarce in Bombay and then send them on by trustworthy and expensive messengers to Shoa.[21] In July 1842 the Governor-General informed Bombay that the Harris Mission should long ago have been withdrawn: 'the situation of the finances of India is such as to make it absolutely necessary to reduce all expenditure . . . not evidently tending to produce important benefit to the people of India'. The Mission reached Bombay in April 1843 after an absence of two years.

Although there was criticism of the way that the Mission had been conducted, Harris was well received in England and knighted in June 1844. He returned to India and died four years later of lingering fever at the age of forty-one, in the same year as Sahela Selassie died.

The Slave Trade

(1840 to 1855)

The French attempts to find a footing in the Gulf of Aden had been arrested by Haines' activities and by the Harris Mission which, by its very extravagance, showed the French that the British were determined to prevent encroachment. D'Hericourt Rochet attempted to reach Ankobar with presents for the King of Shoa from King Louis Philippe of France, but was received with hostility by the Danakils and had to retire to Mocha. From there he wrote to his Government to complain of the opposition of the British and especially of Haines. Rochet did eventually reach Ankobar but by then the situation had changed and he had little influence.

Haines had reported in April 1842 that the number of Frenchmen in northern Abyssinia, their religious missions there and the many French warships visiting the Gulf of Aden made it clear that the views of France towards Abyssinia were not purely scientific and geographic, but that 'the possession of Aden will enable Britain at any time to counteract them'—a fact that was realised by the French naval officers who visited Aden. Captain Page, commanding the French ship-of-war *La Favorite*, who had taken part in the capture of Algiers in 1830, exclaimed: 'Why, Captain Haines, Aden is most decidedly the Gibraltar of the Red Sea and with a better harbour—you are lucky.' He was friendly but refused to salute the British flag as the King of France had not recognised Aden as a British settlement.[1]

While French influence had been strong along the east coast of Africa a little over thirty years previously and there had been French plans for the conquest of India, the Government of India had been careful not to press the Sultan of Zanzibar too hard with regard to the abolition of the slave trade, as the Sultan might have become on even more friendly terms with the French than he was already. But in the 1840's the East India Company was in a stronger position; since Zanzibar was one of the main centres of the slave trade from central Africa to the Persian Gulf, to Mukalla and other ports in South Arabia, it was decided that a concerted effort had to be made to try to deal with the trade.

Haines at Aden, Hennell in the Persian Gulf and Hamerton at Zanzibar were asked to co-operate and to report to Government. These three men backed by the power of the East India Company and the British Government, were the most influential officers in the area, '*les principaux rouages de cette superbe mécanique appelée la puissance anglaise*', wrote Alexandre Dumas in '*L'Arabie Heureuse*', '*et qui domine dans la Mer Rouge, sur le golfe Persique et sur les mers de l'Inde*'. Haines stated that the British possession of Aden had checked slavery in its vicinity though Muslim traders had soon found other ports. Lieutenant Christopher, commanding the *Tigris* had been sent to Massawa, where he found that the annual trade in slaves, mostly Galla children brought down from Abyssinia by Muslim traders for export to the ports of the Yemen, had nearly doubled to about sixteen hundred annually. The main markets for the purchase and export of slaves were Berbera, Zeyla, Tajjura, Massawa, Suakin, Mocha and Mukalla. The trade existed 'to a frightful extent', wrote Haines, and he had seen as many as two to three hundred children arrive at Mocha each month, placed naked in a compound, and from there driven to a well for water twice a day 'like a flock of sheep'.[2]

Abyssinia was one of the chief sources for slaves. In the Shoan markets boys could be bought for 10 to 15 dollars (£2 to £3) and girls cost a little more, reported Harris, while in the interior a boy could be purchased for a pair of Birmingham scissors or ten pieces of salt (two shillings). The law forbade any Christian to deal in slaves but Abyssinians could buy as many as they liked from traders. He argued that in the fifty years since Great Britain had started the offensive warfare against the African slave-trade, it had been 'trebled in amount and increased in horrors tenfold, and this notwithstanding the obstructions thrown in its way by the expenditure of £600,000 per annum [by the British Government] to help put it down'.[3]

Haines was a humane and religious man and was horrified at the sufferings and indignities caused by the slave trade, but he gave a warning of the danger of trying to move too fast. 'We do not want a religious war with the interior. This would inevitably follow a direct attempt to overthrow the traffic in slaves, inasmuch as though the Koran does not distinctly justify the proceeding, yet the conduct of their great Prophet sanctions the possession of slaves, he having one named Belal and another Kumba, the property of his son-in-law Ali'. From time immemorial the traffic in slaves along those coasts had been considered as just as any other trade—and by far the most lucrative. Almost every small harbour was the exclusive property of one independent chief and the trade of their forefathers continued to be considered a legitimate right to themselves individually as well as valuable to the finances of the tribe. 'Slavery provides them good and attached servants from whom the higher classes select their bodyguard, the care of their domestic economy, the tutors of their children, and frequently the *nacodahs* of their vessels are slaves. Their hareems are half filled with chosen beauties from the Galla tribes and Suwahil and much of their domestic satisfaction arises from their possessing an ample establishment of the kind, an attractive slave girl being considered the most complimentary present that can be offered.'[4]

These facts, Haines considered, should be known and taken into account: he wondered, for instance, how far British law could interfere with the trade of independent States, which were not allied to the British; 'although the surrounding tribes can form an appreciative idea of our principles of action on this point, still their feeling regarding freedom and independence is equal, if not greater, than that entertained by more civilised nations'. Slavery was repugnant to every British person and he knew that a British subject connected in any manner with slavery on the high seas or elsewhere, within or without the jurisdiction of the Admiralty Court, might be convicted of felony. He certainly had in mind the extraordinary case of Captain Hawkins who had in January 1830 reported on the island of Socotra as a coal depôt.[5]

The Bombay Government considered the slave trade traffic between East Africa and India was as objectionable as the trade carried out between the western coast of Africa and the West Indies. It had prohibited the export and import of slaves in the Bombay Presidency two years before the Abolition Act of 1807. But it realised that more ships were needed to stop traffic and that there would have to be agreements with a number of rulers such as the Sultan of Zanzibar who was also Imam of Muscat. Nothing could be done as yet with regard to the slave caravans which came annually from Abyssinia through Harar to Berbera and also through Zeyla and Tajjura.

A distinction was drawn between the possession of slaves and the trade in them. The latter might be stopped by naval action, but Hindu custom and Muslim law had accepted the status of slavery for many centuries and the Government of India could not afford to interfere too much with the customs of millions of people. Thus the Act which ended slavery in the British Colonies in 1833 excluded its application to the territories of the East India Company, though it was clear that while slavery existed the trade would continue, since there were never enough slaves to satisfy the demand. In 1843, however, the Government of India proclaimed that slavery could no longer be considered as legal, though it was not until 1860 that it was made a penal offence to own slaves as well as to trade in them, but the courts of India had no jurisdiction over Aden although it was Government territory.

It was well known to the Government of India how little had been achieved in the suppression of the slave trade and it was as concerned about this as was the British Government at home. In 1820 there had been a treaty with Sultan ibn Suggur and other Arab chiefs of the 'Pirate Coast' on the Arabian side of the Persian Gulf (now the Trucial Coast) to forbid piracy and slavery. A sworn bond had been given by the Arab chiefs to General Sir William Keir 'yet up to the present moment,' wrote Haines, 'it has failed to elicit the attention required and the slave markets are supplied as numerously as before'.

Captain Atkins Hamerton had estimated that about two hundred thousand slaves, mostly in Zanzibar, were possessed by the Imam of Muscat, who had stated that if slavery were abolished from the coast of Africa he would lose at least 100,000 dollars (about £20,000). It was not thought that the instructions for the suppression of the slave trade issued by the British Government to the Board of Control (June 8 1841) would be carried out, unless those concerned were made to feel the power of the British and Indian navies. The offer made by the British Government to pay the Imam of Muscat £2,000 a year for three years appeared, for instance, quite inadequate to cover the losses resulting from the abolition of the trade. It was argued that treaties and negotiations were useless, for so many were deeply interested in the continuation of the trade; even the sailors, for instance, who manned the boats of the Arab tribes each received one or more slaves instead of pay.[6]

When the British Government's instructions were communicated to the Sultan of Muscat and Zanzibar, he said 'Now all is over, these instructions and the orders of Azrael, the Angel of Death, are to the Arabs one and the same thing.'[7] The Sultan decided to send his ship the *Sultaneh* to London with a special envoy, Ali bin Nasir, with a petition to the Queen to modify in his favour the order, otherwise 'be thy Majesty informed that these countries will in consequence be totally and entirely ruined'. He sent Queen Victoria two pearl necklaces, two emeralds, an ornament made like a crown, ten cashmere shawls and four horses—'a trifling gift, scarce worth mentioning'; he also sent a petition to Lord Aberdeen the Foreign Minister. Captain Hamerton told the Sultan that the people in England and the British Government would be pleased to receive his envoy but that it would not alter the decision.[8] The Sultan had said to Hamerton: 'I well know the English have the power to stop the conveying of slaves by sea, but it will bring them the curse of the whole of

Islam. Arabs won't work; they must have slaves and concubines, but I see that the English will soon do something.'

'The Imam has not the power to interfere even were he willing to do so, but he is not', reported Hamerton about the situation in Zanzibar. 'Slavery is, in the opinion of all Arabs, a right guaranteed to them by their religion and the Imam would not, nor dare he, appear to coincide with the wishes of Government on this subject.' All his subjects were concerned with the slave trade, each possessing, according to his means, from five to two thousand slaves and they sell according to their financial needs—wealth and respectability depended on the numbers of slaves owned. Having collected a sufficient number of slaves an Arab 'lounges about from place to place with a sword under his arm subsisting on the labour or robbery done by his slaves'; because female slaves could be procured so easily in the bazaar of Zanzibar the Mohammedans had the opportunity 'of indulging to the fullest extent their love of variety in women', and if they had not got much money they could borrow slave-girls from the market and return them later. Hamerton also did not consider that anything could be done by negotiation, but by continually talking to the Sultan he had managed to persuade him to issue an order that the slaves who died should be buried, instead of being left on the beach to be devoured. 'I have seen fifty dead Africans, men and women lying on the beach, and the dogs of the place tearing them to pieces as one sees the carrion eaten by the dogs in India.' The only way to stop the slave trade in that part of the world, he stated, was by intercepting at sea the slave trading ships from Zanzibar.[9]

The Sultan's envoy, His Excellency Ali bin Nasir, was well received in London. He found Lord Aberdeen charming, but relentless, insisting that both the Government and people of Britain wanted the total abolition of this 'odious traffic' and urging that His Highness the Sultan should use every means in his power to 'extinguish the revolting custom of the Slave Trade'.

Ali bin Nasir returned from London through Aden and Haines was asked to accord him every hospitality. It was decided to send him back to Zanzibar in the *Tigris*, commanded by Lieutenant Christopher, who knew Arabic, had long conversations with the envoy and found him very charming and intelligent. But, though Lord Aberdeen had won His Excellency's 'unqualified esteem' and was repeatedly quoted by him, he had found the English attitude to the slave trade incomprehensible. Christopher gave what he described as a verbatim account of one of the conversations he had during the voyage with His Excellency Ali bin Nasir.

H.E.   How is it that though there have been a great many mighty nations and Sultans, no one ever spent money or used their means to subvert slavery but the English.

C.   We are getting wiser every day.

H.E.   No! From of old people were as wise as now.

C.   They were wise in some things, but it was not the wisdom which resulted from a desire to effect the greatest good for the greatest number of their fellowmen.

H.E.   Should the Imam put a stop to buying and selling servants, he would lose himself and be overwhelmed by the fury of the people.

C.   His name would be very great and never be forgotten. We consider that nearly all the criminality of slave dealing rests with the first purchaser.

H.E.   We consider them child murderers—naked, dying in numbers of starvation; we save their children and bring them up with a knowledge of God and teach them religion; they grow up as our children and true believers.

C.   We have a saying that you must not do evil though good may follow. I have heard of nearly five hundred slaves purchased in the interior of Africa for the Cairo market and only seventy-five arrived alive; there is much misery attending slavery.

H.E.   (Smiling at this remark) That is true, but travellers die of hardship of the road as well as servants.

'These are the usual arguments' commented Christopher, 'used by Mohammedans, the great traffickers in human bodies, to dispel their own scruples.'[10]

The Sultan of Zanzibar and Imam of Muscat was an unhappy man when he received his envoy's report, but he managed to obtain one concession from Aberdeen, that British ships would not interfere with the passage of slaves in the Sultan's ships between the ports and islands on the coast of his African dominions. On October 2 1845 the agreement was signed between the Sultan and Hamerton 'for the termination of the export of slaves from the African dominions of His Highness the Sultan of Muscat'. The agreement was to be enforced from January 1847. Hamerton wrote a warning despatch that not a great deal should be expected for the Sultan was the only man in his dominions who wished to meet the views of the British government and he had no means to enforce them on a population of many thousands who depended on slavery for their wealth and considered that God had, through the Prophet Mohammed and the Koran, given them the right to enslave non-Muslims.

Palmerston, who had become Foreign Minister in 1846, thought this attitude was defeatist and was annoyed. 'You will take every opportunity', he wrote to Hamerton, 'of impressing on these Arabs that the nations of Europe are destined to put an end to the African Slave Trade, and that Great Britain is the main instrument in the hand of Providence for the accomplishment of this purpose; that it is in vain for these Arabs to endeavour to resist the consummation of that which is written in the book of Fate. . . . They should hasten to betake themselves to the cultivation of the soil and to lawful and innocent commerce.'[11]

Haines was, fortunately for himself, not in a position to be thus admonished but he was under orders to stop and search ships which were thought to be carrying slaves. He had not enough armed vessels to do this effectively and some ships were seized which belonged to Somali or Arab tribes which had no slave treaties with Britain, so that this action amounted to piracy on the high seas on the part of the British.

With the co-operation of Captain Hennell, the Political Resident in the Persian Gulf, he had one minor success in returning to Berbera four Somali women who had been rescued from the 'Pirate Coast' of the Persian Gulf. They were brought to Aden in H.M. frigate *Endymion* and he sent them on to Ali Sharmakay at Berbera on board the *Constance*, then commanded by Lieutenant Christopher. 'I presented each female', wrote Haines, 'with four German crowns on quitting Aden, also some clothes, so that their appearance when relanding on their native soil might satisfy their countrymen they had been taken care of.' During the voyage across to Berbera, Lieutenant Christopher had shown his usual initiative by taking statements from the Somali women. All had been enticed aboard an

Arab boat either with the idea of meeting a young Somali they might marry or to be shown something to interest them. Somali women were seldom abducted, for they showed too much independence and caused trouble; nor was it considered right for Muslims to enslave other Muslims. Captain Grey, commanding H.M.S. *Endymion*, who had recently sailed from England, accompanied the *Constance* to Berbera and reported that he had hoped the handing over of the Somali women would be greeted as a lesson to the slave traders, but he found that fifty slaves were waiting to be embarked and all the leading men appeared to be so much interested in the trade that he was careful to avoid saying anything to suggest any British intention of interfering in it. 'Indeed, I feel satisfied that any such attempt at the present moment would involve us in quarrels with all these tribes, which would make it necessary to keep up a large force of small vessels for the protection of our trade'[12]—a comment that was sent on to the British Government. There was no doubt that the British war on the slave trade aroused 'a rancorous and implacable' hatred among the Arabs affected. The Turks fared no better. When an order from the Porte prohibiting the slave trade was read at Mecca in October 1855 there was a revolution and the *ulema* proclaimed that the order could not be obeyed as it conflicted with the word of God as given in the Koran.

The degree of success achieved by the British was, however, remarkable. Guillain wrote that their pertinacity displayed 'a manifest greatness in a people which, as one whole body, government and governed alike, is passionately bent on redressing the social crime of Slavery, and pours out its money, its ships, and its sailors and involves itself, day after day, in quarrelling and bloodshed in order to achieve its noble mission'.[13]

Insult and injury: defence or attack?

(March 1841 to June 1842)

British intentions regarding the slave trade were much discussed among the tribes near Aden; stories were being spread, partly by the French, that the British object in taking Aden was to stop the slave trade. This aroused apprehension and anger; contempt was also expressed for the British because they took no reprisals for the insults of Sherif Hussain of Mocha.

There was a strong case for punishment of the Sherif. He continued to intrigue with Sultan Mahsin of Lahej and to announce that he would capture Aden. Prayers for the extermination of the English were said in every mosque, and the Sherif refused to have dealings with the English or to have their flag flying over any Mahommedan town of which he was in control. Sherif Ahmed, his brother, told Cruttenden on one of his visits to Mocha that if an Englishman were found riding a horse in the town 'he would have his legs crossed over his shoulders and lashed at the back of his neck'. Very large sums of money had been unlawfully extracted from Indian merchants who were supposed to be under British protection, and there were some barbarous methods of doing this—a number of them, for instance, were enticed into an enormous wooden chest on the pretext of estimating how much grain it would hold, and then shut in until they agreed to pay large sums to save themselves from suffocation.

Haines had repeatedly recommended that the Sherif should be called on to mend his manners and that if he did not do so Mocha should be bombarded, as had happened in 1820 when the British flag had been insulted. Haines, who had been a member of the 1820 expedition, had seen how effective it had been in coming to an agreement with the Imam of Sana, then in control of Mocha.

At last, in March 1841, Lord Auckland wrote to Bombay to say that, as naval reinforcements were being sent out from England, it would now be possible to make the Sherif of Mocha agree to pay compensation for the property of Hajj Abdulla Roussoul. If he did not comply within a reasonable time Haines was 'to proceed to enforce the demands by naval and military operations' and, if necessary, 'to carry on the operations as far as the temporary occupation of the town of Mocha, the confiscation of all public property and the seizure of the person of the Sherif himself'.[1] Haines was delighted for he considered that such action would be understood by the Arabs and raise British prestige, so that peace and trade would follow. He began to work out a plan with Captain J. W. Grey of H.M.S. *Endymion*.

The Secret Committee, however, had already written in February 1841, a month before the Governor-General had issued his instructions for firm measures to be taken, stating that while there was no objection to vessels of war being sent to Mocha, the Board of Control refused to agree to any force being used. The Secret Committee also wrote on the same lines in July direct to the Bombay Government which had argued in favour of action being taken. These instructions were humiliating to the Government of India. Anguished appeals were being received from the Indian merchants at Mocha and Hodeida who were not allowed to leave the ports and large sums of money continued to be taken from them. The Imam of Sana went on urging Haines to send ships to blockade the port of Mocha while he attacked Sherif Hussain by land. In return he promised a number of advantages with regard to trade and said that the British could make full use of Zeyla once Sherif Hussain had been defeated. Zeyla was the best route to Shoa and Captain Harris had urged the Government of India to acquire it. The agreement made by Moresby was ineffective while the Sherif of Mocha controlled Zeyla and was hostile to the British.

In September the Governor-General in Council decided to write again to try to alter the London decision. The attention of the Secret Committee and of the British Government was drawn to the continuing insults from Sherif Hussain whose career had been marked 'by an undeviating course of hostility to this Government', and pointing out that the presence of H.M.S. *Endymion* would make it possible to carry out the original intention of enforcing reparations.[2] The letter might have had an effect if there had not been two developments: firstly the forceful Palmerston was no longer Foreign Minister, his place having been taken by Lord Aberdeen in September 1841; secondly, the Turkish Government had suddenly decided to revive a claim to the area, and the Sherif of Mocha had been made the accredited Agent of the Ottoman Empire. The Governor-General then suggested to London that the British Ambassador at Constantinople should explain the situation to the Porte and obtain either the removal of Sherif Hussain or allow the British Government to take its own measures for his punishment.

When Haines was informed that he could send warships to Mocha but was not to allow them to take any action, he decided that nothing would be achieved by such an expedition. As there seemed no hope, therefore, of enforcing reparations for Hajj Abdulla Roussoul, Haines reminded Bombay of the written undertaking given to Hajj Abdulla by Captain Moresby ('Government will fully remunerate you for all your losses and protect you to the utmost of their power'), and that the Company was therefore, fully responsible for repaying Hajj Abdulla the value of all that had been seized, which included the property he held as a merchant as well as a private individual. Lists of his possessions were sent and the estimated value was very large.

The Governor of Bombay and the Governor-General turned and

twisted to avoid making any such payment. They pointed out that Hajj Abdulla could have left Mocha when ships had been sent from Aden to warn the merchants to leave with their property to which Haines replied that, like a captain of a ship, the British Agent was expected to stay at his post. Then it was argued that under the protection of his character as a British Agent, he had been carrying on his business as a merchant; but it was just because he was a prominent merchant and so able to obtain information that he had been chosen as a British Agent. But no notice was taken of these points, nor of Moresby's written undertaking on behalf of the Government which was dismissed as 'unguarded', and the Governor-General wrote a classic example of an Establishment letter which ignored all the main points: 'It was notorious that Hajj Abdulla Roussoul carried on an extensive business at Mocha as a merchant and that the situation which he held as British Agent was an object to him in so far as it conferred upon him weight and responsibility. Had he not been encumbered with articles of merchandise . . . and had he possessed no other property but such as was suitable to his station as Agent, it is probable that he would have escaped with little or no loss.'[3] The Government was prepared to make a donation but that did not satisfy Hajj Abdulla. The Government of India had been ready to spend considerable sums of money on sending warships to bombard Mocha and on troops to land and seize the Sherif on the chance that reparations would be obtained, but it would not honour its bond to repay a useful servant of the Government for the losses suffered on official business.

The Sherif continued to be very troublesome and had found a new way of annoying the British. He made special arrangements with some American traders, such as Mr. Webb, master of the brig *Rattler*, allowing them so low an export duty on coffee that they took it from Mocha instead of from Aden as they had been doing. British failure to deal with the Sherif encouraged the Sultan of Lahej to think that he would eventually succeed in capturing Aden. Disturbing stories about the tyranny exercised by Sherif Hussain and his brothers were brought to Aden by the large number of refugees from Mocha. Many of these were artisans and labourers and proved an important factor in the growth of Aden.

The caravans were being interfered with by the Abdalis and the

Fadhli Sultans were also active. In July 1841, the Arab interpreter
to the regiment on duty at the field-works was murdered in a most
cold-blooded manner by Fadhli Sultans within a hundred yards or
so of the Aden defences and within range of British muskets. Haines
was disturbed that 'a body of chieftains coming immediately under
our guns, even our very muskets, and deliberately murdering a man
before our eyes should have escaped', and he referred again to the
advantage of a detachment of irregular cavalry. 'The success of so
daring a scheme of treachery' would be exaggerated in the interior;
it caused a stoppage of all supplies and prevented the return of the
envoy from the Imam of Sana who was visiting Aden at that time.[4]

In the middle of August Haines received one of Sultan Mahsin's
typical letters: 'I am friendly towards you, my heart yearns for you;
you believe things that are told you and people wish to make us
quarrel. I wish much for the friendship of the English. I have no
faults; we have been cool towards each other for nothing. Every day
my men are slain on the road bringing your supplies and it is on your
account that they are killed. . . . If you will give me kindness it is all
that I want.'[5] But the intrigues and attacks continued. On September
11 a caravan of four hundred camels entered Aden with supplies at
two o'clock in the afternoon; there was nothing unusual in the
number, but Haines was suspicious that the Arabs were planning a
Trojan horse operation and told Cruttenden to make sure that the
police had all members of the caravan out of the gates before sunset;
the cameleers were so obstinate about leaving that the police had to
use force to get them out but eventually nearly all were removed
before sunset. At 7-15 p.m. the warning rockets went up in the
field-works and there was rapid fire along the length of the wall, but
the enemy soon retreated when they realised that their plan had
failed. Their next ruse, a few days later, was to arrange with Arabs
inside the fortifications to set fire to the town so as to distract the
troops during an attack, but that became known and was stopped
by an order that no fire or light was allowed in the town after eight
o'clock at night.

Haines felt that he was losing the battle. He could do nothing about
the Sherif of Mocha, no cavalry was being sent and he had not been
allowed to advance beyond the fortifications. He was still convinced
that the only way to deal with the neighbouring tribes was to make

a quick assault on Lahej. He knew, he wrote, that these opinions were contrary to those of the Government but he felt it was his duty to make clear his views; 'it would have convinced all that insult to the British flag did not pass with impunity'.

The Governor-General of India and the Governor of Bombay continued to discuss with their respective Councils whether to pursue a forward policy or to remain on the defensive. At one moment it was agreed to attack and then they became nervous and cancelled the orders. Lord Auckland still considered Haines' proposal to have cavalry was a good one. 'Considering that we have now had this fortress for upwards of two years, maintaining there a large and expensive garrison, it is time that we should determine whether we are to continue to occupy it as a beleaguered town . . ., or whether we shall, by a small increase to the garrison of the place, be enabled to keep those marauders at a distance and thereby give such confidence to our friends and adherents and such protection to our subjects as will render Aden the prosperous sea-port which its position so well fits it to become.' He did not consider it 'creditable to our reputation . . . to allow matters to remain much longer on their present footing'. His Lordship thought that when the European regiment was next relieved an opportunity might occur 'of striking a blow at Lahej that would produce a permanent effect on the policy of the Sultan and other chieftains'.[6] He would also sanction the expense of fifty mounted troops.

By July, three months later, Lord Auckland was wondering whether an attack on Lahej would be wise: 'the effect of such a blow might be only temporary' and the Sultan would then resume hostilities which could in the end 'force us to an occupation of a part of the inland country and be in that manner a source of much embarrassment'. His Lordship wanted the views of Bombay and of Captain Haines 'upon the weight due to this objection'.[7]

It was unfortunate that while Auckland was a good man of business and 'an assiduous reader of all papers' he was also 'much wanting in promptness of decision and had an overweening dread of responsibility'.[8] But Bombay was no more capable of making up its mind than was he, and by the end of August the Governor-General had received no answer. He asked the Bombay Government what it had decided to do 'to convince that Chief [Sultan Mahsin] that, if he persists in his present course of open hostility to the British power, he is not beyond the reach of punishment.'

The Bombay Government finally decided to give Haines permission to attack Shaikh Othman, which was eight miles from the fortifications, but he was told that he was not on any account to advance further. It was left to him to decide on 'the highly important and delicate question' as to whether such an attack on the Arabs 'would be likely to exasperate them still more and so prevent, or render more distant, the establishment of a friendly intercourse with them'. The Government knew quite well what Haines would do, but did not itself want to take responsibility for the decision in case of failure. The Company's frigate *Auckland* was due to leave Bombay on September 22 with five hundred rank and file of H.M.'s 17th Regiment and Haines was told that he could keep the *Auckland* for not more than ten days when she was to return with the troops due to be relieved.

'It took but little time', commented Haines, 'to decide on the execution of the opportunity so favourably offered.' Within twenty-four hours of the receipt of the Bombay Government's letter Colonel Croker, commanding the garrison, had prepared an expedition consisting of four hundred Europeans and twenty native infantry with one gun and eighty artillerymen. Everything was organised so quickly that the townspeople were unaware that the expedition had left at 10 p.m. on October 5 1841. Lieutenant-Colonel Pennycuick of the 17th Regiment was in command and Lieutenant Cruttenden with three guides led the way. A little before daybreak the detachment reached the village of Nobeir Maidee, the residence of Shaikh Maidee, where the Fadhli chiefs met and planned their attacks on Aden. Unfortunately three miles before the village, at Bir Zaad, the detachment came upon two armed guards watering their camels who fled spreading the alarm in all directions; this afforded the Fadhli chiefs and Shaikh Maidee and his family just time to escape before the British surrounded his house. The Shaikh's fort was* blown up and by 8 a.m. the British were marching on to Shaikh Othman. By that time the Fadhlis and Abdalis were on the alert.

---

* The fort, known as Nowbat Shaikh Maidee, had been built after the Arab attack of July 1840 and used as a headquarters for raids on caravans taking supplies to Aden causing great loss in trade.

The Arabs began to appear at first in small parties and at a distance, but gradually their numbers increased and they advanced opening fire upon the rear-guard and the left flank of the column. A constant and sharp fire was kept up on both sides for about two hours during the march through a wood, the Arabs being no sooner driven from one post than they retreated out of range to another near the line of march. 'This they were enabled to do,' reported Lieutenant-Colonel Pennycuick, 'in consequence of a great number of them being mounted on horses or camels and we, not having any cavalry, were not able to follow up the advantage gained by our skirmishers. . . . The number must have been considerable for at one period the front, left flank and rear were being attacked at the same time.'[9] The Arab losses were heavy since the skirmishes were closely fought and severe, but the only losses on the British side were a lieutenant and four privates wounded, and one private dead from sun-stroke. The detachment reached Shaikh Othman at 11 a.m., rested a few hours and returned to Aden in the evening without being again attacked. Pennycuick praised the cheerfulness and gallantry of the troops, reporting that they had marched nearly forty miles in twenty-four hours—a remarkable performance since they also had had to fight for nearly two hours during the hottest part of the day.

The expedition from Aden had been most effective. Shaikh Maidee, whose tower had been blown up, wrote for forgiveness; 'you are a powerful nation and your arm is strong, I say again I wish to study your wishes'. When the Sultan of Lahej heard the explosions, he had feared that the British were coming to Lahej and he went with his family and many of the inhabitants to the British Agent's house at Saffran for protection. 'Thus does a sudden night's surprise, and a specimen of British discipline and coolness during the day cause the Sultan to fly to the British Agent for protection who, not a fortnight before, he had endeavoured to murder.'[10] The Sultan sent an express letter to Haines saying that he wished to visit him: 'I will throw myself on your bed and solicit forgiveness from the Government. You can then either make me a prisoner or grant forgiveness?' He said he could not bring his children as they did not want to come; 'they will not obey me. If I am severe with them they will leave me. You know a father's love for his children?' But Haines was not to be won over by soft words and continued to believe that the only way to deal with a fickle Sultan was to take strong measures. 'With such a man,' he wrote to the Secret Committee, 'nothing but dictating terms to him at Lahej and retaining two of his children in Aden as hostages will quieten the country.'[11]

The Government of Bombay was pleased with the results of the action but their praise was a little reserved, as if it feared that to express enthusiasm might encourage Haines in a forward policy. He had, in fact, written a letter on September 22 about advancing to Lahej which had crossed the instructions from Bombay limiting any advance to Shaikh Othman. Haines had put forward a bold, and not very wise plan, to set up a more subservient Government in Lahej after its capture. It was, on a minor scale, rather similar to the plan that Lord Auckland and the British Government had been foolish enough to carry out when they removed Dost Mohammed from the throne of Afghanistan and had replaced him by the more amenable Shah Suja. Auckland's arguments against Haines' plan were equally valid with regard to his own: 'It appears obvious to His Lordship that although such measures might at first be executed with great rapidity, yet their subsequent maintenance would be attended with constant difficulties and calls for our interference.'[12] It had not been obvious to His Lordship that the Afghans would resent having a puppet king put on the throne and kept there by a British garrison. The Governor-General was yet to learn the details of the revolt in Kabul and of the terrible march back to India which led to the deaths of about five thousand British and Indian soldiers and of ten thousand camp followers.

The expedition to Shaikh Othman was followed by a blockade of Shuqra by the *Euphrates* (Lieutenant Christopher), which was also a success since it forced the Fadhli Sultan to withdraw his tribesmen from controlling the roads to Aden. On November 28 an influential emissary arrived in Aden from Sultan Sallah ibn Abdulla Fadhli to solicit peace and to offer himself as hostage. Haines accepted the terms offered and called off the blockade of Shuqra. In the meantime the Abdali Sultan of Lahej was disturbed that the Fadhli Sultan might reach Aden and come to terms with the British before he did. He suggested to the Fadhli Sultan that he should wait so that they should go together to Aden to confront the Political

Agent, which might have more effect than if they went separately. Having made this very plausible suggestion, the Sultan of Lahej suddenly ordered his attendants to proceed with him at once to Aden, thus ensuring at least four or five days conference with Haines before the Fadhli Sultan could learn of his movements.

Before leaving Lahej the Sultan told Sayyed Hussain Weiss that if he could persuade Haines not to insist on keeping his sons as hostages, the Sultan would give his two youngest daughters in marriage to the Sayyed's two sons, and would also give the first instalment of the stipend money after peace had been concluded. The Sayyed was eager for these marriages as it would make his family more influential and he asked Sayyed Zain Aidrus in Aden to help him persuade Captain Haines to forgo his demand for hostages; but Sayyed Zain refused, saying that he would not again act in any way against the Political Agent.

The meeting between Haines and the Sultan on January 4 was a strange one. After the formalities the Sultan asked in decided tone: 'What have I been guilty of? And what do you demand of me?' When Haines began to enumerate his misdeeds, the Sultan interrupted him with an impatient gesture exclaiming: 'Stop! Stop! Commander Sahib, for heaven's sake don't speak so plainly in the presence of my people.' Haines said that he was only doing what the Sultan had asked and it were better that he concluded his statement to which the Sultan grudgingly signified assent.[13]

The Sultan was overcome by this list of charges which all present knew were justified and for once he was humbled. Indeed, at the next meeting two days later he was still contrite and admitted that all the accusations had been true, except the one concerning the murder of Abdulla Khatif. The murder, he declared, had been committed by his son Hamed but he had acquiesced in it and Sayyed Hussain Weiss had sanctioned it. Haines was amazed at this charge against his Agent and afterwards called the Sayyed to a private interview to tell him what the Sultan had said. This roused him to a state of absolute fury and he abused his father-in-law in the most insulting language, which he later repeated in front of the Sultan and many of the most influential inhabitants, including Mullah Jaffar, and each accused the other of the murder.

While in Aden the Sultan swore on the Koran that he would give two of his children as hostages. Having given Haines that solemn assurance he unbuckled his belt and offered his creese, saying: 'Now kill me or forgive me!' Haines returned the weapon expressing the hope that peace and prosperity might result to him and the British. 'He then advanced towards me and made an effort to salute my brow and my feet in the eastern style, craving pardon in abundance of words. I said that the pardon was granted if he left behind his sons and fulfilled the conditions required.' These were, firstly to solicit pardon publicly, secondly to give hostages and thirdly to restore all the money and possessions to Abdulla Khatif's son and to give back all other property plundered from the inhabitants of Aden.

While these negotiations were proceeding there arrived at the main gate a number of Fadhli chiefs with a large body of retainers to make peace on behalf of their Sultan, who had waited at Shaikh Othman to hear from them before he entered. At the gate someone told them that the Sultan of Lahej was a prisoner and bound in chains, so they refused to pass into Crater until Sayyed Zain Aidrus went to the gate and brought them in to see the Sultan. They found him, a guest in Mullah Jaffar's house, surrounded by every comfort and being served with a large meal. The Fadhli chiefs were angry to find that Sultan Mahsin, after proposing joint negotiations, had stolen a march on them. They left at once to communicate their discovery to the Fadhli Sultan at Shaikh Othman.

This meeting worried the Sultan of Lahej and he did not like any of the terms proposed. He left Aden without making any formal agreement and, although he had promised to give his sons as hostages, his last effort before leaving Aden was to try to bribe Mullah Jaffar to use his influence with Haines that he should not insist on having them. When Haines was told of this by Mullah Jaffar his views on the Sultan's unreliability were confirmed and he almost despaired of ever reaching a final and lasting agreement with the Arabs of South Arabia.

'Their youth is spent in the study of dissimulation and intrigue,' he wrote to London, 'and their older age in practising these vices, and often, when I have considered any treaty with them almost secure, my hopes have been arrested by the unravelling of some artful intention, or palpable falsehood. When explanation for the discrepancy is required, the only reply they will give is: "Yes, we have broken our promise but it is our custom." It is such ignorant stubbornness that requires us to evince our power to *enforce* attention to their promises. Fear alone will control them for a while, until they become familiar with European laws and ordinary attention to their word of honour.'[14]

It was unlike Haines to be so depressed, but he was also anxious lest his account of the Sultan's humility during the meetings in Aden might lead the Bombay Government to think that his promises meant anything. Indeed, only a little time later Haines learned that the Sultan of Lahej was writing frequently to the Fadhli Sultan urging him once more to join him against the English. No new written agreement had been made with the Fadhli Sultan, but he considered that he had given his word to make peace and wrote to Haines. 'I have made peace with the English and though the Sultan [of Lahej] has offered to pay me, still I have sworn and will not break my oath.' But he would, remarked Haines, if he were bribed enough 'bribes are absolutely beyond the principle of a Beduin to refuse, unless restrained by fear'. There was another reason for Haines to feel depressed. The powerful Sayyed Hussain Weiss was now working against him instead of for him, since he had been dismissed from his post as Agent when Haines had learned of the part he had played in the murder of Abdulla Khatif.

The Bombay Government, as Haines had expected, were delighted when they heard of the friendly meeting between Haines and Sultan Mahsin and proposed that, in view of the new situation, the garrison might be reduced and that the expensive detachment of cavalry was not really necessary. That was not at all what Haines had in mind and he pleaded again for the addition of the detachment of irregular horse, which he knew had been agreed to by the Governor-General and by the Court of Directors; as it was, the Beduin could approach the walls without fear since they knew they could escape on their fleet camels. 'Until I had seen the magnificent manner in which these men manoeuvre their camels I knew not what the animal was capable of,' wrote Lieutenant Wellsted, 'they are stopped, turned and in fact kept under control as completely as a horse.' The Governor-General emphasised Haines' point that 'security from annoyance' would in a short time more than counterbalance the expense; nor did he rely on the promises of peace made by the Sultans and it were better to have the cavalry detachment which was designed 'to make us to some extent independent of their enmity or friendship'.[15]

The Bombay Government at last, on February 17 1842, gave instructions for the detachment of horse to be sent from Poona and informed the Governor-General that it would be despatched to Aden immediately. But there was a muddle. The detachment was not ready until too late in the season and so could not be sent before the next favourable monsoon. Then the Bombay Government instructed the committee which was to report on the fortifications in Aden to give its views about the need for the cavalry detachment; the Governor was still worried that it might lead to a collision with the inhabitants of the country 'which it is so very desirable to avoid'. Any question of a military expedition inland reminded officials of the disastrous expedition led by Captain Perronet Thompson in 1820 against the Abu Ali tribe of Oman, fifty miles inland from Sur. Arabs armed with broad swords had destroyed a force of British, Indians and Arabs. Thompson was court-martialled and a second, much larger expedition, sent in retaliation, succeeded in destroying the Abu Ali fort but also suffered very heavily. An attack by sea, however, was regarded generally with favour by Bombay.[16]

When Haines eventually learned that the Governor-General had asked the British Foreign Office that the case of the Sherif of Mocha should be taken up with the Porte and that the British Government had agreed to this, he protested in a long despatch to Bombay. He pointed out, as he had done before, that the Turkish Government had no justifiable claim to the Yemen whose rightful sovereign was the Imam of Sana.[17] The Bombay Government, which was still annoyed at not being allowed to send an expedition to Mocha, 'passed Haines' arguments on to London, pointing out that the action taken by the Foreign Office at the Porte had been a mistake and had tied the hands of the Government of India. The Foreign Office agreed that the Turkish Government made claims to territories, as in the case of the Yemen, which had not been part of their dominion since the departure of Turkish Armies in the sixteenth century. At the same time it could be argued that Mohammed Ali Pasha, as the Ottoman Sultan's Viceroy, had given the Turks a claim by the

Egyptian occupation of the seacoast of the Yemen in the 1830's. The British Government, however, did not pursue the question of sovereignty closely with the Porte but decided that if Turkish troops were in control of any area it would recognise at any rate the *de facto* authority of the Turkish Government. This avoidance of the issue led to difficulties later when the British tried to control the slave trade in the Red Sea; 'if they recognised the authority of firmans sent from Constantinople to Turkish officials in southern Arabia to suppress this trade, they automatically recognised the sovereignty of the Porte in the area'.[18]

The British Government by referring the question of the Sherif of Mocha to the Porte certainly gave some recognition to Turkish authority there, but nothing was achieved with regard to the Sherif of Mocha. The Turkish Government sent a high official, Eshreff Bey, with instructions to remove the Sherif from office as a punishment for the repeated insults to the British. The Turkish commander at Jedda had insufficient troops to enforce the dismissal, and Eshreff Bey received a large bribe from Sherif Hussain so that he recommended to the Porte that the Sherif should be left in charge of Mocha. This advice was eventually accepted by the Turkish Government several months later and in the meantime Haines was not pleased to have Eshreff Bey in Aden as a guest of the British Government to await orders from the Porte.

These uncertainties made it very difficult for Haines to deal with the tribes neighbouring Aden and he believed that British loss of prestige would have a long-lasting effect. Indeed, a later political resident, Brigadier Coghlan, commented twenty years later: 'Though proverbially inconsistent themselves, and frequently indulging in threats they have no power to fulfil, the Arabs appreciate consistency in others, and the want of it which so unhappily characterised Captain Haines' administration, though not the fault of that officer, has had the most prejudicial effect in lowering our prestige.'[19]

The uncertainties had been partly due to Lord Auckland's lack of decision. He was recalled by the Court of Directors at the beginning of 1842 and it was hoped that his successor, Lord Ellenborough, would be able to handle affairs better. At the beginning of his rule he was successful in re-establishing British prestige in Afghanistan and then carrying out a withdrawal. His main concern

Insult and injury: defence or attack?

was with the affairs of the Indian continent and he showed no interest in Arabs and Somalis or understanding of the importance of the areas they held on the shores of the Gulf of Aden and of the Red Sea. He had a weakness for display, arranging extravagant and sometimes rather ridiculous ceremonials—carried away by the lingering shadows of former Mogul splendour.

'For what object is Aden occupied?'

(November 1842 to April 1843)

Edward Law, Earl of Ellenborough, had announced that his mission was 'to restore peace to Asia' but he had to contend with war during the two and a half years he was Governor-General before he was also recalled. He was an able administrator and took a special interest in the development of government in India, considering that the British Government should take over the entire administration of India from the Company so that aims could be properly co-ordinated, but that was not done until after the Mutiny of 1857.

Ellenborough was more emphatic than Auckland and expected orders to be carried out. He was annoyed, for instance, to find that nine months after the Bombay Government had said it was sending the cavalry detachment to Aden nothing had been done and he insisted that the detachment should leave at once which it did in December 1842.[1] The Governor-General wished to follow up the initiative taken by Lord Auckland to try to intimidate the Sherif of

Mocha but he, too, was bound by policy settled in London and caught up in the labyrinth of Ottoman politics.

It was clear, wrote Sir Stratford Canning (later Lord Stratford de Redcliffe), the British Ambassador in Constantinople, that Eshreff Bey had not carried out his orders but he could do nothing through diplomacy. The Porte had little power to enforce its orders and Stratford Canning was clearly surprised, being an autocrat himself, that the Governor-General of India had not done what he wanted to do at Mocha without asking the Ottoman Government. 'I venture to submit,' wrote Canning, 'whether it might not be better for the Indian Government to employ in certain cases a more active influence for the protection of British subjects and British commerce on the banks of the Hejaz and the Yemen as well as in the neighbouring seas.'[2] This advice, which must have been infuriating to Ellenborough, arrived from the Secret Committee with a warning that the Governor-General must not act on Canning's statement.

So many people were taking a hand in the affair of the Sherif of Mocha that Ellenborough wrote in pique to the Bombay Government: 'Mocha is not really within our sphere of action, diplomatically. It is nearer to England than Calcutta and everything done there has a bearing upon European politics.' Considering how close Mocha was to Aden and how important Aden was to Bombay, this must have seemed to the Bombay Government a very strange attitude.

Ellenborough considered that the cost of the defences and the upkeep of the garrison made it too expensive a port. 'For what object is Aden occupied?' He himself could see no object in holding Aden except as a coal depôt and a supply station for steamers, and he was not sure that it was even necessary for that. Larger steamers should be able to go all the three thousand miles from Bombay to Suez, but if not, was there not another place where steamers could anchor in security and good water be obtained.[3] There were a number of other questions which ignored four years of development in Aden and must have caused distress and annoyance to officials in Bombay.

In October of the same year, 1843, Lord Ellenborough was again considering adversely the problem of Aden and its government. Haines had reported that Hajj Ali Sharmakay had taken possession of Zeyla from the Arab troops of the Sherif of Mocha. 'I secretly determined, as a Somali Chief,' he wrote to Haines, 'to teach them a lesson by removing the Arabs from the land of the Somalis, Zeyla is mine without bloodshed.' If he could have the protection of the British flag Zeyla could be British, and he would suppress slavery, reduce the customs duties to five per cent and make the road safe to Harar. These were all proposals that the British and Indian Governments had wanted for a long time. Yet Lord Ellenborough saw nothing but disadvantage in it, and reacted vigorously with a diatribe against interference in the disputes of the chiefs of Africa and Arabia. Relations with them would continue to be 'commercially of very minute importance and politically of no importance at all'. The British Government retained Aden 'for the purpose of protecting a depôt of coal, not for that of promoting intervention in the affairs of the neighbouring chiefs of Africa and Arabia, and of gradually extending its possession in that quarter'.⁴ But after the capture of Aden there had been no question of extending territory and the Government of Bombay replied rather crossly to the Governor-General: 'from the tone of your letter it should be imagined that this Government has been favourably disposed to an aggressive intermeddling policy either in the Red Sea or Persian Gulf or in any other quarter'.

Even to protect a depôt for coal it was good policy to seek allies among powerful neighbouring Arab chieftains in the Yemen as well as around Aden, and Ellenborough carried his indifference dangerously far. When three of the British Agent's servants were murdered on the verandah of his house at Tajjura, the Government of India refused to let Haines punish the Sultan of Tajjura who was suspected of having encouraged the murders to curry favour with the Sherif of Mocha. When the Imam of Sana sent his many envoys to Haines asking for British help in removing the Sherif of Mocha, the reaction from Calcutta was: 'the Governor-General has no wish to mix up the British Government with the unimportant affairs of the Imam of Sana'.⁵

The Governor-General thought that to have any officer at Aden 'nominally charged with what are termed political functions' was detrimental since it encouraged 'a disposition to meddle in matters wherein we really have no interest, no right of interference and in which the most ample and unequivocal success would hardly compensate for the charge of the officer's salary for a single year'. This letter of October 7 1843 was circulated as a guide to Government of India policy and sent to Haines by the Bombay Government without any friendly gloss. What was he to make of it, or Captain Hennell in the Persian Gulf, or Major Rawlinson at Baghdad, each of whom received copies?

But however many statements the Government might make to the contrary, the Political Agents had to be involved with the tribes, especially those near Aden which had become an important port to them. The links between every tribe in the Yemen were so close that all were aware of the intrigues in the area; events at Mocha, Jedda or Sana, and even at Cairo or Constantinople, had repercussions up to the walls of the Aden fortifications. Rumours were so many and so exaggerated that, if Haines had not maintained a good intelligence service, the commander of the garrison would have been asking Bombay for reinforcements when they were not necessary and at other times have been caught off his guard.

It sounded well when Ellenborough wrote that he would deeply regret the necessity of using 'coercion for the protection of our interests in the Arabian and Persian Gulfs and more especially in the Red Sea'. But the British Government had ordered that ships were to be searched for slaves to stop the trade which entailed the possible use of force and, if Indian merchants were to be protected, force had to be employed every now and again in regions where there was lawlessness.

It might have been thought that Ellenborough was influenced by such anti-imperialist views as were expressed at the time in an article in *Blackwood's Edinburgh Magazine*: 'Events in Kabul opened the eyes of our statesmen both in India and England to the moral and political delinquency of the system we have so long pursued—of taking the previous owner's consent for granted whenever it suited our views to possess ourselves of a fortress, island or tract of territory belonging to any nation not sufficiently civilised to have had representatives at the Congress of Vienna. Whether our repentance is to be carried to the length of universal restitution remains to be seen; if so, it is to be hoped that the circumstances of the capture of Aden will be duly borne in mind.'[6] Perhaps Ellenborough was indeed influenced by these views as far as Arabia and Africa were concerned, but he carried on an active and aggressive policy to maintain and increase British prestige in India. It was not, however, very sensible or practical to pursue a policy of regional Liberalism.

Haines did not allow the Governor-General's views on Political Agents to depress him and carried on with his job governing Aden; he liked being 'the point of reference for all' and, with the growth of the town, work increased. The flow of passengers who stopped in Aden on their way to and from England had more than doubled; a second monthly service had been started through Aden at the beginning of 1845 by the Peninsular and Oriental Company picking up mails and passengers from Hongkong, Singapore, Ceylon, Calcutta and Bombay on their way to and from Suez; the other monthly service continued with steam packets of the East India Company to and from Bombay.

More and more passengers landed from these ships, shopped at Crater bazaar and went for a ride round Aden. Every camel, horse, mule and donkey for hire had a brass badge on his headstall with a number stamped on it, and a regular scale of fares was laid down for visitors from boats and for members of the garrison. A notice was posted in the hotel and at the police station at Steamer Point, cautioning passengers and all strangers to take a note of the number of the animal they hired before leaving any property in the hands of the individual attendants. As more Arabs from the interior flocked into the town, a system of registration was adopted for them also; each man on entering Aden was supplied with a copper ticket while his name was entered in the Police Office. If there were any sign of trouble the newcomers could be assembled and sent out of Crater town. At night every person after evening gun-fire had to carry a lantern when out of doors, as was the rule at Mocha and Hodeida, and there was a nightly patrol of mounted police.

The Police, the Post Office and the coal wharf were looked after by Cruttenden who was also continuously short of staff. When a steamer arrived with mails, Cruttenden often had to sort the letters from Bombay himself, make up the mail for England and then sometimes go down at dawn to arrange for the coaling of the ship. When he was away or ill it was impossible to prevent everything falling into arrears—and Cruttenden was away a great deal, sent by Haines to deal with Somali troubles at Berbera, or to Zeyla, Tajjura, Mocha, Socotra and the East coast of Africa; when the *Memnon* was wrecked in August 1843 off Cape Gardafui while on the mail service to Suez, Cruttenden was sent to help with the salvage of the ship and spent nearly ten months in Somaliland.

Thieving took up a great deal of the time of the Police, an efficient and well-trained force of Muslims from Bombay. The young Somali boys made a profession of stealing from the shops and Haines found himself faced with new problems. 'The best mode of punishment has not yet been discovered. To put them in jail amongst their fellows is merely to confirm them in vice, and the certainty of obtaining their food regularly, coarse though it be, is almost an inducement to be sent there. Whipping is a punishment that causes no disgrace and is unheeded, being endured by the youngest lads with the most stoical indifference. It is a matter of very great difficulty to award a punishment commensurate with the extent of a man's rational powers or degrees of civilisation and still make the award serve as an example. With the Somali the disgrace is not because he is a robber, but because he has been detected and taken, and the readiness with which they frequently avow themselves to be the offenders plainly shows that they consider it no crime but rather a distinction.'

Despite the pressure of work and difficulties with Bombay Haines remained good-tempered and in good health. He was interested in his mixed population in Aden, he enjoyed the company of Arabs and was intrigued by their way of life, which appeared anarchic and yet had controls built up within the tribal system and developed over the centuries. He enjoyed administering a growing town and keeping in touch with the interior through his intelligence sources. Every day there were letters in Arabic and Hebrew from various places in the Yemen and South Arabia passing information which had to be translated and evaluated.

But there was one job which had irked him from the beginning of his administration and that was looking after the Treasury. He knew nothing about accounts when he first came to Aden and he had to deal with about one hundred thousand pounds a year helped by a low-grade and underpaid staff, whose salaries he supplemented out of his own pocket. Out of the Treasury he made advances monthly to the naval, military and civil establishments at Aden, keeping accounts of receipts and disbursements which had to be sent monthly in duplicate—sometimes three copies had to be made and even five copies when concerned with ships of the Royal Navy. There were also the stipends for the chiefs and expenses of hospitality when they visited Aden. A large supply of dollars had to be kept, as the Arabs outside Aden had not yet accepted rupees as currency, and Walter Plowden, the British Consul in Abyssinia, needed supplies as well as the Harris Mission. There were occasions when the Treasury was very short of coin and he took advantage of the fact that Indian merchants used to have from thirty to fifty thousand rupees ready to send to Bombay by each ship, and he obtained permission to give bills on the Bombay Government at twenty days sight in exchange for these rupees. He also made an arrangement with an Indian merchant firm to transact bills for him.

Haines felt bitter against the Government of Bombay for not sending him and his assistant sufficient staff to deal with the accumulation of work. He was also annoyed when he was accused of spending too much money on the entertainment of chiefs and their followers visiting Aden. He replied that he had been as economical as possible, but that some chieftains came from as much as three hundred miles away to pay a complimentary visit; it was the custom in South Arabia that a visitor should be entertained at the host's expense and if a present were not given on departure it was considered an insult. Even the Sultan of Lahej, 'though avaricious in the extreme', had to spend large sums in entertaining chiefs and several hundred followers. 'It would be unwise policy and ill become me as the Government representative to behave either uncourteously or inhospitably. The British character for generosity and liberality would be sullied, and the future and rapidly rising prosperity to Aden be destroyed.'[7] The Government did not like the tone of this letter and considered it 'perfectly uncalled for'. As usual Government wanted the best possible service at the least expense, and made it clear that it was not prepared to agree to the payment of large sums of money for entertainment. Haines felt obliged to continue as he had been doing and paid some of the expenses out of his own pocket to avoid trouble.

The new attitude adopted by the Governor-General towards Arab and African affairs in general and to Political Agents in particular had an effect on the Bombay Government; it began to be more critical and, at times, to distrust Haines' judgement, believing that it knew better than him how to handle South Arabian affairs. Haines, of course, was more than a Political Agent. He was the first Governor of a newly created and growing town for which he had to work out the system of administration with little help from British officials in England or India who were mostly ignorant of the problems. The Bombay Government considered that his duties were not 'in any way heavier than those which usually devolve on other officers holding similar situations', and there were no grounds for adding to the very heavy charges by increasing his staff. There was, in fact, no officer of his rank who did hold a similar situation throughout the whole administration of the East India Company, or had as much responsibility.

Haines wrote bitterly that the Afghan campaigns with the storming of Ghuznee had led to Aden being almost forgotten. 'How differently, however, has the first conquest [Aden] and the other terminated. Aden has thrice successfully repulsed united Arab endeavours to retake it, is now a peaceful settlement and a valuable brilliant in the British Diadem, requiring only a European War to develop its true value, while Ghuznee, for which so many were rewarded, and a medal adorns the breast of many a soldier now in Aden, has been lost, retaken by the late General Sir William Knott, and destroyed.'

Aden was indeed a peaceful and growing settlement but there were many setbacks. At the end of December 1842, for example, it rained so heavily that the water from the mountains rushed along the Valley of Aden drowning men and animals and destroying property. Haines and his wife were secure in the new house on the cliff above Steamer Point. Damage from the floods could still be seen in March 1843 when a visit was paid to Mary Haines by her brother, who was on his way from England to Calcutta where he was a Chaplain on the Bengal Establishment. Haines wanted channels to be dug to deflect any future floods which might again endanger life and property but the Government was not prepared to spend the necessary funds and there was further damage in subsequent years.

'I have lost everything: you have Aden.'

(November 1842 to November 1847)

For a long time Haines had been criticised by a clique in the Aden garrison for being too hard on the Sultan of Lahej, and the Bombay Government began to argue on the same lines. In his many letters to Haines the Sultan often made his appeal indirectly to Government, and tried to divide so as not to be ruled. There was a letter from him in November 1842 which made little impression on Haines, for he considered it full of hypocrisy, but on the Government it had its effect: 'I have lost everything—you have Aden and I must wait patiently. I do not act with treachery. I remained in my house while the Fadhli crept in (as the serpent tempted Eve) and tempted me. I was bewildered and committed myself. If I had been friendly to you it would have been to my advantage. You have heard untruths and discard me. I am fallen, others are elevated. The injury done on the roads by murder and plunder is not good; there is a difference between us and my men will not obey me; you have neglected me and they disrespect me. If God pleases and you are willing to be friendly with me, then will the road to Sana be open to you and it will be crores [of rupees] to your treasury and Aden be a grand emporium. Look to this, examine into the probable benefits and be friends.'[1]

Bombay urged Haines to conclude peace—as if he were the only obstacle. The Government felt confident that it could be done, if the Sultan's overtures were received in a conciliatory spirit and if in his correspondence with him, Haines would 'carefully avoid any allusion likely to irritate that chief'; if the demand for hostages was the only reason for failing to conclude a treaty of peace they should not be insisted upon. It was not a sound argument, for there was no difficulty about concluding a treaty, the problem was to ensure that the Sultan honoured it. Haines regretted that Government did not like the way he wrote to the Sultan, but the expressions he used were the result of 'a long and attentive examination' of the Sultan's character, and whenever he had been conciliatory in the past, the invariable consequence had been a new aggression 'owing to his inability to distinguish between a true and honourable reconciliation and a cowardly vacillating spirit'.[2]

Then a letter came signed by both the old Sultan and his son Hamed, which was more straightforward and practical than previous letters and which did, in the end, lead to the signing of a peace treaty. The Bombay Government thought that this new approach was the result of the advice it had given, but Haines had not written again to the Sultan and it was more likely to have been due to the arrival of the cavalry detachment. Another factor was the success of British forces in China, including the capture of Hongkong, and in Afghanistan which had awakened a more lively sense of our merits, whereas the earlier disasters of 1841 had considerably lowered British prestige throughout the area. The Sultan was now over seventy and appeared to be deferring more to his son, who was anxious for agreement with the British. 'I now confess that I can keep nothing concealed from you and that you know everything,' he wrote. 'Between the English and ourselves friendship and alliance have existed for two hundred years. By the will of God the English have obtained possession of Aden and on my part no fault has been committed; better far is it to burn oneself than to lose one's fatherland. Therefore I have tried various schemes to recover mine but after all I have found no friends but the English. I now say you are my true friend. I am now even as the sheep and you are the knife and I throw myself on your protection and implore pardon. Give me pardon from your heart. I have now appointed Sayyed Alowi as my agent between you and me.'[3] 'If in your heart you wish to make peace,' replied Haines, 'I think it would be better arranged in person. Come then Sultan with some of your sons and counsellors to Aden under the bond I enclose guaranteeing perfect safety, honourable and friendly treatment and a safe return to Lahej whenever you wish.'

The Sultan arrived at the Main Gate into Crater on January 28 1843 with forty shaikhs and a large retinue; he was received with honour and respect but was so nervous and agitated that he refused at first to enter the fortifications; he may well have expected to be taken prisoner, but he gained confidence with the arrival of Lieutenant Cruttenden, whom he recognised from his visit to Lahej eight years previously. It was customary for an important visitor to rest for a day or so and Haines made his first call on January 30. So much had happened since he had last seen the Sultan that he wondered what his reception would be, but he was reassured. When he entered the room in full uniform the Sultan and all the chiefs rose to greet him. The Sultan assured him that his fears of the British had subsided and that he had returned to Aden a wiser man than when he left it. The next day Haines received a letter from Sultan Hamed who had been left in control at Lahej: 'I beg you to treat my father with respect and esteem. Our hearts will be without a spot and our union be strengthened'. Unfortunately the Sultan suddenly became very ill and was anxious to leave Aden for home. A whole day was therefore occupied in conference to conclude the articles dealing with peace as quickly as possible and the treaty was signed and sealed between the Sultan and Haines on February 11 1843,[4] while each chieftain made it clear that he was in agreement. 'The old chieftain betrayed evident symptoms of severe suffering and was considerably changed before twenty-four hours had elapsed.' Haines presented him with a comfortable palanquin on which he was carried for the first six miles of his journey home by twelve Indian bearers lent by Colonel Croker. All the members of the Sultan's party were given presents and food for the journey, and the Sultan left 'perfectly delighted with the attention and the honour shown him. Thus I hope we shall soon be on more certain terms. The appearance of horse, which has been magnified to an immense extent, has I believe done much to effect this our end.' Haines was extremely relieved that the Sultan had not died in Aden for the Arabs might ' "measure our corn by their own bushel" and consider us liable to the influence of treachery equally with themselves'.

The Government of Bombay was so pleased with the treaty, and had such a pressing need for troops, that it wrote to Aden again to say that the garrison was to be reduced.[5] But there was strong objection to this from Aden. Haines did not expect the Sultan would keep to his bond, but at the same time he was determined to follow through with the policy of friendship and to try to establish confidence with the Sultan's family.

The Sultan had repeatedly asked for a visit from Cruttenden, and Haines decided to let him go, not fearing for his safety as he was much liked by the Arabs. Colonel Croker provided a guard of irregular horse as far as Khormaksar which was then the boundary of the British sphere, and from there to Lahej Cruttenden was escorted by fifty mounted Beduin. He was met near Lahej by the Sultan's three sons and another escort of two hundred mounted men, and, as the camelcade came into view of the palace, guns were fired from the four fortified buildings. He had a warm welcome from the old Sultan, reclining on a bed, who invited him to stay in his palace. To avoid any possibility of giving offence, Cruttenden called separately on the three sons—Hamed, Abdulla and Ali. The Sultan was still ill and believed that he was dying; he said that he wanted to leave his sons bound in firm alliance with the English, promising peace and no interference with trade to Aden. He did not ask directly for his stipend but he complained bitterly of the feuds between his own tribe and the Fadhli and Haushabi tribes, who taunted him with the loss of his port and his present weakness in contrast with his former strong position as Sultan of Aden. 'You have made yourselves masters of my port by the strong hand and the will of God and if I cannot obtain your assistance to shield me from my enemies, to whom am I to apply?'

On the third day of his stay in Lahej, Cruttenden fell so ill that he became unconscious and there was great alarm at the palace that he was going to die. 'My name will be broken', exclaimed the Sultan, 'for everyone will say that I poisoned him.'[6] But Cruttenden after a few days recovered sufficiently to be carried by twenty-four men in the same palanquin that Haines had presented to the Sultan when he was taken ill at Aden, and he was escorted by seventy men among whom were the Sultan's three sons and Sayyed Zain Aidrus; from Shaikh Othman he was able to ride and soon recovered.

Not more than a month later, however, Haines became suspicious that the old Sultan was intriguing again, for he had given orders to the mounted guard at Shaikh Othman to limit supplies coming into Aden and some of the Abdali cameleers were turned back. The fact that he had also granted land at Lahej worth 5,000 dollars to Sayyed Zain Aidrus was suspicious. 'In this part of Arabia the Sayyeds mix as much (nay more) with politics than religion', wrote Haines. 'Indeed I consider that the Sayyeds have far more to do in creating petty blood feuds than the Sultans themselves, and they are but too frequently secretly the instigators of them. Their lives being almost sacred from the superstition of the Beduin, they fear not retaliation, but coolly look on at the bloodshed caused by their own intrigue and, having caused it, they in their sacred office appear as mediators.' Another aspect of the intrigue was, he considered, charges brought by Sayyed Zain Aidrus against Mullah Jaffar, which had been carefully investigated.[7]

It was a complicated and typically fantastic Arab case. Haines acquitted Mullah Jaffar on the evidence and he suspected that some of the charges were manufactured because of Mullah Jaffar's influential position as his interpreter and because he was of the Shia faith while the accusers were Sunni. The Bombay Government thought that Haines was probably right to acquit but disliked one aspect of the case—that Mullah Jaffar had bought a boat from the Sultan of Lahej soon after the capture of Aden for 2,000 dollars (£400) against a bond which had not been fully redeemed. Instead of insisting that the full amount must at once be paid the Government ordered the interpreter's dismissal. This meant that the enemies of both Haines and Mullah Jaffar had triumphed and that his departure was a blow to Haines, who was told that as he and Cruttenden knew Arabic there was no need for another interpreter in his place.

'I have lost everything: you have Aden'

The Sultan of Lahej was active, once more plotting not only with people in Aden but also with the Sherif of Mocha, Hussain ibn Ali Hyder, who had been proclaimed formally by the Ottoman Government in July 1843 as ruler of Mocha and all the seaports on the Yemen coast and of the Tehama in return for an annual tribute to the Porte. It was a disappointment to Haines who remarked that as the Sultan had spent his life in dissimulation he could not find happiness without it.

In August and November the Sultan was in constant correspondence with Sherif Hussain. Haines saw a letter from a chieftain who resided twelve miles from Mocha, to the Chief of Bir Hamed, which announced that the Amir of the Assir tribe, Sherif Hussain, and the Sultan of Lahej had 'united to remove the infidels from Aden; God be praised and may the infidels be defeated'. The rendezvous was to be at Lahej, and Sultan Mahsin arranged a meeting for November 3 1843 with chiefs of the Haushabi, Yafa'i and Fadhli tribes to discuss these developments. Haines immediately advised Bombay that in view of the excitement among the chieftains and the influence of the unfriendly Sherif of Mocha, it was not prudent to reduce the garrison until a relief had arrived, especially as the 10th and 16th Regiments of Native Infantry had not more than six hundred fighting men, a hundred having been sent back to Bombay as unfit or sick.

By the end of November a large Arab force began to collect and the garrison guards were strengthened. The Sultan of Lahej pretended that the tribesmen had collected to protect him from attacks from the Fadhli tribe.[8] Sultan Abdulla of the Fadhli made it clear, however, that he was not prepared to combine with the Abdali to stop the trade from the interior which he was finding profitable. He reminded Sayyed Hussain Weiss—now working for the Sultan of Lahej—of what had happened when previously he had broken his bond and Shuqra had been bombarded: 'Look at my castle at Shuqra and now you wish to bring upon me a repetition of that. No! No! The English have kept their word and I will not become on bad terms again.'[9] There was no further move towards Aden and the tribesmen dispersed, so it was decided to grant the Sultan of Lahej his stipend on a monthly basis. A new bond was entered into which was signed on February 20 1844.[10]

Another threat, however, developed from Sana. The Imam,

Mahommed Ibn Ahmed, had died on January 8 1844, and the new Imam, Ali Mansur, wrote to the Sultan of Lahej demanding tribute and telling him to join the *jehad* against the foreigners with money and men; 'as soon as you send the money I will descend from the hills'. The Iman's army advanced towards Lahej but his uncle, who had been left in charge during his absence, usurped the throne and the Imam hurried back to Sana; having recovered his throne he declared that after Ramadan he would move south to Lahej again with a strong force. The Bombay Government decided after all that there could not be any reduction of the garrison which should not anyway exceed one thousand seven hundred men and that the fortifications should be strengthened further.

In August 1846 the work of building up the fortifications and the construction of the new town of Aden was brought to a standstill by another danger. A fanatic from Mecca, called Sayyed Ismail, marched south through the Yemen collecting tribesmen to turn the infidels out of Aden. Many people left Aden believing that the British could not resist his superhuman powers. The Sayyed wrote to Haines about his divine mission, telling him that 'the whole army of God from all parts of the world' would empty Aden of atheists and unbelievers. On August 17 a small advance force of four hundred tribesmen approached and opened fire on the field-works; fire was returned and twenty-two Arabs were killed including their leader, Sayyed Ibrahim. At 8 a.m. on August 26 about two thousand Arabs led by an Assir Chief advanced across the bridge of Khormaksar preceded by an advance-guard with banners. Fire was opened from the field-works and from the *Sesostris*, commanded by Lieutenant Benjamin Hamilton who took advantage of the tide to bring the ship close inshore to shell the approaching army, which retired through the swamps after suffering heavy losses. The Arabs remained in the neighbourhood, but the Abdalis and others were anxious to harvest their fields and the assembled tribes gradually broke up. The army brought by Sayyed Ismail, ignorant of the country, tried to return to Mocha by the sea-coast and two hundred died of thirst on the way. The Sayyed had lost his magic and when he asked for help from the Imam of Sana the comment was 'why should a man possessed of supernatural powers rely so entirely on earthly assistance'.

These disturbances had interfered with supplies from the interior for the garrison and the townsmen of Aden. They were dependent for their fresh meat on the supplies of sheep and goats from Somaliland and these supplies had been much reduced by fighting between the Somali tribes which had continued for about two years. Tribal warfare had also affected the annual Berbera fair which was important to Indian merchants, who came in their large ships to barter for the goods brought by the big caravans from Shoa and Harar with slaves, ivories, skins, coffee and millet. In good years many thousands assembled in Berbera and the trade was worth about thirty lakhs of rupees (£300,000). Cruttenden was sent from Aden and after long discussions with the Somali tribes he settled their differences; Aden began to receive supplies and the fair revived. In January 1848 Cruttenden found that the fair was once more in full activity; but the caravans from Shoa had had to fight their way through owing to the Galla rebellion which had followed the death of the King, Sahela Selassie. About twenty thousand people had come to Berbera but as usual everyone had dispersed inland and the ships had left by the beginning of April, 'beasts of prey now take the opportunity to approach the sea; lions are commonly seen at the town well during the hot weather, and . . . but a week after the fair had ended I observed three ostriches quietly walking on the beach'.[11]

Death of Sultan Mahsin
of Lahej

(November 1847 to October 1853)

'I am an old and feeble man', wrote the Sultan of Lahej in his last
letter to Haines. At nine o'clock in the evening of November 28
1847, he died.[1]

For nearly ten years Haines and the Abdali Sultan had carried on
a strange contest; Haines firm, sure of his ground since he was kept
well informed of the Sultan's intrigues, often exasperated but on the
whole remaining calm and prepared to be friendly; the Sultan,
tireless in his efforts to retrieve the position he had lost and, jealous
that Haines had become 'Sultan of Aden', he used his wealth in
forming one coalition after another but was always repulsed before
the fortifications of Aden or attacked by his lifetime foe the Fadhli
Sultan. Even when he was over seventy and had lost the use of his
legs he was still trying to beat the English. He was shrewd, cunning
and obstinate, not the imbecile Haines had at first thought him.

If it had not been for Haines' optimism and ability, the Sultan could have succeeded, for there were periods when it looked as if the Government of India might give up the expensive struggle. The growth of Aden suffered greatly from the repeated attacks, and Haines regretted that he could not have persuaded the Sultan that it would have been in his best interest to co-operate with the English since, with stability and trade, the whole area would have benefited; but Haines also knew that to the Beduin honour was more important than prosperity, and that the Sultan suffered a blow to his pride from the jibes of his rivals at his loss of Aden.

On the death of the Sultan of Lahej, his son, Hamed Mahsin, was elected to succeed him. Hamed made it clear that he wished to be friendly with the British and keep the roads open: 'Wisdom has again been restored to me', he wrote. There had certainly been a change in his attitude since the time he had tried to kidnap Haines and refused him entry to Aden nearly ten years before. Many of the tribesmen had become accustomed to the British, to appreciate the prosperity that trade could bring and to find that the order introduced into the administration of Aden made it a very much more pleasant place to visit. Arab and Indian merchants were buying plots of land from the Government on which to build shops and houses; immigration continued from Mocha, which had been ruined by the extortions of Sherif Hussain, and the population of Aden had increased to over twenty thousand.

The pattern of Haines' duties remained much the same during his last few years in Aden but the death of the old Sultan removed some of the excitement and interest. Sultan Hamed was prepared to be co-operative and it was decided that there should be a new agreement. He insisted on retaining almost all the high transit dues his father had imposed on goods passing between Aden and the interior. It was agreed that Hamed should be responsible for paying the stipends to all the other tribes except the Fadhli, which had been the system adopted before the capture of Aden. Sultan Hamed was given by the Government 2,308 rupees annually (£230), but his request to be placed under the protection of the British was refused as this amounted to an offensive and defensive treaty which was at that time unacceptable to the East India Company in London. The agreement was signed on December 21 1847.[2]

The Fadhli tribe continued to be as aggressive as ever and the Fadhli Sultan considered himself now to be the most powerful chief in the neighbourhood, while the Abdalis still felt vengeful at the heavy losses they had suffered in the last attack on Aden which they regarded as largely the result of Fadhli treachery.

On January 20 1849, only two years after his father's death, Sultan Hamed succumbed to small-pox. He was succeeded by his brother Ali which resulted in the enmity of Abdulla, who was a rival to the succession as he had been born at much the same time but of another mother. Ali was twenty-nine years old, handsome, of medium height and energetic, while his brother Abdulla was crafty, treacherous, revengeful and bigoted and intrigued with Sayyed Hussain Weiss to overthrow Ali.

In May 1849 a new agreement was made by Haines with Sultan Ali on the same lines as the previous one with Sultan Hamed, though the transit dues were reduced. Ali was very dependent for advice on Haines and was apprehensive as a result of threats from the Imam of Sana that he intended to advance on Lahej and Aden, but the Turkish Government sent troops and took over the coastal area of the Yemen. The Turks failed, however, to advance into the mountains and were repulsed when they sent an expedition by sea to try to capture Mukalla.[3] The Turks forced Sherif Hussain to retire to Abu Arish and took over Mocha which had become a ruined and deserted town as a result of Sherif Hussain's extortions, and between three and four thousand people had left Mocha to settle in Aden.

The most acute problem that Haines had to deal with during his last years in charge of Aden was a series of murders of British service men. In May 1850 an unarmed boat from the steamer *Auckland* was attacked when it landed west of Aden and a seaman was killed.[4] In March 1851 Captain G. I. D. Milne, Deputy Assistant of the Commissariat in Aden, was murdered by a Sayyed at night in his tent at Wahut while on an expedition to shoot bustard with a party of officers who were guests of Sultan Ali.[5] The same month Abdulla, Sultan Ali's brother, sent an assassin into Aden to murder Haines. As Haines and his wife were driving in their carriage from Steamer Point to the town in Crater they noticed a man with 'a repulsive expression' who stared at them from the roadway but the Arab let the carriage pass and a little later attacked a British officer who killed him with the Arab's own dagger.[6] In July there was an attack on the coal brig, *Sons of Commerce*, and two British seamen were killed.[7]

Haines told Sultan Ali, who was now responsible for order among the tribes, to seize the murderers. Ali had collected a force and entered the Aqrabi town of Bir Ahmed whose Shaikh, Hyder ibn Mehdi, was responsible for much of the trouble, but he failed to reduce the fort without aid and asked for artillery. Haines wanted to destroy the fort with a small expedition of European troops and artillery which would have pleased Sultan Ali and would have been regarded by the Arabs in general as a fair enough revenge for the murders committed. The Governor-General of India, too, was in favour of this but the Court of Directors opposed any idea of destroying property and thought such action would lead to further trouble. Instead, they insisted that Haines must make Sultan Ali deliver up the murderers. Haines knew that Ali could not do this without some help from Aden, for Arabs argued that Muslims who killed infidels could not be handed over to infidels, and the tribesmen might have become angry with Sultan Ali which would have given Abdulla an opportunity to lead a revolt against his brother. It was true that Captain Milne had been a guest of Sultan Ali at Wahut which made him responsible, but the Sayyed who had committed the murder had sought asylum with the Fadhli Sultan who refused to give him up and wrote to Haines: 'We Arabs have our laws and customs; only Sayyeds can judge Sayyeds. No one can drive a man back, he must go by himself. Why do the soldiers of the Government roam about this country, whilst there is peace between us?'[8] That was a question asked by the Government of India. Haines was blamed by some for allowing the officers to go on a shooting expedition inland and the officers were blamed for dismissing their escort at night.

The Government ordered Haines to stop Sultan Ali's stipend but he succeeded in having this countermanded, for he realised that the only solution was to help Ali to govern 'his refactory and turbulent people who are incapable of estimating the value of good government'. He wrote bitterly that they were indolent, proud and vain, believing that they were a favoured race because the Yemen had received the Law of Mahommed without compulsion and that they were forever blessed; 'justice or right feeling is unknown among them and a Sayyed may apparently commit any crime with impunity, being holy'. In his annoyance he added: 'I have visited nearly every part of Arabia and the tribes in the neighbourhood of Aden are more treacherous and false than any other.'⁹ Long after Haines had left Aden the British were trying to have the murderers delivered to them but never succeeded.

In the Yemen the Turks were soon in difficulties with the Arab tribes as Haines had expected and he was not sorry, for he did not consider that they had any right to be there. They had also ruined trade by imposing huge taxes and large customs dues, contrary to the agreement between the British Government and the Porte in 1838 which allowed only five per cent on British goods. The result had been to throw most of the trade into Aden, but the Indian merchants in the Yemeni ports were in great distress and Aden would have benefited if the Yemen had been prosperous. The Turkish Governor of Mocha had written a peremptory letter to Haines stating that Aden could not remain a free port, which it had been since 1848, because, it was ruining the trade of Yemen.

Nearly all the coffee trade was by 1852 coming through Aden and amounted in that year to four thousand camel-loads, each load being a little over three hundred pounds in weight. This attracted to Aden the large American trade which was over twenty-eight thousand sterling in 1852 and nearly double that the next year. (The gross value of the total trade of Aden was by then nearly £600,000 annually.) About ten or thirteen American merchantmen, mostly from Massachusetts, visited the port each year bringing cotton piece-goods which they exchanged for coffee, guns and hides. Aden's merchants were prepared to buy from them on the expectation of selling in Lahej, Mocha and Hodeida, so that the American captains could get rid of their merchandise without the wear and tear of the journey into the Red Sea. They could also have their ships refitted in Aden and receive mail from America by steam in as little as forty-five days.¹⁰

It seemed as if Haines had laid the pattern for the successful future development of Aden and that the Government of Bombay had curbed the power of the Military Department. It wrote to the Quartermaster-General of the Army in September 1853: 'Government cannot altogether consent to the position that Aden is to be held only as a military post. The Peninsula has been a British possession for thirteen years, and, by encouragement given to trade, a town has risen up which contains more than twenty thousand inhabitants. It is too late to enquire whether the policy adopted has been right or wrong; the effect is evident, and the fact that there is a flourishing town to be protected, in security of which the British national faith and honour are involved, cannot be ignored. . . . The measures of Government must be governed by a due consideration for the people of Aden, as well as for the preservation of the proper efficacy of the garrison.'

The Fall of Captain Haines

21

Haines is dismissed from Aden

(May 1852 to February 1854)

Aden was on its way to becoming an important asset to the Government of India, both financially and militarily, and Stafford Haines could congratulate himself that he had made a great success of his mission. All, except some of the military, praised him for what he had achieved. At such moments of high success Fate sometimes strikes a crippling blow; in this case, as if it resented Haines' motto: *Deo non Sorte*—God not Fate.

The Military Department had reacted strongly to the Government view of the civilian importance of Aden and brought all their guns to bear. The Government completely reversed its policy and in October 1853 established that 'the military importance of Aden is to be considered paramount to its commercial improvement, and should be the first object in view'. The reason for this sudden change was almost certainly due to the fact that the Government no longer felt that it could rely on the strong and enthusiastic support of Haines. He was in trouble because a military committee had discovered a very large deficit in his Treasury.

The Fall of Captain Haines

There was a Government rule that a Political Agent's Treasury should be checked once a month by a military committee and that should have been done in Aden since the beginnning of 1839, but the Accountant-General did not think of it until May 1852—a lapse of about thirteen years or one hundred and fifty checks. The Bombay Government sent instructions to the Officer Commanding troops in Aden in July 1852, but forgot to inform Haines, who was responsible for the Treasury. All the same, when he was told by the military, he arranged that the examination should take place on September 1.

A few days beforehand Haines prepared for the counting with Mr. Francis Moreas, who had served as a clerk in the Treasury since 1841. They opened all the wooden boxes and about six or seven, containing from 5,000 to 10,000 rupees each, were found to be rotten at the bottom so they asked two Aden merchants to help count the rupees and to put them in bags of 2,000 rupees each. The Military Committee duly carried out their inspection on September 1 in the presence of Haines, counting the notes but not the rupees because it took too long. When all the German crowns, rupee notes and coin— annas, half annas and pice—had been counted and estimated, the total was 189,335 rupees. Haines' cash account of the same date showed that there should have been 471,315 rupees, making a deficit of 281,980 rupees (£28,198). He showed no emotion when he countersigned the statement as a correct count of what was in the Treasury on that date—he would never have allowed himself to show any emotion in such circumstances before military gentlemen. He had certainly known that there was a deficit when he had made his rough count with the clerk, and probably was aware of it some time before, for though he had not, understandably, counted the contents of the boxes on their arrival he must surely have counted the boxes themselves every now and again and that should have shown him there was a shortage. But he argued that he was too busy even to count the boxes and he once told the authorities that there were more important things to do in Aden than count money.

Now he was brought face to face with a large deficit—a fact that would be known not only in Government but also in military circles in Bombay. He asked the Government for permission to visit Bombay for twenty-six days in order to look into the accounts to find the errors, which could not be done by reference to the Aden accounts alone, 'for some grand mistake there certainly is'. His request was not granted although he had had no leave for thirteen years. In a personal letter to the Accountant-General he again asked for time to go through the accounts; 'I was considering myself a man tolerably well off and thinking of England. I fear, alas! I shall be poor enough unless I can find out the errors.' He realised that he was responsible for the accounts and would 'have to make up any deficiencies on leaving'.

Besides the rule that a military commission should count the Treasury monthly, there was also a Government form to be signed by the person appointed to examine the Aden Treasury each month, declaring that he had counted the money and found that the amount agreed with the balance entry in the books; but nobody had apparently paid any attention to these forms. Dr. Malcolmson, who was the first to inspect the Treasury after the capture of Aden, signed without counting, as did Cruttenden later, who stated that he thought it was a matter of routine involving no personal responsibility. The Government of Bombay considered these excuses to be 'in the highest degree unsatisfactory' and wanted to court-martial both Dr. Malcolmson and Lieutenant Cruttenden, but the Legal Department stated that there were insufficient grounds to charge them.

The Government of Bombay severely reprimanded Haines for not having carried out orders and he was told to censure Cruttenden; but he did not do this, nor did he tell him of the results of the count by the military committee. Cruttenden learned that there was a deficiency in the Aden Treasury, from a Bombay newspaper of January 1853 and that his name was implicated. On April 9 he wrote Haines a private letter: 'I can no longer rest in the state of anxiety I have been suffering under for the last month—now especially as each day brings additional strength to the rumours that have of late been rife regarding Aden affairs. . . . I have heard that the "routine work" of signing the Treasury books, is likely to prove most disastrous to myself, and that the matter is already before the Court [of Directors] in England. I am not alone in the world now. I have one who looks to me for everything.' He wanted to know the worst so that he could at least prepare in some measure for what might happen. 'I dare not tell my wife anything about it in her present condition.'

Haines' reply showed a complete lack of understanding of the gravity of the situation. He had an admiration for Cruttenden's ability and an affection for the younger officer who had served with him loyally for about eighteen years, but it was not doing Cruttenden a kindness by making light of the situation. 'When I found your name included for signing without counting I at once took all the blame myself'; he had understood from P. M. Melvill, one of the Secretaries to the Government, that he himself would have a 'reprimand' for not having had the money counted and he hoped to save Cruttenden even from "a wig".* 'I shall have to pay what I cannot discover in error and omission, still I hope to trace all. One fortunate thing; I have been prudent and am not without means to assist me in meeting the Government check [*sic*]. . . . Of course I have much upon my mind, and where the error is I will yet trace; and if I do trace it all I shall be inclined to give up the berth, unless they relieve me of the responsibility of the Treasury.'¹ The indications are that this was not bravado but that he really believed that the choice was his.

Nearly ten months passed and little was achieved in finding errors and omissions. Haines offered a reward to the clerks in his department if they could find any mistakes but the senior clerk was ill and the others were dealing with the current accounts. Haines himself was very busy with political affairs, such as the murders of British servicemen, threats from Sana or from mad fakirs. At the same time the French were trying to obtain possession of Kamaran Island; Walter Plowden was having trouble with the Abyssinians and an armed vessel had to be sent from Aden to Massawa; an Egyptian envoy arrived on his way to Bahrain with smallpox on board the ship and one of his concubines had to be removed and looked after in Aden; the Fadhlis launched several strong attacks on Aden's new water supply at Koorsi, defended by the Abdali and gunboats

* Melvill had written to Haines in Aden a number of private letters warning him of the dangers of his situation and when later he learned of what had been said to Cruttenden he could not understand what Haines could have meant. He had never stated, Melvill told the Bombay Government, that a big deficit in a public treasury was an affair to be settled by a wigging or a reprimand; 'looking to Haines' antecedents, to the high character he has always borne, and the good service he has rendered to the Government, I have all along believed and hoped that he would prove to be innocent'.

from Aden. Haines was also urging the Government to make a new survey of the Red Sea and the threat of war between Russia and Turkey in the autumn of 1853 caused general unrest among the Arabs in the Yemen who were intent on exploiting Turkey's difficulties. The Turkish Governor of the Yemen coastal area sent a regular messenger from Mocha to Aden to meet each steamer from Suez and, having obtained the latest information of the Turco-Russian crisis, returned as fast as possible to relay the news to Hodeida and Jeddah. In October 1853 Haines informed Bombay that the Supreme Pasha of the Hejaz had asked that an English vessel of war might be sent to Jeddah in the event of war between Turkey and Russia, as there was fear that the Arabs might revolt. The troops employed there, he said, were mostly Egyptian as all Turkish troops had been recalled to Turkey. In December the Arabs in Yemen were in open revolt and no Turks or Egyptians were safe outside the walls of the towns.[1]

It was not easy for Haines to concentrate on his accounts, covering fourteen years and totalling about one and a quarter million pounds sterling in various currencies. He suspected that some of the errors could well be the fault of the Bombay accountants who had made a number of mistakes in the past. Haines had not yet begun to take the matter very seriously—there had been deficits before in different establishments in India and there was at the time a deficit in the military establishment in Aden, which the officers of the commissariat had been working on for three years and about which no one seemed to bother unduly.

On July 29 1853 the Government of Bombay told Haines that a Commission was being sent, consisting of Major Scobie of the 29th Infantry Regiment, and Mr. Archibald Robertson of the Bombay Civil Service. The Governor-in-Council wished him to understand that the Commission was 'simply one of enquiry' to help Government decide what to do, and that it was to work 'in such a manner as to avoid interference with, or weakening' his authority as Political Agent. That seemed all right to Haines; the Commission was going to give the help with the accounts which he had so often requested. But, in fact, it was not to be merely an enquiry, but amounted almost to a police investigation.

When the two Commissioners arrived in Aden on September 10

1853, Haines invited them to stay in his house, but they did not accept nor did they seem particularly friendly. After a few days Haines was outraged to learn that they were making enquiries from Cruttenden and from Arab and Indian merchants as to whether the Political Agent took any part in trading on his own account and questions were being asked about his private conduct which Haines described as 'disgusting'; such enquiries undermined his position as Political Agent and were contrary to their orders. Haines was questioned about the accounts in such a way that he thought it must have been due 'to the wantonness of a little brief authority'; but he wished to be helpful and answered as best he could. The questions needed careful study and with his account books in the possession of the Commissioners, he could only make random answers.

Haines considered that the Commissioners knew nothing about the rather complicated customs of South Arabia with regard to finance, and that the only person who could have helped them was himself. But they declined his services. The Commissioners, for instance, were puzzled and suspicious because merchants left rupees at the Treasury in exchange for dollars or bills and then reclaimed them later; but rupees were a new currency and useless at first for trade inland where German crowns, or Maria Theresa dollars, were the accepted currency. Haines argued that in order to encourage trade he had to simplify matters—'he might as well have commanded the wild Beduin to don the hat and coat of an Englishman as to have required them to comprehend the intricacies of a European Finance Department'.

In order to help him deal with the various payments that had to be made Haines had used Damjee of the Indian mercantile firm of Veerchund Ameerchund, as banker; the same man that he had employed in 1838 to deal with the property of the *Duria Dowlat*, and who had given the first warning about the kidnapping plot. Haines explained to the Commission that he gave Damjee orders for cheques to pay shipping, commissariat, entertainment and expenses; these cheques were brought on the twenty-first of each month when he saw that all had been accounted for and duly settled. 'This month on the *Elphinstone* requiring money,' he told the Commissioners, 'I overdrew from Damjee Rs 3,000 and paid him on the 12th. He also kindly assisted me with 1,500 German crowns for H.B.M.'s Consul

Passengers from England crossing the Isthmus of Suez to take ship for India or Hongkong

The steamship *Berenice* at Bombay

Portrait of Sahela Selassie, 1795–1847, King of Shoa, grandfather of the Emperor Menelik II who was the great-uncle of the present ruler of Ethiopia

Abyssinian scene from a painting by Bernatz, a member of the Harris Mission to Shoa

in Abyssinia, for which I lodged with him Rs 3,000 of my own savings, to be returned when I paid the 1,500 German crowns.' Exception was taken to the fact that Haines used a banker without having informed Bombay and that advances were being made in this way.

The Commission questioned Haines about frequent entries in the rough cash account of deductions from his pay and whether he made advances to members of the establishment. He replied that he always kept a private balance in the treasure chest in his favour to meet contingencies; he had, for instance, made advances to assist the establishment in building their houses, but these advances were always adjusted from the private money he had deposited. Francis Griffs, one of the clerks, told the Commission that he owed the Political Agent 2,000 rupees. 'When my establishment have been sick,' wrote Haines, 'or when marriages, births, or deaths have happened in their families, I have assisted them with small sums, and they have repaid it by instalments. I have already, gentlemen, informed you I have given bills, but never until I had sufficient money of my own lodged to meet the same; Government money has not been used on such accounts, or by me.' The Commission was disturbed to find that advances had been given to assist the merchants of Aden; Haines stated that these were made against the dollars they placed in the Treasury and which were redeemed when they had repaid the rupees. He had, for instance, wanted to improve the one hotel in Aden and when he found that the proprietor, Sorabjee Cowasjee, was paying nine per cent compound interest for the money he had expended, 'I promised, on his bringing me regularly every month Rs 1,000 or upwards, that I would give him a bill to the extent of my pay monthly, that he might pay off his debts in Bombay. This I did, I think, for fifteen months, to meet which I paid the whole sum into the Treasury.'

A government today might well consider it wise and sensible to advance money for the development of an area or of a new town, and Haines' great ambition was to see Aden develop; but he was pursuing a dangerous course in using public money, even though he said that he backed it with his private money. From the answers he gave to the Commission it did not appear that he had kept careful and detailed statements of all these expenditures. An examination of Damjee's books showed that bills on Bombay had been purchased with government money for more than 14 lakhs of rupees (about £140,000). How thoroughly these accounts were studied by the members of the Commission it is difficult to say. They were all in Gujerati which Robertson could understand when spoken but could not read, so he made notes as the items were dictated to him.

Haines found Robertson's attitude insufferable throughout and complained to the Government of the insults he had received and of Robertson's 'utter defiance of his authority as Political Agent'. The Government of Bombay did not like this criticism of its representative and Haines' letter was never answered. Lord Falkland, who had been sympathetic to Haines, had been succeeded in October 1853 by Lord Elphinstone, a former Governor of Madras. Elphinstone took a very severe attitude towards Haines from the beginning. After the Bombay Government had studied the report of its two Commissioners it decided that the large discrepancy in the accounts was not due to honest error and that Haines had embezzled. The Commission, however, was not a properly constituted body to deal with the guilt or innocence of the Political Agent and no such decision should have been taken based on a Commission which was not given that authority or on a report which Haines had not seen.

Haines was peremptorily informed, in a letter of February 22 1854, that he was removed from his appointment in Aden 'on the report of the Commission', and he at once asked to be informed of the contents of the report, so that he could have an opportunity of making his defence. The Government also informed him that he was responsible 'for the whole amount of the public money deficient in the Aden Treasury'. He agreed that he was responsible for any proved deficit but argued that the accounts had not yet been properly examined and audited. Lieutenant Cruttenden, too, was removed on the ground that he had every month incorrectly certified that he had examined the Treasury. Lieutenant Colonel Augustus Clarke of the 8th Regiment Madras Native Infantry, who was commanding troops at Aden, was directed to take temporary charge of the Agency.

Haines decided to dismantle his house at Steamer Point, which he had built at his own expense and where he had lived as virtual Sultan of Aden. He must have realised then that it was very unlikely that he would ever return to Aden, except as a passenger on a ship to go home to England, perhaps to join his wife and son who were already there. An oil painting of his wife and another of his son were taken down from the walls; glassware and crockery which had gone backwards and forwards between Bombay and Aden with his family were packed; also a small chess table which had seen many nights of play and a box of silver spoons which Mrs. Haines had had in Bombay in 1852 and had taken with her to Aden; the bright and valuable sword given by the Court of Directors which was worn by the Captain on important public occasions; a dressing case with epaulettes; a tin box with 'likenesses' of his family and relations; his case of pistols 'worn in several skirmishes'; the plate chest of silver with the 'Victoria pattern' which he used for dinner-parties in Aden when his wife was there or when he was entertaining visitors, and the silver with a 'common pattern' which he generally used when he was by himself. All his clothes were neatly packed by his servants including '33 new shirts, 13 antimacassar white jackets, 49 trowsers, 60 white nearly new, 34 pairs of socks, 7 sheets, 13 pillow-cases'; especially careful packing was needed for his valuable chronometers, barometers, his geological specimens, his many shells and stuffed birds.

In the official correspondence there is no account of Haines' departure from Aden but he must have had many friends among English, Arabs, Indians and Jews to see him off. Cruttenden had already been ordered to Bombay; the clerks of his office whom he had so often helped financially and befriended must have come, and presumably also Colonel Clarke, who was taking over from him temporarily as Political Agent, and surely some of the officers who knew that they had depended much on Haines' remarkable intelligence service for warnings of attacks. He sailed for Bombay suffering under what he considered was a great injustice, and on board the ship wrote: 'The receipt of the Government letter ordering my immediate removal from Aden clearly convinces me I have been most unjustly suspected without a hearing or being able to defend myself or explain matters, and without knowing on what count my integrity is doubted.'

22

Mystery of the missing funds

(April to August 1854)

The effect of Haines' dismissal from Aden had caused a sensation in South Arabia and the Arabs were puzzled. They concluded that the past had been forgotten and that there was to be a new deal so that preposterous claims were made on the bewildered Acting Political Agent, Colonel Clarke, who had had experience of administration in Mysore but had never had to deal with Arabs. Sultan Ali of Lahej, for instance, produced a forged document, which purported to have Haines' signature to it, promising to give the Abdali tribe military support for the capture of the fort of Bir Ahmed.

The removal of the strong control exercised by Haines very naturally led to a good deal of trouble and it lasted a long time. He had exercised power by diplomacy and through the strength of his own personality which had won him the respect of the tribes. He did not follow strictly the instructions from London that there must be no intervention. Clarke, who was promoted Brigadier, carried out those instructions literally and followed 'without partiality the principle of non-intervention whether by sea or land'. He recommended that all tribes should be left to themselves to fight out their own quarrels; they would benefit by the system of non-intervention 'and gradually weaned from predatory practices'.

When Haines arrived in Bombay Clarke's reports from Aden were shown him for his opinion. 'I would agree with Brigadier Clarke had he Europeans to deal with, but he has Arabs who are most difficult to control and manage. Our European ideas of equity and politics will not be comprehensible.' Once Arabs realised that the man in charge knew what was in their minds and what they planned to do, they had respect for him. 'This united with frankness, firmness, decision and consistency will secure an Englishman his point and he will have moral power over them and be respected and feared and they will afterwards give him little trouble.'[1] Some years later General John Jacob of Jacobabad echoed, 'it is moral more than physical force which is required to control predatory tribes'.

The fact that the Government referred Aden affairs to him encouraged Haines to believe that after all the Government was not unfriendly to him. He made the mistake of waiting for it to communicate with him instead of taking the initiative and pressing immediately for an enquiry. The Government had been informed that a naval court-martial was not in order because the only offences covered when committed on shore were mutiny, desertion or disobedience to a lawful command issued by the Superintendent of the Navy. But a general commission or court-martial of senior officers could have been set up by the Government to investigate the matter.

While Haines waited developments the Bombay Government, having decided already that he was guilty, pursued a hostile policy towards him in secret without allowing him to know what was being planned. If Haines had had as good an intelligence service in Bombay as he had had in Aden he could have discovered the Government's intentions, and at least consulted a lawyer, but he continued to trust the Government for that had been his training over a period of thirty years.

During the fifteen years that Haines was in charge in Aden the equivalent of over one million and a quarter pounds sterling had passed through his hands and the alleged deficit was a little over five per cent of the total. It was, indeed, puzzling to everyone how so large a sum of money had disappeared, but embezzlement was not the most likely explanation considering Haines' character. Over the thirteen years money could have slipped away in various ways. The Treasury chests were kept first in the *Coote*, then handed over to Major Bailie during Haines' illness, brought ashore to Crater, and moved to an insecure building where locks were tampered with on at least two occasions; without a proper count whole chests could have disappeared; clerks, Indian bankers and Arab merchants might have cheated, and perhaps there were shortages in the money sent from Bombay or unaccounted expenditure by Haines in entertaining Arabs and other visitors. He considered that any money spent for the good of Aden was money well spent and he was lax in keeping proper accounts.

There are many questions that can be asked and not answered. How far was Haines wise in trusting to the Banians and did he in the pressure of business always note down what had been advanced? The well-travelled Henry Salt recounts the trouble he had in settling his accounts with the Banians of Aden: 'though these traders possess a remarkable suavity in their manners, and an immoveable command of temper, yet there are no individuals in the world more keen, artful and rapacious in their dealings, and consequently in all communications with them undue exactions must be expected and carefully guarded against, notwithstanding there may be an appearance of minute and scrupulous accuracy in their accounts'.[2] Could Haines' wife, perhaps, have been extravagant, spending freely in Bombay and England, but if so it would have been remarked on in official correspondence. His son was given a good education in England and later became a clergyman but there was nothing exceptional in that. Haines invested much of his savings in having houses built in Aden and there is no indication that he salted away large sums of money in England, for this would have come to light after his death.

Haines continued to appear unaware of the danger he was in. He complained, for instance, of his reception in Bombay where all his luggage was retained at the customs until he paid freight and dues. He wrote to the Commissioner of Customs to point out that it was all private property 'long in use by an old officer ordered to move about from one station to another' and he saw no reason why he should pay anything. He asked that his letter should be sent to Government; in it he had mentioned two tin boxes 'of official papers, records and valuable memoranda of the past 36 years, of value to me but to no-one else'; he also mentioned a davenport with papers. Government noted this and instructed the Commissioner of Customs to detain any official papers, though it had no right to have private papers taken from a person's baggage at the customs; but the Legal Department did not think that Captain Haines would be so ill-advised as to complain against the proceeding and if he did bring an action against Government, the Court would only grant nominal damages. Thereupon the Government wrote to Haines that in view of the unsatisfactory state of the accounts produced before the Commissioners, the absence of documents which ought to have been forthcoming and his objectionable practice of mixing up private and public transactions, all his accounts and papers were to be examined by a Commission in his presence. Haines replied the same day (April 22 1854) that 'however painful and degrading' such an examination would be he would cheerfully submit to the order in the hope that justice would be done. He asked again to be permitted to take charge of the books and papers which the Commissioners had had in their possession since they came to Aden in September, and to see the report of the Commissioners, so as to continue his examination of the accounts. 'I make this appeal truly and conscientiously feeling that some error must exist and will yet, I hope, be discovered. . . . I beg to assure the Right Honourable Governor-in-Council that though *deeply* grieved at the change so evident in the sentiments of Government towards me . . . I fear no enquiry; my conscience is clear, as I have never acted otherwise than as a true and faithful servant and, to the best of my ability and judgement, to benefit Government and the settlement over which I presided.'

The Commission this time included a naval officer, Captain Powell I.N., but Mr. Robertson, who had, Haines considered, behaved so insultingly in Aden, was also a member. The examination began at 10-30 a.m. on April 25 and ended in the afternoon of the following day. The Commission reported to Government they had found such a vast mass of paper, both private and relative to money transactions, thrown into the boxes without any arrangement, that it would have been a work of considerable time and labour to have separated them, therefore all the boxes had been resealed. The fact that Haines' papers were still in disorder was certainly strange. It showed either indifference or, as the Government argued, he was trying to conceal the facts by creating confusion.

The Government told the Commission to resume their investigation and a Major G. Pope was added as a member. When they met at the town hall to re-examine the boxes Haines handed them a letter in which he stated: 'After the treatment I have received in the presence of numerous subordinates (a culprit could not have been compelled to submit to greater insult) I most respectfully and firmly protest against my private books or papers, being again looked at, or removed from my boxes.' If they were removed after his protest, he would consider it an act contrary to law and nothing could justify it 'but well substantiated treason against the State'. His past conduct in submitting to examination would show the world that he understood obedience, but for the honour of himself and family he could not allow his private letters to be re-examined—'nothing but force shall compel me to submit to it, though their content could only rebound to my credit'.

He was willing, however, to place before them any public documents or papers which threw light on the deficiency; the private letters sent abroad that he had lent to the Commissioners at Aden 'for perusal only to disprove false rumours' had been retained without his authority and he wished them to be restored. He had intended to work hard on the accounts once he had been given the documents and he could not understand the proceedings that were being followed, 'for if there is any public or private accusation against me, let it be produced openly and permit me an Englishman's privilege viz. a knowledge of my accuser, the charge alleged and the opportunity of disproving the same. Justice demands this.'

The letter was passed to the Government and the members of the Commission stated that, as it had been understood that the examination was to be carried out with Captain Haines' agreement, they had not proceeded further.

Haines' reactions are understandable but his letter was unwise and gives the impression that he had not yet sought legal advice. He was now in such a critical situation that he should have moved very cautiously and not been concerned with such minor problems as that his papers had been examined by officers who were inferior to him in rank and that one, Major Pope, was 'almost a stranger'. But he also knew from past experience that papers were not released once they were in Government's hands.

The Advocate-General advised that Haines should be charged before the senior Magistrate of Police with an offence under Act 13 of 1850; on that the Magistrate could issue a search warrant and detain all Captain Haines' papers at the Custom House. That meant a prosecution in the Supreme Court before a jury on a criminal charge; 'we have no alternative', minuted the Governor on May 1. One alternative would have been to send a member of the Council or the Government's solicitor, or a private individual to talk to Haines and to point out, before proceedings were started, what would happen if he did not reconsider his attitude to the examination of his papers. As Government had not yet heard from the Court of Directors there was no immediate hurry, but it made no attempt to make personal contact with Haines.

Without any warning Haines was summoned on May 2 to the office of Mr. A. K. Corfield, the senior Magistrate of Police, and had to tender bail for rupees to the equivalent of £2,000. Haines was amazed and horrified to find that he was faced with a most serious charge—of having appropriated the public money. He told the Government that he had been unaware until his papers had been seized and examined that they entertained the slightest suspicion of his integrity. 'Had I for a moment thought this possible, I should not have waited until the present moment to solicit, as I now earnestly do, the fullest enquiry into my conduct by a Commission'—something he should have done two months before, when he was dismissed from Aden. He begged the Government not to subject him to so degrading a proceeding as that of vindicating his character in a police court, before it had been ascertained whether he could clear it before a commission of his fellow officers. 'I am willing to submit to the fullest enquiry to allow every scrap of paper I possess to be inspected by the committee'; he wished to withdraw the protest about the investigation of his papers which he had made 'under excited feelings and without due consideration'. Before a Commission of Enquiry he was confident he could clear himself, but to make him face a criminal trial, before his case had been properly investigated, would, whatever the result, 'inflict an irreparable wound' on himself and all who were intimately connected with him.

Elphinstone was exasperated by this letter and wrote that the Government had almost overstepped the limits of forbearance—an unjust and dictatorial reaction to the plea from an officer of the Company. Before the law had been invoked it would have been possible for the Government to have constituted a high-ranking Commission of Enquiry and allowed Haines several months to concentrate on the study of the accounts with members of the Accountants Department and under their supervision. Haines' guilt had not been proved. It was not only his reputation that was at stake but also that of the Government. The humbler Haines became in his pleas—and once he had realised the danger he became humble— the harder the Government struck, and the members of Council looked for signs of guilt in everything he said or did; their interpretation of Haines' actions seemed to them logical because they had from the first assumed him guilty and they had a case to make. The Government was not prepared to accept that it bore any of the blame by refusing Haines the necessary staff and failing to carry out the regulations for a monthly check by a committee. One newspaper argued later that a guilty conscience drove on the Government —'anger at their own shortcomings. . . . If they had hitherto failed in their duty as supervisors, they would not do so as the detectors and pursuers of delinquents. Their own error should be expiated, but Captain Haines must be their scapegoat. So that gallant officer was carried off to Bombay with every mark of indignity, as though his guilt had been already proved'.[3]

Lord Elphinstone was quite confident that all the guilt lay with Haines. He pointed out that he had twice been given the opportunity of handing over all his papers but had failed to do so, 'and yet this is precisely the investigation which a man in his position, conscious of his own integrity, would have courted. . . . It is Captain Haines himself who has driven us to take the step which he now deprecates by "emphatically protesting" against that very mode of examining his papers which he now solicits'; Captain Haines should be informed that Government could not recede from the position 'to which he has driven us'. It was the Government that was being 'driven', not an officer of the Indian Navy who had been offered no advice or warning of the legal net which was gradually being drawn around him.

Mystery of the missing funds

Lord Elphinstone might have paused a moment to consider whether a man whom he believed had consistently over the years been cunning enough deliberately to defraud the Government of £28,000 would have behaved in the way that Haines had done after the deficit was known, for Haines himself closed every loop-hole of escape by stating that none of his establishment could have taken the money for they were poor and honest; he did not exploit the fact that the Treasury was notoriously insecure having been entered by Somali robbers on one occasion, a lock broken on another and floods having made the whole building unsafe even to work in. From the first he accepted that it was his responsibility and that he alone would have to pay for any deficit that was proved.

The Governor made his own personal assumptions; he was a strong character in a powerful position and he had already made it clear to members of the Council that he did not think that anyone could hold a view of Haines' guilt different from his own. A more sensible and humane approach was adopted by Mr. J. G. Lumsden, senior member of the Council, who wrote in an official minute that it might be as well to find out from the Legal Department whether the proceedings with the police officer could not be suspended and the investigation before a Commission resumed, 'before we commit ourselves to a course which may perhaps lead hereafter to the imputation that we have not shown a fitting consideration to the previous high character and long service of Captain Haines'. The Governor grudgingly accepted but doubted the propriety and expediency of retracing their steps.

The Advocate-General advised that proceedings could not be stopped, nor the papers taken out of the legal custody of the Magistrate. Haines was informed that his application for a Commission to investigate the accounts had come too late and that there could be no further correspondence direct but only through the Government solicitor.

Haines realised at last that he had a serious battle to face. He went to live with a friend in Bombay and asked for a few things to be brought from the customs to which the Government agreed. These consisted of a couch, one small ship's dressing table, two worn carpets and an iron chair. His wife and son were in England and he hung the oil paintings of them in his room. He kept away from

Bombay society. Once it was known that the Governor and his Council considered Haines was guilty, members of the civil service took the same view and worked to bring about his downfall; many malicious stories were going the rounds for it was not possible for a naval officer to be 'Sultan of Aden' for fifteen years without creating enemies. Some described him as a 'Sultanised Englishman' or that he had 'gone Arab'; the military said, correctly enough, that he had even argued that the word of his interpreter, Mullah Jaffar, was as good as the word of a British officer!

There was, however, a large body of opinion in Bombay who supported Haines and he had friends who tried to draw him out of his despondency, for he was shattered by the attitude taken by the Government of Bombay and was apprehensive of the outcome. 'It is unanimously believed,' he wrote, 'that where powerful enemies in Bombay, shielded by the might of Government, are permitted to oppress, neither innocence of offence, nor law of his country, are of any effect in protecting an officer against this mighty antagonism— all must yield to the strong arm of the reigning power for good or evil, according to the will and not the justice of Government.'

Bombay society could be malicious enough to ruin a man's career. Richard Burton had 'stood aghast in its presence' and wrote that the rank climate of India, which had a marvellous effect on the growth of vegetation, seemed to have the same effect on the Anglo-Indian character which 'shot up, as if suddenly relieved of the weight with which society controls it in England'.[4]

Richard Burton had been reading some of Haines' reports from Aden while staying with Mr. J. G. Lumsden, in order to prepare himself for an expedition from Aden across Somaliland to Zanzibar and then in search of the source of the White Nile in central Africa. Burton had left for Aden a month after Haines had arrived in Bombay following his dismissal and had found the Government of Aden in great difficulties with the tribes. He approved entirely of Haines' argument that it was necessary to advance every now and again outside the Aden fortifications in order to obtain the respect of the tribesmen.

'For half a generation,' wrote Burton, 'we have been masters of Aden, filling southern Arabia with our calicoes and rupees—what is the present state of affairs there? We are dared by the Beduin to come forth from behind our stone walls and fight like men in the plain—British protégés are slaughtered within range of our guns, our allies' villages have been burned in sight of Aden, our deserters are welcomed and our fugitive felons protected, our supplies are cut off and the garrison is reduced to extreme distress. . . . Our forbearance to attack is universally asserted and believed to arise from mere cowardice.'[5] That was the view, too, of Colonel James Outram who arrived in Aden in June 1854 appointed as Political Agent and Commander of the garrison. Outram wrote long despatches emphasising the importance of Haines' arguments against confining the garrison always to the defence of the fortifications, and attacked the Bombay Government's policy as 'vacillating'. He wanted power to act against the tribesmen as he thought necessary but Lord Elphinstone replied that the Court of Directors had forbidden any expeditions inland; the cost of the garrison was £75,000 annually but London had repeatedly refused to allow these troops to be used outside the walls of Aden.

Outram's prestige and his forcefulness might have led to a modification of the policy, but he found the climate of Aden bad for his health and he had to leave in October 1854 after only four months there. Burton left on his lone expedition to Harrar two months later having had no help from Outram for his main expedition to Zanzibar. Colonel Coghlan took over in Aden and showed considerable ability. Haines' excellent intelligence service was missing and Coghlan did not have the prestige with the tribes that Haines had acquired, but he was fortunate in having as his assistant Lieutenant Robert Playfair (later Sir Robert) and two excellent Arabists in the Reverend Percy Badger and his brother-in-law, Hormuzd Rassam, who had been appointed to a post in Aden after his excavations at Nimrud and Nineveh. 'Haines' success in dealing with the Arabs was due almost entirely to his own uncanny ability to understand the Arab mind; Coghlan's success was due unquestionably to his intelligent use of able advisers.'[6] It had also been to Haines' advantage that, while he understood the Arabs, he remained always a bluff sailor. 'Amongst the English,' wrote Richard Burton in *Scinde or the Unhappy Valley* (1851), 'there is no man so attractive to the Orientals, no man who can negotiate with them so effectively, as a good, honest, open-hearted and positive naval officer of the old school.'

Trial and acquittal

(May to August 1854)

Neither the Governor-General of India, Lord Dalhousie, nor the Court of Directors questioned the method followed by the Bombay Government in dealing with the Haines' case. The Company was prepared to swallow the costly Afghan war started by Lord Auckland or the elaborate and expensive durbars and wars of Lord Ellenborough's time, and though both were recalled by the Court of Directors, Ellenborough was created an earl and was voted the thanks of Parliament while Auckland, after a few years, became First Lord of the Admiralty.

But when there was any loss of money which could be blamed specifically on an individual the East India Company became vindictive. To that enterprising man, Stamford Raffles, who created the valuable trading centre of Singapore, it behaved with outstanding meanness and charged his widow £10,000 for expenses which should have been ignored. In the case of Haines, who had, as he said, created Aden out of rude and unpromising material and had saved the Government ten times the amount unaccounted for, the authorities jumped to the conclusion, in spite of his past loyalty and achievements, that he had deliberately robbed the Company.

The Court of Directors agreed that Haines should be arraigned before the Supreme Court of Bombay, if it were thought that a conviction could be obtained, and it blamed the officers dealing with the Bombay accounts for not having had the Aden Treasury in-

Trial and acquittal

spected earlier.[1] By the time this letter of June 14 1854 reached Bombay preparations were already being made for Haines' trial before the Supreme Court of Bombay.

Haines had arrived in Bombay in April 1854, the decision to put him on trial was taken at the beginning of May and the trial planned for July, which did not allow him time to prepare adequately for a complicated case. He had great difficulty in finding a good barrister who was at liberty to defend him, for anyone who did work for the government was not allowed to take a case in opposition to it. Eventually a Mr. Geoffrey Taylor was persuaded to come from a hill station where he was on sick leave and an assistant, Mr. Standen, was found, whose first brief it was in India.

The trial aroused very great interest. It was not the first time that officers had had to fight for their freedom in cases brought by the East India Company.* Captain Haines was arraigned on an indictment which included twenty-two counts charging 'malversation and embezzlement to the extent of 27,851 rupees between March 1 and September 1 1852'. He pleaded not guilty.

The Chief Justice, Sir William Yardley, addressed the jury of twelve local businessmen, drawing attention to Article 11 of Act 13 of 1850, under which Captain Haines was to be tried, and particularly to the sentence, 'proof of a gross deficiency in the accounts of any such trustee or public servant shall be evidence of the offence charged, until such deficiency is otherwise explained'. The result of the enquiry might, he said, turn upon this Article which he considered was so loosely worded as to be almost unintelligible and seemed to be the reverse of what was intended, but the Article could make no alteration in the law of England—that before embezzlement could be substantiated it had to be proved that the accused had misappropriated and applied to his own use certain specific sums of money. Proof of a general deficiency was not sufficient. 'Indeed, it would be a most dangerous position for a public officer to be placed in, if a deficiency was always considered a felony. No matter how difficult it might be, the prosecution were bound to produce conclusive proofs.' Much of the prosecution's case had been set down by Mr. Archibald Robertson, and Sir William

* See note 5, chapter 16, and Low's *History of the Indian Navy* for other examples.

observed that the greater part of his depositions appeared to be made up of inferences drawn from certain facts which had come to his knowledge in Aden and however competent Mr. Robertson might be to draw inferences and conclusions it was absolutely necessary that the jury should draw their own conclusions.

The Chief Justice fell ill and another Judge, Sir Charles Jackson, presided over the trial which started on July 25 1854 and lasted four days. The case for the prosecution was conducted by Mr. Le Mesurier, the Advocate-General. A large number of witnesses for the prosecution had been brought from Aden including clerks, the Arab merchant, Ali Bu-Beker, whose father had been in charge of Aden under the Sultan, and one or two Banians, but their evidence seemed to be more in favour of the prisoner than against him. Except perhaps in the case of Ali Bu-Beker, who probably did not realise that he was creating a bad impression when he said that Haines used to make him temporary loans of 25,000 or 28,000 rupees which were not entered in any books as there was complete trust; 'it is usual between Arabs', he said. The prosecution stated that Haines had disobeyed orders by not having the boxes opened and the money counted each month; the count was a protection 'against the errors and frauds of his establishment and, by throwing away this protection, Captain Haines was placing himself in the dangerous position of having an enormous treasury at his absolute command, without any supervision or control'. The monthly cash reports sent to Bombay, not only stated the balance but gave the amounts in notes, rupees, half-rupees, annas and pice, so that the prisoner was in the dilemma that if he did not carry out a count the reports were fictitious and if he did, then his statement that he did not must have been false. Other arguments were that Haines had used his position and Government funds to carry on trade, for the improvement of the hotel in Aden and to help build himself a house. Mr. Robertson stated that in a number of cases he could not find vouchers or entries to show that Government funds had been repaid or disbursed and he had disallowed such amounts. There had been a large number of remittances to Mrs. Haines either in London or in Bombay and it was pointed out that whereas Haines' salary was 24,000 rupees annually (£2,400), his remittances each year were more than double that amount. The Judge gave a warning that such

Governors-General of India during the period of Haines' administration of
    Aden and his imprisonment:

George Eden, Earl of Auckland, 1836–1842   Edward Law, Earl of Ellenborough, 1842–
                                                1844
Henry Hardinge, 1st Viscount Hardinge of   James Andrew Broun Ramsay, 1st Marquis
    Lahore, 1844–1848   of Dalhousie, 1848–1856

View of Bombay in the middle of the nineteenth century

Bombay harbour in the monsoon

inferences could not be depended upon and that the jury would have to decide how much consideration should be given to them.

Lieutenant Cruttenden, against whom no action was being taken by the Government, made some surprising statements which were not helpful to the prisoner; for instance, he said that the Treasury was a secure building and could not be robbed, that Haines was not hard worked and that he was a good accountant.

Counsel for the Defence pointed out that there was no evidence that Haines had taken part in trade. It was true that sums of money had been advanced but these had been backed by amounts paid into the Treasury from Haines' own salary. 'I myself put into the money chest deductions from Captain Haines' pay,' stated one of the Aden clerks, 'sometimes 800, 1,000 or 1,500 rupees; he used frequently to bring money from Steamer Point in the buggy and put money in the Treasury.' Counsel argued that it was wrong to quote haphazard replies prisoner had given to the Commissioners in Aden as evidence; they were not final or decisive answers since Captain Haines had not been able to refer to his accounts, which were in the hands of the Commissioners, and he was not on trial at that time. The Commissioners had disallowed certain items because they were unsupported by vouchers, but that was not a reason to convict the prisoner of embezzlement. There had been an attempt by the prosecution to make out that Captain Haines was systematically guilty of daring robbery, but for what object after thirty-five years of service and considering that he was in a position to retire at any time on a pension of £800 a year?

After the Judge had read over the evidence from his notes, the jury retired and returned in an hour and twenty minutes with a verdict of 'Not Guilty'. 'Then,' wrote a local newspaper, 'one loud burst of approbation broke out amongst the crowd who thronged the Court, a demonstration which His Lordship immediately checked.'[2]

Haines' supporters were delighted, but amazed to find that the Government was in a position to make further charges in another trial before the Supreme Court before a different jury. The second trial started on August 1, also before Judge Sir Charles Jackson, and was concluded three days later. As the Advocate-General was temporarily indisposed, Mr. Howard of the Legal Department conducted the prosecution and concentrated on 'four distinct acts of embezzlement' between August 25 1850 and February 19 1851. He argued that if it were once admitted that officers could use public funds for a temporary purpose without exposing themselves to penal consequences, the most serious results might ensue, and half the revenues of the country might disappear. As this was a new trial many of the previous arguments were repeated and a strong case was made by the prosecution.

Counsel for the Defence argued that there was not sufficient information in the evidence produced by the prosecution. It was true that the entries made by Captain Haines told against him because they were incomplete, but if he were an embezzler would he not have kept his accounts very carefully so as to protect himself from suspicion? 'Would he have inserted in his books every possible evidence against himself and stopped short, omitting the only entries which could operate as his protection? A fraudulent man would have made his accounts appear perfect, and on paper at least have rendered his detection impossible.'

The Judge in summing up stated that evidence had been given of Government funds having been drawn out by Captain Haines and the proceeds applied to his own use. It was for the jury to decide on its weight and effect. The jury retired for an hour and a half and it, too, returned a verdict of 'Not Guilty'. The Judge was informed that the prosecution was abandoned and a verdict of 'Not Guilty' was recorded against the remaining indictments. Once again great enthusiasm at the result was shown by the large crowds in the Court. 'The prisoner on hearing the verdict could not control his feelings', stated the local newspaper which gave very full reports of both trials. 'He bowed respectfully to the Judge, the Jury and the spectators around him. On going out of the dock he was congratulated by his friends and others.'[3]

Haines left the Court a free man. He received reports that the Advocate-General, Mr. Le Mesurier, was in a fury at the result and had declared that he would see that Haines lost his commission and remained in prison. But Haines was confident. 'How frivolously and captiously,' he commented, 'has the smallest error been caught at and handled till the astounding charges of breach of trust and embezzlement were plotted with.' The Government had instructed him to see that the commercial advantages of Aden must have primary consideration, yet his obedience was turned into a charge against him, and his anxiety to encourage commerce was taken as proof that he traded for his own gain. In the prosperity of Aden, he said, lay the vindication and living demonstration of his exertions, and in direct contradiction to the calumnies by which he had been oppressed. He considered that the verdict of the Supreme Court had cleared him entirely: 'he had been proved wholly innocent of any criminal connection with the erroneous balance—he had been relieved of it in consequence'. It was a generous interpretation of the verdict which the Government could have made, but had no intention of doing so.

A debtors' prison

(August 1854 to December 1856)

The Advocate-General produced a printed report of sixty-four pages which was given wide circulation and was intended to prove that Haines was guilty in spite of the verdict of the Supreme Court.[1] The report shows, indeed, that there was a strong case against Haines, but selection can make an effective case for either side in so long and complicated a trial. The arguments about figures and lack of vouchers depended to a great extent on Mr. Robertson's own views and there are indications that his evidence was not so effective under cross-examination as it seemed on paper. Much that was apparent to the members of the juries in both Courts cannot be recaptured, such as the general atmosphere of a crowded court-room, the Judge's attitude, the demeanour of witnesses and whether those conducting the prosecution gave the impression that the Government was pursuing an officer of the Company in a fair or in a vindictive way.

The Bombay Government was angry at the result of the trial and determined that the acquittals should make no difference. It made excuses to the Court of Directors that the trial had been before a

Petit Jury taken from a class of men who were not as competent to deal with so complicated and important a trial as juries taken from those on the Grand Jury list. 'Looking at the terms in which both the juries appear to have been charged by the presiding Judge, as also to the evidence on which those charges were founded, we cannot but apprehend that to treat Captain Haines as a servant whose character has been cleared by the investigation, or even to allow him to retire from the service, would have a most demoralising effect!'

That the jury did not accept the Judge's guidance may have been true, but to pay no attention to the verdicts must have had an even more demoralising effect on officers, civil servants and members of the Indian population who followed the trial. The Government would have shown justice and good sense if it had sent Haines back to sea or retired him on his pension, but it pursued Haines to the end. Its letter to the Court of Directors concluded: 'As we were informed [presumably by the Advocate-General] that it was clearly shown at the trial that Captain Haines had employed the public money for his own private purposes, a civil action was commenced against him for the recovery of the unexplained deficiency.'

This was the worst of all conclusions for Haines. The Court of Directors had stated in their letter of June 14 1854 that if there were insufficient grounds to have Haines charged before a Civil Tribunal he should be tried before a general court martial. The Bombay Government was reminded that Act 27 of the Indian Legislature of 1848 provided that if there were not a sufficient number of officers of superior rank to form the court martial, officers of the Royal Navy and of the Army could be drawn upon. Haines had asked for such a trial (though he called it a Commission of Enquiry) but as he had been acquitted by the Supreme Court he could not be court-martialled. The result of that would certainly have been more favourable to him than a civil case for debt since in those days prisoners languished many years in jail.*

A story was being circulated in Bombay that Haines intended to

---

* The anomaly that naval officers could not be tried by naval officers at a court martial for alleged offences committed on shore, with certain exceptions, was corrected a few years later, in 1856, when a Bill was passed by the Supreme Legislative Council which laid down that a naval officer charged with fraud could be tried by a naval court martial.

take passage in a ship to England and the Government arranged that bail should be demanded for the enormous sum of 200,000 rupees (£20,000), a sum that it knew he could not pay, so that, only three weeks after Haines had been acquitted, he was arrested and detained. 'Wherefore did the Government,' wrote Haines, 'ignore the decision of the Supreme Court when it had itself chosen the same as the most degrading to which an officer could be subjected. What could have led to the ungenerous action for debt that instantly ensued?'

It was true that Haines had from the beginning accepted responsibility for any deficit that could be proved, but now the Government was, as he argued, 'converting an erroneous and unaudited balance into a civil claim' and still he had been given no opportunity to inspect the accounts. 'Where everything is in the Plaintiff's hands what possible chance has a Defendant?' He continued to believe that he could find the errors, but he had been treated as 'an automaton to be disposed of in the manner best adapted to the will of the Government party.' Besides, argued Haines, supposing the Government were correct in stating that there was no way of accounting for the deficit, would there have been any harm 'in following the just course and allowing the Defendant to understand whether the money sued for was actually missing?' Haines did not trust Mr. Robertson's figures or the deductions made from them and in a memorandum to the Court of Directors Haines quoted Article 5 of the Legislative Act 37 of 1850: 'When the charge shall be brought by an accuser, the Government shall require the accusation to be reduced to writing and verified by oath, and if the oath is false and malicious the person making it is liable to punishment for perjury.'

Haines was not in a position to pay much more than half the amount which the Government said was the deficit, and once he was put into a debtor's prison there would be little hope for him. His legal advisers made some soundings in official quarters and proposed that he should make an offer to Government—to hand over all his property in Aden and elsewhere and that that should be accepted as full settlement of the amount claimed. Haines made the offer, adding that he wished to retain his collection of stuffed birds, the sword presented to him by the Court of Directors for the capture of Aden and Mrs. Haines' jewels. He had sent a long list of what he possessed with estimates of the value of the items, but Lord Elphinstone placed no reliance on this and believed that Haines had property hidden away in England or elsewhere.

The Governor-in-Council suggested that if action were taken through the Insolvency Court it might be possible to discover what Haines really did possess and whether he had contrived to hand over property to third parties. The Legal Department pointed out, however, that Haines could not be examined as to his means; the Commissioner of the Insolvency Court would decline to enter into the question as to whether the debt was contracted fraudulently or not and would 'treat the verdicts of two successive juries as decisive on the point'. It recommended that the Government should accept Haines' offer as the best chance of recovering some of the money for 'if proceedings are carried on hostilely against Captain Haines, very little of his property may eventually be available to Government and even that portion may only be secured after a tedious and costly litigation'. The Governor-in-Council, after much discussion, agreed to accept that advice but there was one proviso—that it should be made clear to Captain Haines that acceptance did not mean that the Government had changed its mind about him; it would not 'in the slightest degree influence the consideration of his conduct as a public officer'.

Haines should have been thankful that the Government had agreed to accept his offer. It would have been a way out of the pit into which he had fallen, for his only salvation was to leave India where he was at the Government's mercy. At fifty-two years of age he could have started another career at sea with the Peninsular and Oriental line, as Robert Moresby had done; there was a demand for naval officers who knew the Red Sea and the Indian Ocean. Having been acquitted in two trials, and having entertained so many ships' captains at his house at Steamer Point, he might well have obtained a good commercial post. But Haines rejected that means of escape. Often he had lectured the Arab Sultans on their failure to see what was in their best interest, but they could not alter their ways or change their ideas—and nor could Haines. He was a loyal servant of Government and he could not imagine himself as anything else; if Government continued to reject him, he would have to stay and try to solve the mystery of the accounts to clear his name. He replied to the Government's letter accepting his offer that in view of the 'very harsh conditions' which Government had placed upon acceptance he had no alternative but to withdraw it. The harsh conditions were that Government was not prepared to alter its view of his conduct.

The Court of Directors put the wrong interpretation on his refusal, stating that what Haines must have objected to was the clause that he should give a full statement of the property he possessed and the withdrawal of the offer by Haines was 'a strong indication that it was not made in good faith'.

That clause certainly had added to his feeling of humiliation since it was a further proof of the Government's distrust; but it was the proviso that touched him to the quick; he considered it a terrible indignity that he should have to continue to prove that he was an honourable man. 'Why in every step,' wrote Haines later, 'was insult and severity thus recklessly hurled at an innocent man? For, even supposing the erroneous balance to be utterly irreparable, surely the misfortune might have been more courteously and generously reviewed.' It was another echo of the old Sultan of Lahej—'if you will give me kindness it is all that I want'. Haines' refusal to compromise and his trust in his employers prevented him from fighting as hard as he should have done in the early stages of the proceedings. He wrote at the end of his life that, instead of having his case taken up by the Press in England, he had sought justice first from the Bombay Government and then from the Court of Directors 'with the utmost folly of devotion'.

Haines informed the Government through his solicitors that he would not contest the fact that he held himself responsible for any deficit in the accounts, and it is possible that the Government believed that he did not intend to contest the case, or that the Advocate-General was secretive about the date that the case would be called, determined to have no more failures. Haines, however, had every intention of contesting the figure arrived at by the Government in their claim, but his solicitors were given no warning that his case was to come before Sir William Yardley, the Chief Justice, on January 4 1855, and no time was allowed for witnesses or argument. The case was disposed of in fifteen minutes and a verdict given in favour of the East India Company for 278,971 rupees and costs, an amount only a little less than the original total of about £28,000, in spite of the sum realised by the sale of some of Haines' property.

This judgement gave the Company the right to issue a writ enabling the Sheriff to seize and sell any of Haines' property within the jurisdiction of the Supreme Court. As he had not sufficient property to cover the deficit, he was arrested and imprisoned in Mazagon Jail in Bombay. The jail had a dense population of Indians on three sides and a burial ground with a stagnant pool on the third with the result that it had been condemned in various reports for its insufficient ventilation and lack of room for exercise for prisoners. It was the most terrible experience for an active man, wrote Haines, to be enclosed in the walls of such a jail in a tropical climate.

One blow followed another. On March 9 1855 Haines learned through a newspaper report that his name had been removed from the list of the Indian Navy, wiping out, as it seemed, the whole of his distinguished career. He was outraged too, because the announcement suggested that he had been dismissed for fraudulence which he considered came under the law of libel. His person was secured under a writ of *Ca Sa* (*Capias ad Satisfaciendum*)[2] and his property taken and sold considerably below its value; he was reduced to living on 4 annas (sixpence) a day supplied by the Government and on the charity of friends. Under the law only his property within the jurisdiction of the Supreme Court could be seized and this did not include his possessions in Aden. He had invested his savings in houses because they were needed and to provide a place in which he himself could live since nothing had been built by Government for a 'Residency'. When he was put into prison he had counted on the rents from these houses in Aden for the support of his wife and son but the Government disregarded the law and in March 1855 began to sell Haines' property in Aden, which he had had valued by a 'competent engineer' at 50,000 rupees. The property was sold for 17,800 rupees. Haines recalled the way that Government had treated Hajj Roussoul, the British Agent at Mocha, and his own interpreter, Mullah Jaffar; 'it may have been the custom of this Government to drive unfriended natives to servile measures, but an Englishman must appeal to the laws of his country. If domestics in our country homes were liable to be robbed of their earnings on the capricious change in the minds of their employers, England would soon become a land of anarchy and despotism.'

Overwhelmed by these calamities, Haines became both physically and mentally seriously ill and his wife and son were sent for from England. In July 1855 the medical officer of the Bombay jail, Assistant-Surgeon Robert Haines (who was not a relation) reported to Government that it was 'essential' to release the prisoner temporarily from confinement to re-establish his health. The Sheriff was informed that he could allow Haines to reside temporarily outside the jail, 'under such surveillance as may prove as little irksome as possible to the prisoner, while consistent with its perfect efficiency'. Haines was shown the letter and was informed that the Sheriff's peons would be placed in and about the house where he would lodge. He accepted, grateful for the change; indeed, he believed that the Government intended to give him his full freedom. He walked from the jail to his former coachman's house but, having been over six months in prison, he felt faint from the unusual exercise. When he reached his room, where Indian servants were making his bed, he asked them to leave as he was beginning to feel very ill, but they refused to go, saying that their orders were not to lose sight of him— they were, in fact, the Sheriff's peons, 'no privacy', wrote Haines, 'being permitted by day or night'. The surveillance became insufferable and an appeal was made to Lord Elphinstone who arranged that the peons did not have to stay in the rooms watching Haines while he ate and slept, but could remain outside close to the verandah.

The Bombay Government was trying to be more lenient. It wrote to the Court of Directors to say that Haines' health was reported to be so seriously affected that his life might possibly be endangered, if he were again put into the jail, and that it was recommended that he should be permitted to proceed to England for the recovery of his health. If a medical commission confirmed this, would the Court agree to Haines going to England or remaining free in Bombay, even though he would be unable to pay any, or only a small portion, of the debt.

On August 3 1855 three surgeons were appointed from the Bombay Medical Establishment—Stovell, Leith and Arbuckle—to report whether Haines' life would be endangered if he were sent back to prison, and whether his health would be restored if he were permitted to proceed to Europe. The Medical Commission considered that Haines appeared to be in an impaired state of health both bodily and mentally, and that 'mental suffering often leads to mental and bodily disease and even to death in all places and in all climates'. The Commission concluded, however: 'we are of opinion that a fatal result would not be more likely to appear in the Bombay gaol than in any other place'.[3] It was a stupid and wicked decision, amounting to a sentence of death.

Having received this report the Government of Bombay on August 22, a little over a month after Haines had been allowed to live outside the jail, directed the Sheriff to have the prisoner returned to Mazagon. Immediately Dr. Robert Haines heard of this, he wrote to Government to say that his opinion remained unchanged and that to put the prisoner back 'might, at the present period, be attended with dangerous consequences'. The Bombay Government countermanded their order to the Sheriff and allowed Haines to remain in the bungalow of a friend to which he had moved from the coachman's house, while it awaited instructions from London. With him were his wife, Mary, and his son, Stafford, aged sixteen.

It was three months before Bombay received the reply from the Court of Directors. It was not generous. To let Haines come to England would be, in their view, legally equivalent to a relinquishment of the debt due to the East India Company; whatever might be the state of his health, Haines had no ground for expecting that he would be released, unless he applied to the Insolvency Court, the regular mode of obtaining release. The fact that he had not made application to the Court could only be interpreted in a discreditable manner. The Court of Directors noted that the Assistant-Surgeon of the Bombay jail had reported that there were no signs of bodily diseases and that the danger was from mental causes, and it was not prepared to accept his opinion against that of three experienced medical officers. Therefore, unless Assistant-Surgeon Haines could satisfy the Medical Committee of the soundness of his opinion Mr. Haines was to be returned to jail.[4]

Dr. Robert Haines * again protested to Government that the prisoner's health was not strong enough to stand life in jail, as did his wife and son, but Government followed the orders of the Court of Directors and, after just over four months of

---

* Haines' son, Stafford, was later to state that Robert Haines 'was a kind and good friend—*Sans peur et sans reproche*'.[5]

'freedom', on December 3 1855 it ordered the prisoner to be again confined in Mazagon jail.

His family and friends urged Haines to obtain his freedom by making an application to the Supreme Court to be discharged out of the custody of the Sheriff of Bombay, on the argument that he had already been released with the agreement of the Government. The application was opposed and very fully argued before the Chief Justice, Sir William Yardley. In the Supreme Court on December 21 Sir William stated that 'if a Defendant be allowed to go at perfect liberty for ever so short a time by the detaining creditor, he cannot again be taken in execution upon the same judgement'. But the application was dismissed because it was considered that Haines was in the custody of the Sheriff throughout the time he spent out of jail.[6] Haines then appealed to the Privy Council in England, and the application was dismissed on the same reasoning that Haines had remained in custody.[7]

25

Freedom and death

(1857 to 1860)

The prisoner in Mazagon Jail was almost forgotten during the years of the Crimean War and of the Indian Mutiny. His petitions were ignored or he was told that they were full of mis-statements and the Court of Directors declined all his requests to review his case. The outbreak of the Indian Mutiny might have been considered a good opportunity to release an officer who could have been of service but no such move was made.

Haines' resilience was remarkable. After four years in prison he was still fighting hard and still pinned his hopes on the Court of Directors and for that reason, he said, he had continued to refrain from publishing his story in the English newspapers. On August 19 1858 he wrote his fifth and longest petition to the Court of Directors, consisting of ninety-one foolscap pages with one hundred and eighty-three paragraphs.[1] But he was gradually losing strength and hope. 'Should your Honourable Court refuse to extend its protection to an oppressed officer what remains to him to free himself from the fatal grasp of a despotic Government?' There is once more an echo of the old Sultan of Lahej—'if I cannot obtain your assistance to shield me from my enemies to whom am I to apply?'

Haines had been told that the only way to free himself was to apply to the Insolvency Court, and he had seriously considered doing this when first imprisoned, but after studying the law very carefully he had decided that he would be worse off than before if he applied to a Court and he looked on any such proposal from the Government 'with the bitterest suspicion'.

'If the Insolvency Court were desired as a channel of freedom,' he wrote, 'has your Honourable Court no power of itself to bestow that freedom and to cancel an erroneous claim? Has no generous mind among the members of the Honourable Court been yet induced to regard with sympathy the punishments already inflicted for no specified or intentional offence.

'The life of your Petitioner now alone remains to him and is it the will of your Honourable Court that that also shall be forfeited by this harsh imprisonment, unless your Petitioner subscribes to the Insolvent Act, which both his reason and his pride forbid—his reason perceiving in the proposal some new grievance, and his pride resenting the idea of slave-like submission to false debt assumed by his enemies.' There was no precedent that 'on secret report an officer's character may be whispered away'.

Haines had only two more years to live when he wrote his tragic appeal; he refused to give in or to compromise; 'an Englishman cannot be arbitrarily cast away after years of patient labour', he wrote in the final sentence of his last petition.

On June 9 1860 the new Governor of Bombay, Sir George Clerk, ordered Haines' release from prison, and he was taken on board a merchantman, the *Poictiers*, bound for London. He was at last a free man after nearly six years in the Bombay prison. 'By taking Haines in execution upon the Judgement,' wrote the Acting Advocate-General, 'and by his subsequent discharge with the consent of the Plaintiffs, the Judgement was as fully satisfied as if he had paid the debt and costs in full, and there remains no further remedy whatever upon it, either against his goods or lands or otherwise howsoever.'[2]

But Haines had no goods left. They had all been taken by the Government and he had gained nothing by refusing the Government's agreement to his offer six years earlier to hand over all his property in return for his release. He had then been vigorous and healthy and could have made a new life, but after six years in the damp heat of a Bombay prison he was in a pitiable condition.

A week after embarking on the ship that was to take him to England, he was taken ill with dysentery and died on board in Bombay harbour on June 16 1860 at the age of fifty-eight. His body was taken to the Colaba Church and he was buried in the cemetery there with a tombstone which bore only his name and the date of his death. Local newspapers noticed his death in a few lines, though one wrote a fine epitaph which was a violent attack on the Bombay Government for the injustice committed.[3]

It was, as Haines had written from prison, 'the waste of a strong life in the Service of the East India Company', but he did have a memorial—the town of Aden which he had created.

Notes

Unless otherwise stated the notes refer to the correspondence in the India Office Records, Orbit House, 197 Blackfriars Road, London S.E.1. They are based on the classifications in existence before the records were moved from Whitehall to Blackfriars at the end of 1967, but there should be no great difficulty in tracing them under the reclassification which is now being devised. They are nearly all drawn from the following lists of records: Political and Secret Department, Bombay Proceedings, Factory Records Persia (F.R.P.), and Financial Department. Bombay Enclosures are given as B.E.

INTRODUCTION *pp. 1–8*
1 *Arabia and the Isles*, by Harold Ingrams, p. 16, London, 1966 edition.
2 *The Yemen*, by Harold Ingrams, pp. 3–4, 77–81, London, 1963.
3 Ibid., p. 5.
4 In *The View from Steamer Point* (London, 1964), Sir Charles Johnston opposed Ingrams' arguments against Federalism and objected to his support for the T. E. Lawrence precept 'Arabia must be left to fight out its own fatal and complex destiny'. Sir Charles considered that it was the duty of the British to help the Arabs by giving them British institutions; the Arabs were odd, but no odder than the Spanish, Irish or English. Unfortunately for British plans Arab 'oddness' took the form of a passion for independence and objection to any policy which increased the influence of the Sultans and separated South Arabia from the Yemen. The Federal Constitution was pressed through and passed by one Arab vote in 1962, just at the time that a Republican Government was being declared in the Yemen for which there was great enthusiasm among Aden nationalists. The debate with Sir Charles Johnston was carried further by Harold Ingrams in his introduction to the 1966 edition of *Arabia and the Isles*.
5 *Kings of Arabia*, by Harold F. Jacob, pp. 54, 57, 63, London, 1923.
6 'Why Aden Scorns the Chance of Peace', by David Holden in *The Sunday Times*, September 10 1967.
7 *Kings of Arabia*, p. 153.
8 Ibid., p. 66.
9 Article for centenary of death of Captain Haines, 'Through Imperialism to Nationalism in the Outposts', by Harold Ingrams in *Commonwealth Challenge*, vol. 8, No. 4, July 1960.

CHAPTER I *pp. 11–18*
1 *The Administration of the East India Company*, by J. W. Kaye, 2nd ed., London, 1853.

Notes

2   *British Routes to India*, by H. L. Hoskins, p. 3, London 1928; also *On Steam Communication between Bombay and Suez, with an Account of the 'Hugh Lindsay's' Four Voyages*, by J. H. Wilson, Bombay, 1833.

CHAPTER 2   *pp. 19–31*

1   Stafford Bettesworth Haines applied for a Cadetship in the East India Company while a boy in England and was nominated by John Inglis of Middlesex, a Director of the Company. Haines passed into the Company in December 1817 and sailed the same year for India on the *Duke of York*. Having joined the Bombay Marine, as it was then called, he became a Midshipman in May 1818, a Second Lieutenant in April 1824, a Lieutenant in March 1827, a Commander in April 1835 and a Captain in October 1841. He served aboard the East India Company's brig *Antelope* 1818–21 and saw action against pirates in the Persian Gulf in December 1818; served in the *Discovery* 1821–22, the sloop *Benares* 1822–24 and in the sloop *Elphinstone* 1825. He was Assistant Surveyor in the Persian Gulf in 1826.

2   *Travels to the City of the Caliphs along the Shores of the Persian Gulf and the Mediterranean including a Voyage to the Coast of Arabia and a Tour of the Island of Socotra*, by J. R. Wellsted, 2 vols., London, 1840.

3   See Haines' remarks in *Journal of the Royal Geographical Society (R.G.S.)*, vol. 15, p. 107; also for account of survey of Socotra and interview with Sultan Omar ibn Tawari.

4   An agreement which is described as with the 'Sultan of Socotra' dated 1834 is given in *A Collection of Treaties, Engagements and Sanads* compiled by C. U. Aitchison, No. 95, Calcutta, 1892. A slightly different account of the negotiations is given by Mr. H. L. Hoskins in *British Routes to India*, p. 189. I have kept to Haines' account.

5   *History of the Indian Navy (1613–1863)*, by C. R. Low, vol. 2, pp. 75–6, London, 1877.

6   Secret Letters from Bombay, 1st series, Bombay Government to Secret Committee, April 26 1837, vol. 6.

7   See report from *Bombay Times* quoted in Low's *History of the Indian Navy*, vol. 2, pp. 137–8, showing the strength of the Indian Navy at the beginning of 1841.

8   Ibid., pp. 55–6, 58–60.

9   *Journal of the R.G.S.*, vol. 9, 1839, 'Memoir to Accompany a Chart of the South Coast of Arabia from the Entrance of the Red Sea to Misenat', by Captain S. B. Haines; vol. 15, contains part 2 of the Memoir continuing east to Ras el Hadd. There is an account of the Kuria Muria Islands which are also described by Dr. Hulton of the survey-ship *Palinurus* covering February and March 1836 in the *Journal of the R.G.S.*, vol. 11, 1841. Mr. C. J. Cruttenden, Midshipman, described an expedition he made from Morbat to Dyreez in *Transactions of the Bombay Geographical Society*, vol. 1.

10 *Journal of the R.G.S.*, vol. 9, 1839, memoir by S. B. Haines, pp. 144–5; 'Narrative of a Journey . . . to the Ruins of Nakab al Hajar in April 1835', by Lieutenant Wellsted, *Journal of the R.G.S.*, vol. 8, 1837.
    Dr. G. Lankester Hardinge describes Nakab al Hajar as one of the very

Notes

few ancient walled towns in South Arabia; the date is uncertain but it might be as early as the first century B.C. Hisn Ghorab was the ancient and prosperous port of Qana (Cana) which was an important port for the incense trade and is described in the *Periplus* as existing in the 1st century A.D. *Archaeology in the Aden Protectorate*, by Dr. G. Lankester Hardinge, H.M. Stationery Office, 1964.

The once famous Cana, mentioned in the Bible, is now inhabited mainly by crows and is for that reason called by the Arabs, Hisn or Husn Ghorab, the Crow Castle.

11 *Voyages and Travels to India, Ceylon, the Red Sea, Abyssinia and Egypt 1802 to 1806*, by Lord Valentia (later Lord Mountnorris), 3 vols., London, 1809.

12 *The Periplus of the Erythrean Sea* was written by an anonymous Greek trader and navigator about A.D. 60. It is the first detailed record of the ports on the Somali coast, such as Malao (Berbera) and Opone (Dante) and on the South Arabian coast, such as Arabia Eudaemon (Aden), and Cana (Hisn Ghorab). These were entrepôt ports for the important trade carried on from India and Ceylon with Egypt, Rome and Byzantium; from there, too, frankincense and myrrh were exported from the area of Cape Gardafui and South Arabia to the temples of Egypt and Rome and for the Christian Churches of the Byzantine Empire.

Cana and Aden (Eden) are referred to in a verse of the Bible (Ezekiel): 'Harran and Canneh and Eden, the merchants of Sheba, Asshur and Chilmad, were thy merchants. These were thy merchants in all sorts of things, in blue cloths, and broidered work, and in chests of rich apparel, bound with cords, and made of cedar. . . .'

13 Bombay Secret Proceedings, vol. 95, Haines to Rear-Admiral Sir Charles Malcolm, March 7 1838.

14 *A Voyage to Abyssinia . . . in the Years 1809 and 1810*, by Henry Salt, London, 1814.

15 Treaty of Commerce concluded with the Sultan of Lahej, September 6 1802, *Treaties, Engagements and Sanads*, No. 33, compiled by C. U. Aitchison, Calcutta, 1892.

16 *Travels in Arabia*, London, 1838, and *Travels to the City of the Caliphs*, 2 vols., London, 1840, by J. R. Wellsted.

17 Factory Records, Persia, vol. 58, Colonel Patrick Campbell, British Consul-General in Egypt, to Lord Palmerston, Foreign Minister, Alexandria, November 1 1837.

18 *Britain's Imperial Rôle in the Red Sea Area 1800–1878*, by T. Marston, p. 31, Connecticut, 1962.

19 *East Africa and Its Invaders to 1856*, by R. Coupland, p. 362, Oxford, 1938.

20 Ibid., p. 365.

21 Palmerston to Campbell, March 1 1837, FO 78/318.

CHAPTER 3   *pp. 32–36*

1 *The Founder of Modern Egypt*, by Henry Dodwell, pp. 162 and 106, London, 1931.

2 Palmerston to Campbell, August 12 1837, FO 78/318.

Notes

3 Palmerston to Campbell, May 24 1838, FO 78/342.
4 Ponsonby to Campbell, May 24 1833, FO 78/227 and Campbell to Ponsonby, August 21 1834, FO 78/246.
5 Sir Henry Lytton Bulwer's *Life of Palmerston*, vol. 2, pp. 144-5, quoted in *The Founder of Modern Egypt*, p. 123.
6 Campbell to Foreign Office, FO 78/227, June 11 1833, quoted p. 44 *Britain's Imperial Rôle in the Red Sea Area.*
7 'Journal of an Excursion to Sanaa the Capital of Yemen', by C. R. Cruttenden, *Transactions of the Bombay Geographical Society*, August 1838 to May 1839, vol. 11, article 1, v.
8 Report of Captain Mackenzie, January 6 1837, FO 78/3185

CHAPTER 4   *pp. 37-46*

1 Hutchinson to Henry Salt, January 25 1823, see *Britain's Imperial Rôle in the Red Sea Area*, pp. 39-40, 65.
2 Sir Robert Grant's memorandum, Secret Letters Received from Bombay 1st series, vol. 6, September 23 1837. On October 21 the Bombay Government sent to the Court of Directors a memoir drawn up by Commander Haines on Cape Aden.
3 Government of India to Bombay, October 16 1837, Secret Letters from Bombay, 1st series, vol. 6, (1830–38).
4 Long Report from Haines to Sir Charles Malcolm January 20 1838 enclosing letters from Sultan Mahsin, Bombay Secret Proceedings, vol. 95, January 10 to March 28 1838.
5 Sultan Mahsin's important letter of January 22 1838 was not included by C. U. Aitchison in his collection of agreements, but a text was published in *Treaties, Agreements and Engagements* by R. Hughes Thomas, Bombay, 1851. Papers relating to the negotiations with Sultan Mahsin for the sale of Aden were tabled in the House of Lords and Lord Melbourne, the Prime Minister, stated on March 11 1838 that Aden had been 'ceded' to the British by the Sultan, so that when the son refused to hand over Aden at the end of that year the Bombay Government had considered it was justified to take Aden by force in January 1839. This was in reply to criticism of the action by Lord Lyndhurst. (Hansard, Parliamentary Debates, third series, vol. 46, 1839.)
   Apart from this brief exchange scarcely any notice was taken of the affairs of Aden either in Parliament or in the Press until the 1860's when Aden became an important staging post for troops from India with Sir Robert Napier's expedition against King Theodore of Abyssinia.

CHAPTER 5   *pp. 47-52*

1 Haines to Sir Charles Malcolm, February 3 1838, Bombay Secret Proceedings, vol. 95.
2 Haines to Ibrahim Pasha (known as 'the Little' was the Viceroy's nephew), February 8; Ibrahim to Mohammed Ali Pasha, February 12, F.R.P., vol. 59.
3 Campbell to Palmerston, March 27 1838, F.R.P., vols. 59 and 60.
4 Ibid., June 9 1838, F.R.P., vol. 60.
5 Lord Auckland, Governor-General of India, to Mohammed Ali Pasha, Viceroy of Egypt, Simla, April 16 1838, F.R.P., vol. 60.

Notes

CHAPTER 6 *pp. 53–59*

1 *The Bombay Courier* of February 24 1838, reported that Aden had already been surrendered by the Sultan in exchange for an annual payment, quoted in *Asiatic Journal*, N.S., vol. 26, 1838, part 2, p. 83.
2 Bombay to Secret Committee, August 27 1838, Secret Letters received from Bombay 1st series, vol. 7.
3 *Blackwood's Edinburgh Magazine*, April 1843, vol. 53.
4 Mr. James Farish, Acting Governor of Bombay, in his minute of September 5 1838 in Bombay Secret Proceedings, vol. 10, which includes other reports quoted up to October 1838.
5 Bombay Government to Secret Committee, August 27 1838, Letters received from Bombay, vol. 7.

CHAPTER 7 *pp. 60–69*

1 *Asiatic Journal*, N.S. 28, part 2, p. 202.
2 Enclosures to Secret Letters from Bombay, vols. 11 and 12 give most of the correspondence in this chapter.
3 Campbell to Palmerston, Alexandria, June 9 1838, F.R.P., vol. 60.

CHAPTER 8 *pp. 70–78*

1 James Farish's minute, March 24 1839, Bombay Enclosures, vol. 12.
2 Haines' report given in Low's *History of the Indian Navy*, vol. 2, p. 119. For Major Bailie's report see *Asiatic Journal*, N.S. 29, part 2, pp. 167–7.
3 'Captain Daniell hopes to leave the sword, valued at 100 guineas, presented to him for his services at Aden, as an heirloom to his children; I hope to leave mine a legacy they will consider more valuable, viz., an unblemished character for truthfulness.' That was the conclusion of a memorial sent to the Under-Secretary of State for India in May 1864 by Captain Benjamin Hamilton who contested the story of the attack on Sira Island given by Captain Daniell.
4 Throughout January and February Haines signed a large number of agreements with neighbouring tribes which are contained in *Treaties, Engagements and Sanads* compiled by C. U. Aitchison, vol. 11, part 3, 1892. They included agreements with the Abdali (No. 34), the Subaihi (No. 43), Agrabi (No. 55), Haushabi (No. 67) and the Yafa'i (No. 65).

CHAPTER 9 *pp. 79–89*

1 Secret Department Bombay to Secret Committee, vol. 6, February 25 1839.
2 Bombay Secret Proceedings, Haines to Bombay Government, April 13 1854, quoted in *Britain's Imperial Rôle* etc., pp. 205–6 and *Kings of Arabia*, pp. 253–4.
3 *Asiatic Journal*, N.S. 29, 1839, part 2, p. 104.
4 Ibid., p. 280.
5 Ibid., pp. 176–7.
6 Haines to Bombay, February 28 1839, B.E., vol. 13.
7 'Account of Aden', *Asiatic Journal*, N.S. 28, 1839, part 1, pp. 317–21.
8 *First Footsteps in East Africa*, by Sir Richard Burton, note p. 53, edited by Gordon Waterfield, London, 1966.
9 Haines to Bombay, February 25 1839, B.E., vol. 13.

10 Text of agreement given in *Treaties, Engagements and Sanads*, vol. 11, part 3, No. 44, dated March 10 1839.
11 Haines to Ibrahim Pasha, Commanding the Egyptian troops in the Yemen, February 25 1839, F.R.P., vol. 64.
12 Haines to P. Campbell, British Consul-General in Egypt, February 28 1839, F.R.P., vol. 64.
13 Government of India to Bombay, March 25 1839, B.E., vol. 13.
14 Sultan Mahsin's letter to Government of Bombay, sent from Aden March 16 received Bombay April 4 1839, B.E., vol. 13.
15 Minute by James Farish, March 24 1839, B.E., vol. 12.

CHAPTER 10   *pp. 90–100*
1 Haines to Bombay, April 10 1839 on board H.C.S.S. *Berenice*, B.E., vol. 13.
2 Minute by Governor of Bombay, subscribed to by Anderson, April 12 1839, ibid.
3 Captain Foster's report on fortifications of Aden, sent to Bombay Government April 15 1839, ibid.
4 Lord Auckland, Governor-General, Simla to Bombay Government, April 18 and 22 1839, ibid.
5 Government of India, Simla, to Bombay Government, April 11 1839, ibid.
6 This agreement, No. 35, and the other agreements with the Yafa'i, No. 65, the Haushabi, No. 66, and with the Fadhli, No. 49, are quoted in *Treaties, Engagements and Sanads*, by C. U. Aitchison, vol. 11, Calcutta, 1892.
7 Haines to Bombay, July 11 and 12 1839, F.R.P., vol. 65 and B.E., vol. 15.
8 Bombay Government to Haines, August 10 1839, B.E., vol. 15.
9 Bombay Government to Adjutant-General of the Army, September 27 1839, B.E., vol. 17.
10 Government of India to Bombay, October 14 1839, ibid.

CHAPTER 11   *pp. 101–112*
1 Haines to Bombay, October 20 1839, including confidential correspondence of Sultan Hamed, B.E., vol. 18.
2 Haines to Secretary of Secret Committee of the East India Company in London, November 11 and 12 1839, F.R.P., vol. 67 and B.E., vol. 17.
3 Haines to Secretary of Secret Committee, December 8 1839, F.R.P., vol. 67.
4 Haines to Bombay, December 15 1839, enclosing letter from Sultan Mahsin, B.E., vol. 19 and F.R.P., vol. 68.
5 Government of Bombay to Haines, November 28 1839, B.E., vol. 17.
6 Haines to Bombay, including circular letter from Fadhli Sultan, December 15 1839, F.R.P., vol. 68.
7 Haines to Bombay, December 30 1839, ibid.
8 Haines to Bombay, February 1 1840, containing letter from Sultan Hamed, ibid.
9 Haines to Bombay, November 18 1839, B.E., vol. 19.
10 Haines to Colonel Hodges, British Consul-General in Egypt, February 1 1840, containing report from Company's Agent in Mocha about the correspondence between Mohammed Ali Pasha and the Imam of Sana, F.R.P., vol. 68.

Notes

11 Colonel Hodges to Lord Palmerston, Alexandria, February 22 1840, ibid.
12 Captain Hennell, Political Agent Persian Gulf, to the Court of Directors, London, February 18 1840, ibid.
13 Haines to Secretary of the Secret Committee, February 7 1840, (reached London March 23), ibid.
14 *Kings of Arabia*, by Harold Jacob, p. 56.

CHAPTER 12 *pp. 113–118*

1 Reports to Bombay from Haines and Colonel Capon from January to March 1840, B.E., vol. 20.

CHAPTER 13 *pp. 119–128*

1 Haines to Bombay, March 1 1840, B.E., vol. 20.
2 Bombay Government to Haines, February 26 1840, B.E., vol. 19.
3 Government of India to Bombay, March 7 1840, B.E., vol. 20.
4 Haines to Bombay, March 23 1840, enclosing letter from Fadhli Sultan, ibid.
5 Haines to Bombay, May 21 1840, including other reports on the Arab attack against Aden, B.E., vol. 23.
6 *The Asiatic Journal*, vol. 33, N.S., September to December 1840, part 2, p. 3, also Low's *History of the Indian Navy*, vol. 2, p. 128.
7 Haines to Bombay, June 2 1840, B.E., vol. 23.
8 Haines to Military Secretary to the Government of Bombay, June 3 1840, enclosing letter from Colonel Capon.

The following analysis from the office of the Quarter-Master General in Bombay gives the number of troops in Aden at that time, May 1840, as totalling 2,275.

	Europeans		Natives	
	Officers	*N.C.O.'s & O.R.'s*	*Officers*	*N.C.O.'s & O.R.'s*
2 Batt. Artillery	3	112	2	32
Golundauze Battalion	1			97
Engineer Corps	2	3	1	55
H.M.'s 6th Regiment	14	272		
Bombay Eur. Regiment	13	332		
10th Regiment N.I.	11	1	17	921
16th Regiment N.I.	3		7	376
Total	47	720	27	1481

9 Government of India to Bombay, July 6 1840, B.E., vol. 23.
10 Haines to Bombay, July 9 1840, with enclosures reporting on the third attack on Aden, B.E., vol. 24.
11 Captain Foster's report on defences to Bombay Government, August 8 1840, ibid.

CHAPTER 14 *pp. 129–136*

1 Colonel G. Lloyd Hodges, British Consul-General in Egypt, to Sir James Rivett Carnac, Governor of Bombay, March 19 1840, B.E., vol. 20.

Notes

2 Abdulla Roussoul, East India Company Agent at Mocha, to Haines, March 23 1840, F.R.P., vol. 68.
3 Government of India to Bombay, May 11 1840, B.E., vol. 23.
4 *The Founder of Modern Egypt*, by Henry Dodwell, p. 189.
5 Hodges to the Earl of Auckland, Alexandria, April 18 1840, B.E., vol. 21.
6 *The Life of Henry John Temple, Viscount Palmerston*, by Sir Henry Lytton Bulwer, vol. 2, p. 293.
7 Lieutenant R. Ethersay, commanding the *Elphinstone*, to Haines, July 23 1840, B.E., vol. 25.
8 Hodges to Governor of Bombay, Alexandria, August 17 1840, B.E., vol. 24.
9 Captain H. Johnson, Deputy to the East India Company Agent in Egypt, to the commanders of E.I.C. ships at Suez, October 5 1840, and Alexandria, October 19, to Government of Bombay, B.E., vol. 27.
10 Thomas Waghorn to the Earl of Auckland (under 'flying seal'), Alexandria, October 16 1840, ibid.
11 Minute by Governor of Bombay agreed to by Council, September 18 1840, B.E., vol. 24.
12 Government of India to Bombay, October 26 1840, B.E., vol. 27.
13 John N. Larking, British Consul-General in Egypt, to the Earl of Auckland (under 'flying seal'), November 19 1840, B.E., vol. 28.
14 Circular to Egyptian officials in the Abdine archives quoted in *The Founder of Modern Egypt*, by H. Dodwell, pp. 199–200.
15 *Voyage dans l'Inde*, by Victor Fontanier, French Vice-Consul in Egypt, quoted in *British Routes to India*, by H. L. Hoskins, p. 286.

CHAPTER 15 *pp. 137–155*
1 *Documents sur l'Histoire ... de Madagascar*, by Captain Guillain, Paris, 1845, vol. 1, pp. 26–31, quoted pp. 457–8, *East Africa and its Invaders—1856*, by R. Coupland.
2 East India House (signed by W. B. Bailey and George Lyon) to Haines, July 2 1840, B.E., vol. 25.
3 Haines to Bombay, August 12, 24 and 28 1840, enclosing reports from Captain R. Moresby, ibid. The commercial treaty with the Sultan of Tajjura is given by Aitchison, no. 79, August 19 1840.
4 Cruttenden to Moresby, August 25 1840, B.E., vol. 25.
5 *First Footsteps in East Africa*, by Richard Burton, pp. 52–3, 1966 edition, London.
6 Moresby from Mocha to Haines, September 4 and 8 1840, B.E., vol. 25. Text of treaty between Moresby and the Sherif of Mocha, Aitchison, no. 77, September 1 1840.
7 Sherif Hussain, Governor of Mocha, to the Governor of Bombay, September 3 1840 (received Bombay September 21), B.E., vol. 25.
8 Aitchison, No. 80, Commercial treaty with the Governor of Zayla, September 3 1840.
9 French travellers published a number of books at this time; Edouard Combes and Tamisier, *Un Voyage en Abyssinie*, four volumes, Paris 1838; Theophile Léfebvre, *Voyage en Abyssinie, ... 1839–43*, six volumes and three volumes of atlases, Paris, 1845–54; Charles E. d'Hericourt Rochet, *Voyage sur la Côte*

Orientale de la Mer Rouge, Dans Le Pays d'Adel et le Royaume de Shoa, Paris, 1841, and *Second Voyage* etc., Paris, 1846. (He first called himself Charles Rochet and later added the name d'Hericourt); Antione Thomson d'Abbadie and his brother Arnaud Michel published a large number of articles on Abyssinia but the general account of their travels in Abyssinia was not published until 1868, *Douze Ans dans la Haute-Ethiopie*. An article, 'French and English Rivalry in East Africa', was published in the *Foreign Quarterly Review*, April 1844, vol. 33.

10 Dr. J. L. Krapf was later, in 1860, to publish *Travels and Researches and Missionary Labours during Eighteen Years in East Africa . . . with an appendix respecting the snowcapped Mountains of East Africa*. The main letters referred to, sent by Dr. Krapf from Ankobar in Shoa to Haines in Aden, are contained in Haines to Bombay, September 25 1840, B.E., vol. 25, with letters from Krapf of May 30 and July 22 1840; Haines to Bombay, February 25 1841, B.E., vol. 31, enclosing letters from Krapf to Haines of November 27, December 2 and 17 1840; Haines to Bombay, July 20 1841, enclosing letter from Krapf from Ankobar of June 8, acknowledging two letters from Haines of February 28 and March 15 which had reached him on June 7 in Ankobar.

11 Memorandum by Willoughby, Secretary to the Bombay Government, April 21 1841, B.E., vol. 31.

12 Secretary to the Bombay Government to Captain Harris in command of the Mission to Shoa, April 24 1841, ibid.

13 Minute by Governor of Bombay, Sir James Rivett Carnac, April 24 1841, ibid.

14 *The Highlands of Ethiopia, described during Eighteen Months Residence. A British Embassy at the Christian Court of Shoa*, by Major W. Cornwallis Harris of the Hon. East India Co.'s Engineers, 3 vols., London, 1844.

15 Lieutenant Horton's diary (May 31 to September 9 1841) sent by Harris to Bombay October 29 1841; sent on to the Governor-General of India, December 15 1841.

16 Harris to Bombay, May 27 1841, B.E., vol. 33.

17 Haines to Bombay, July 20 1841, forwarding despatches from Harris, B.E., vol. 35.

18 Harris to Haines for Bombay from Ankobar, August 24 1841, despatch of over two hundred pages, B.E., vol. 37.

19 Harris to Haines for Bombay, October 6 1841, ibid.

20 Harris to Haines for Bombay, Ankobar, February 1 1842, B.E., vol. 43.

21 This coin was dated 1780 and bore the head of the Empress Maria Theresa and had a star near the edge; this was popular in Abyssinia because many considered that it was the head of the Virgin Mary. The dollars which carried the heads of Emperors were not considered to be of much value in Abyssinia though they were current in the Yemen and South Arabia.

CHAPTER 16 *pp. 156–164*

1 Haines to Bombay, March 30 and April 1 1842, B.E., vol. 44.

2 Haines to Bombay, July 5 1841, B.E., vol. 34.

3 Harris to Bombay, Ankobar, July 20 1842, report of two hundred pages, B.E., vol. 51.

Notes

4 Haines to Bombay, December 22 1841, F.R.P., vol. 65.
5 When Commander John Croft Hawkins, commanding the *Clive* with a crew of ninety-six Europeans, was sent by the Bombay Government in January 1830 to report on the anchorages of Socotra, he was also instructed to proceed to the east coast of Africa and to find men and boys from the native population who would be suitable as seamen for the Company's ships. He was given no warning that there were certain procedures he would have to follow in order to avoid the danger of infringing the Slave Laws which had been passed by the British Government. When Hawkins returned to Bombay with negro boys from the coast of Africa he was arrested for having technically transgressed these laws. He was regarded as one of the ablest and most considerate officers in the service and the negro boys had all been well treated, so that when he was sentenced by the Supreme Court of Bombay to transportation for seven years to Australia, there were violent protests from his fellow officers and others.

Hawkins was put on board the sloop-of-war *Coote* which sailed for Australia in May 1831. At Batavia, however, Commander Pepper, the captain of the sloop, found that there were important despatches waiting to be forwarded by the first ship to England. Courageously, on his own responsibility, he decided to take the despatches as an excuse to get Hawkins to England where he thought he would receive justice. Instead of going to Australia, therefore, he sailed for England. In London Hawkins was granted a free pardon and the Court of Directors severely criticised the Government of Bombay for its handling of the case, and Hawkins returned to the command of his ship. In 1848 he became Acting Superintendent and Commander-in-Chief of the Indian Navy on the death of Sir Robert Oliver. (*History of the Indian Navy*, vol. 1, pp. 505–520.)

6 Lieutenant-Colonel H. D. Robertson, acting Resident Persian Gulf, to Bombay, March 4 1842, B.E., vol. 45.
7 Atkins Hamerton, Political Agent Zanzibar, to Bombay from Zanzibar, January 5 1842.
8 Hamerton to Bombay, February 10 1842, Bombay Enclosures, vol. 45.
9 Hamerton to Bombay, January 2 1842, B.E., vol. 44.
10 Lieutenant Willmott Christopher to Haines, January 5 1843, Letters from Aden, vol. 27, 1843. In 1848 he became Assistant Superintendent of the Indus Flotilla and acted with great bravery at the siege of Mooltan where he was killed. (*History of the Indian Navy*, vol. 2, pp. 218–19.)
11 Palmerston to Hamerton, December 18 1846, British and Foreign State Papers 35, 1846–7, 639, quoted *East Africa and its Invaders—1856*, by R. Coupland, p. 519.
12 Captain J. W. Grey to Governor of Bombay, February 2 1842, B.E., vol. 42.
13 Guillain, vol. 2, pp. 124, 52–3, quoted *East Africa and its Invaders*, p. 523.

CHAPTER 17 *pp. 165–179*
1 Government of India to Bombay, March 22 1841, B.E., vol. 30.
2 Governor-General in Council to the Hon. the Secret Committee of the Hon. the Court of Directors September 20 1841, B.E., vol. 36.

Notes

3 Government of India to Bombay, July 16 1841, B.E., vol. 33.
4 Haines to Bombay, August 2 1841, B.E., vol. 35.
5 Haines to Bombay, August 15 1841, ibid.
6 Lord Auckland, Governor-General, to Bombay, April 12 1841, B.E., vol. 32.
7 Lord Auckland to Bombay, July 19 1841, B.E., vol. 35.
8 Comment by H. T. Prinsep, who was Political Secretary to the Governor-General in the time of Lord William Bentinck, quoted in *British Government in India*, by Lord Curzon, vol. 2, p. 197, London, 1925.
9 Pennycuick to Colonel Croker, October 7 1841, B.E., vol. 36.
10 Haines to Secretary Secret Committee of Court of Directors, October 12 1841, B.E., vol. 37.
11 Haines to Secretary Secret Committee, November 10 1841, B.E., vol. 39.
12 Governor-General to Bombay, December 6 1841, B.E., vol. 36.
13 Haines to Bombay, January 4 1842, B.E., vol. 40.
14 Haines to Secretary Secret Committee, January 10 1842, B.E., vol. 40.
15 Government of India to Bombay, January 10 1842, ibid.
16 An account is given in *The Pirates of Trucial Oman*, by H. Moyse-Bartlett, London, 1966, and in *The Pirate Coast*, by Sir Charles Belgrave, London, 1966.
17 Haines to Bombay, June 27 1842, B.E., vol. 48.
18 Chapter 25 of *Britain's Imperial Rôle in the Red Sea Area* deals with the sovereignty question of 1874.
19 *Kings of Arabia*, p. 61.

CHAPTER 18 *pp. 180–187*

1 Government of India to Bombay, November 9 1842, B.E., vol. 53.
2 Secretary of Secret Committee to Government of India, February 5 1843, enclosing letters from Sir Stratford Canning, British Ambassador at Constantinople, of March 31 and April 25 1842, B.E., vol. 62.
3 Government of India to Bombay, April 9 1843, B.E., vol. 58.
4 Government of India to Bombay, October 7 1843, B.E., vol. 62.
5 Governor-General to Bombay, May 7 1843, B.E., vol. 58.
6 'Occupation of Aden', an anonymous article, April, 1843, *Blackwood's Edinburgh Magazine*, No. 330, vol. 53. In another passage it is stated: 'Even if the tact and *savoir faire*, which Captain Haines must be admitted to have displayed in an eminent degree in the execution of his instructions, had succeeded in intimidating the Arabs into surrendering the place without resistance, such a proceeding would have amounted to nothing more or less than the appropriation of the territory of a tribe not strong enough to defend themselves, simply because it was situated conveniently for the purposes of our own navigation: and the open force by which the scheme was ultimately carried into effect, imparts to this act of usurpation a character of violence still more to be regretted.'
7 Bombay to Haines, June 24 1842 and Haines to Bombay, September 21, B.E., vol. 53; further references to entertainment of chieftains, Haines to Bombay, April 20 1843, vol. 60.

Notes

CHAPTER 19 *pp. 188–195*

1 Haines to Secretary of Secret Committee, November 11 1842, B.E., vol. 53.
2 Haines to Bombay, November 22 1843, B.E., vol. 54.
3 Haines to Bombay, February 3 1843, including letter from Sultan Mahsin.
4 The text of the treaty of ten articles is given in Aitchison, No. 36. Article 5 stated: 'Should any British subject become amenable to the law, he is to be made over to the authorities at Aden; and in like manner are the subjects of the Sultan to be made over to his jurisdiction.'
5 Bombay to Haines, July 15 1843, B.E., vol. 60.
6 Haines to Bombay, July 29 1843, vol. 61.
7 Haines to Bombay, August 31 1843, vol. 62.
8 Haines to Bombay, November 29 1843, vol. 64.
9 Haines to Bombay, January 1 1844, vol. 65.
10 Aitchison, No. 37. In Article 2 Sultan Mahsin solemnly declared 'that in all things relating to the peace, progress and prosperity of Aden, I will use every effort to avert calamity, and lend my utmost aid to support the interests of the British flag'. Articles 3 and 4 gave further details of his duties under the bond.
11 'A Memoir on the Western or Endoor Tribe of the Somali Coast', *Journal of the R.G.S.*, vol. 19, 1849. Haines to Bombay, Cruttenden's report enclosed, November 27 1847, B.E., vol. 91.

CHAPTER 20 *pp. 196–201*

1 Haines to Bombay, 10 p.m. November 30 1847, B.E., vol. 90.
2 The agreement signed with Sultan Hamed was dated December 21 1847. It was similar to the Treaty signed with Sultan Ali on March 7 1849 and given in Aitchison, No. 38.
3 Haines to Bombay, June 13 1850, B.E., vol. 102.
4 Ibid., June 12 1850.
5 Haines to Bombay, March 13 1851, vol. 106, and June 13 1851, vol. 108.
6 Haines to Bombay, April 6 1851, vol. 107.
7 Ibid., July 19 1851, vol. 109.
8 Fadhli Sultan to Haines, May 19 1851, vol. 107.
9 Haines to Bombay, August 25 1851, vol. 108 and August 11 1852, vol. 112.
10 Haines to Bombay, May 29 1852, Letters from Aden, vol. 32. *Britain's Imperial Rôle in the Red Sea Area*, pp. 159–60.

CHAPTERS 21 to 25 are based on Bombay Financial Letters and Enclosures, 1854, L/F/3/635; Political Letters to Bombay, 1854, vol. 16, contains a letter from the Court of Directors in London, June 14 1854, answering Bombay Government's Financial Letters of July 29 (No. 46) of 1853 and letter of February 28 (No. 19) 1854 in Political Letters from Bombay. These cover the early part of the story of the case against Haines.

The year 1855 is dealt with in Bombay Financial Letters and Enclosures L/F/3/636; this includes the legal proceedings before the Supreme Court of Bombay and the Advocate-General's report on the two trials with the Judge's notes; Political Letters to Bombay, vol. 17.

Bombay Financial Letters and Enclosures, 1856, L/F/3/637.

Notes

There were a number of Petitions from Haines in prison to the Court of Directors—February 6 1854, February 2 1856 and March 23 1857 (the last two given in L/F/3/630). The main source used is his last petition of August 19 1858 in Bombay Financial Letters and Enclosures, 1858–9, L/F/3/639.

CHAPTER 21 *pp. 205–213*
1 Haines to Bombay, November 17 1853, Letters from Aden, vol. 32.

CHAPTER 22 *pp. 214–223*
1 *Kings of Arabia*, by Harold Jacob, pp. 253–4, 48. *Britain's Imperial Rôle in the Red Sea Area*, pp. 205–6.
2 *A Voyage to Abyssinia*, by Henry Salt, p. 119, London, 1814.
3 *Allen's Indian Mail*, August 6 1860, quoted in *History of the Indian Navy*, vol. 2, pp. 527–8.
4 *The Life of Captain Sir Richard F. Burton*, by Isobel Burton, vol. 1, p. 103, London, 1893.
5 *First Footsteps in East Africa*, by Sir Richard Burton, pp. 21–2, 1966 edition.
6 *Britain's Imperial Rôle* etc., p. 210.

CHAPTER 23 *pp. 224–229*
1 Court of Directors to Bombay, June 14 1854, Political Letters to Bombay, vol. 16.
2 *The Bombay Times and Journal of Commerce* published six columns on the trial on July 31 1854.
3 Ibid., about the same coverage of the second trial, August 5 1854.

CHAPTER 24 *pp. 230–238*
1 Bombay Financial Letters and Enclosures L/F/3/636.
2 *Ca Sa* or *Capias ad Satisfaciendum* is a writ or process after judgement has been given commanding the Officer of the Court to arrest the defendant and to imprison him until the plaintiff's claim is satisfied. Imprisonment for debt was abolished by the 1869 Act except in certain cases which include a debt to the Crown, but even so no person could be imprisoned for more than a year.
3 Bombay to Court of Directors, August 29 1855, Political Letters from Bombay, 1855, vol. 47.
4 Court of Directors to Bombay, October 24 1855, Political Letters to Bombay, vol. 17.
5 Quoted in *Memoir of Richard Haines 1633–1685—A Forgotten Sussex Worthy*, by his seventh male descendant C. R. Haines, London, 1899. This book sets out to be a history of the Haines family. There is hardly any mention of Stafford Bettesworth Haines.
6 Reported in *Bombay Times and Journal of Commerce*, January 7 1856.
7 Moore's *Indian Appeals*, vol. 6, p. 467.

CHAPTER 25 *pp. 239–241*
1 Haines' last petition, August 19 1858, Bombay Financial Letters and Enclosures L/F/3/639.
2 M. R. Westropp, Acting Advocate-General, to Bombay Government, September 3 1861. The Bombay Government still thought that Haines might

Notes

have left a will which would enable the Government to recover some of the losses, but no will was discovered. Bombay Financial Letters and Enclosures, 1861–2, L/F/3/641.

3 'A dark chapter in the history of the Bombay Government has at length come to a conclusion', stated an article in *Allen's Indian Mail* of August 6 1860 (quoted in *History of the Indian Navy*, vol. 2, pp. 527–8). 'A gloomier page, indeed, will scarcely be found anywhere, except, perchance, in the records of Neapolitan misrule. A mere debtor—if, indeed, he were that— had been for nearly six years confined in jail, in a deadly climate, at the suit of the Government he had served with pre-eminent zeal and ability. What more could have been done to him had he actually been found guilty of the fraud and embezzlement which were so strenuously charged against him?' An account was given of his distinguished career and how he became virtually the dictator of Aden. 'His power no one disputed, for no one denied that it was justly and wisely exercised. . . . No man was then more honoured by the Court, not one of their many able and conscientious servants was held in higher regard. But Captain Haines, though an excellent administrator, was an indifferent book-keeper. Probably he knew nothing about double entry, and was no better acquainted with finance than financiers usually are with navigation. As the commerce of the place, however, increased, so did the necessity of having a properly trained and experienced official to super-intend the treasury. Repeatedly did the Political Agent urge his worshipful masters to place the financial department upon a larger and securer footing. It was all in vain. They were busied about many things and had no time to spare a thought upon the burning rock of Aden, or its over-worked Govern-ment. . . .'

Index

Abbadie, Arnaud d', 144, 150, note 9 (Ch. 15) p. 250
Abbadie, Thomson d', 144, 150, note 9 (Ch. 15) p. 250
Abdali tribe, 29, 43; attitude to transfer of Aden, 54, 59, 67, 68; relations with Fadhlis, 64, 65, 121; war with Haushabis, 94, 95; attacks on Aden, 105, 122, 126, 127; interference with caravans, 168; attack Shaikh Othman, 171; attack Bir Ahmed, 199, 214
Abdul Mejjid, Ottoman Sultan, 131, 132, 133
Abdulla ben Mahsin, son of Sultan Mahsin, 95, 191; intrigues against brother, 198; attempts to murder Haines, 198
Abdulla Khatif, steward to Sultan Mahsin, 78; witnesses Aden treaty, 96; corresponds with Sultan Hamed, 102; negotiations with tribes, 103–104; acts for Sultan Mahsin, 87, 107; plot to murder, 108; murder of, 123–125, 174–176
Aberdeen, Lord, relations with Sultan of Muscat, 160, 161, 162; succeeds Palmerston, 167
Abu Ali tribe, 177
Abu Arish, Sherifs of, 139
Abyssinia, 6, 15; French activities in, 143–144, 147, 156–157; Krapf on, 144–147; Harris mission to, 147–155; slavery in, 157, 158, 159
Aden, purchase of, 1, 2, 28, 39–46, 67–68; 'Eye of the Yemen', 3, 112; as commercial centre, 4, 5, 6, 50, 201, 205; descriptions of, 25–27, 81–82; as coaling station, 29; claimed by Egyptians, 32–36, 111–112; Palmerston's views on, 34, 69; arguments on taking of, 37, 38, 39, 53–59, 70–71; plunder of *Duria Dowlat* by people of, 38; Lahej's sovereignty over, 44, 54; article in *Blackwood's* on, 55; skirmishes in, 65–67; capture of, 70–78; fortifications, 83; health in, 83–84; Captain Foster's

report on, 93; building in, 93, 97; climate, 99; attacks on, 103–112, 119–127, 168–169, 194; population in 1840, 113; free access into, 114; interference of military in, 115–118; strategic position of, 128, 137–138, 201, 205; French interest in, 138; Lord Ellenborough's views on, 181–184; developments in, 184–185; Richard Burton on, 222, 223
Admiral Gardner, East Indiaman, 13
Afghanistan, 54, 55, 68, 173, 178, 224
Ahmed, Sherif, brother of Sherif of Mocha, 165
Ahmed, Sultan of Lahej, relations with British, 27, 37, 54
Aidrus mosque, Aden, 75
Airston, John, traveller, 145–146
Alawi tribe, 96
Alawi, Sayyed, son of Zain ben Aidrus, 68, 117
Albuquerque, Alfonso d', 74
Aleppo, 17
Alexandria, 32, 133, 134
Algiers, 157
Ali, son-in-law of Prophet Mohammed, 34, 35, 158
Ali al Mansur, Imam of Sana, visited by Cruttenden, 35–36; succeeds as Imam, 194; threatens Sultan of Lahej, 198 (see also Sana)
Ali ben Mahsin, son of Sultan of Lahej, 95, 191; succeeds his brother 1849, 198; agreement with Haines, 198; murder of Captain Milne, 199; forges document, 214
Ali bin Nasir, envoy of Sultan of Muscat and Zanzibar, on mission to England regarding the slave trade, 160–162
Ali Bu-Beker, Arab merchant in Aden, 226
Ali Ghalib, Sultan of Yafa'i tribe, 94, 99, 103, 121
Ali ibn Abdulla, Amir of Aden, 59, 60
Ali Salaam, 77
America, trade, 6, 30, 200; financial treaty with Muscat, 31; war with, 37

257

Index

Index

Bourbon (see Réunion)

Britain and British, relations with Aden and Lahej, 1, 2, 3, 4, 7, 8, 40, 43-44, 55, 63, 64, 71, 95, 96, 177; at war with France, 17; rivalry of French, 7, 156; relations with East India Company, 12; competition of Russia, 23; war with North America, 37; Egyptian expedition to Yemen, 51; relations with Egypt, 56, 85, 130-136; abolition of slave trade, 157-160, 163-165; relations with Turkey, 177-178, 200

Bunder Kassim, 140

Burma, 16, 68

Burton, Sir Richard, 84, 114n., 141, 154, views on Aden, 222-223

Bushire, 15

Byzantium, 6

Cain, grave of, 128

Calcutta, 15, 16, 17, 24

Campbell, Colonel, Consul-General in Egypt, recommends taking Aden, 29-30; correspondence with Palmerston, 33, 51, 56, 85; good relations with Mohammed Ali, 34, 130; receives reports on Haines, 68-69; removed from Egypt, 110

Canning, Sir Stratford (Lord Stratford de Redcliffe) British Ambassador in Constantinople, 181

Cape of Good Hope, 6, 17, 30

Capon, Colonel, appointed to command of Aden Garrison in succession to Major Bailie, 100; report on Arab attack, 105; quarrel with Haines, 115-118; fault of Bombay Military, 115; reprimanded, 118; concern at further Arab attacks, 121-124

Carless, Lieutenant T. G., 20

Carnac, Sir James Rivett, Governor of Bombay, 128, 129, 149

Carnatic, Nawab of, 38

Caspian Sea, 23

Ceylon, 6, 13

Charger, 23, 126

Chesney, Colonel, 23

China, trade of, 6, 13, 16, 25, 31; Arab colonies in, 6; Chinese in East Africa, 7; surveys in, 19; war with, 130

Christopher, Lieutenant, commanding *Tigris*, explores Shebelli river, 154; dealings with slave trade, 157, 163; talks with envoy of Sultan of Muscat, 161-162; blockades Shuqra, 173

Clarke, Midshipman, 141

Clarke, Lieutenant Colonel Augustus, acting Political Agent, 212-215

Clerk, Sir George, Governor of Bombay, 240

Clive, 18

Clive, Robert, 12

Coghlan, Brigadier, 178, 223

Colonial Office, 3

Combes, French scientist, 144, 147

Constance, 163, 164

Constantinople, 17, 23, 34, 131

Coote, sloop, 39, 87, 91, 92, 216; in Aden, 41, 45-48; 51, 56, 58, 60, 62-65; capture of *Ateeh Allah*, 66

Corfield, A. K., magistrate, 219

Court of Directors, rules laid down by, 12; headquarters, 13; formation of Secret Committee, 14; rivalry with Board of Control, 14-15; resist change from Cape route, 17; against steam navigation, 18, 23; persuaded to support steam, 24; on the taking of Aden, 40, 58, 59n., 63n.; present Swords of Honour, 77, 213, 232; capture of Aden, 77; relations with tribes, 95; Haines' correspondence with, 98; reinforcements for Aden, 176; Lord Auckland recalled by, 178; opposed to destroying fort at Bir Ahmed, 199; Haines' deficit in Treasury, 207, 219, 224; forbid expeditions inland from Aden, 223; agree to arraign Haines, 224; trial of Haines, 230, 231, 232; attitude to Haines' offer of repayment, 234; order Haines' return to jail, 236-237; refuse to review case, 239 (see also East India Company and Secret Committee)

Crater, district of Aden, 47, 48, 59, 75, 175, 184, 190; description of, 81-82; Haines has house in, 84, 90; main gate into, 100; British troops in, 127

Crete, 33

Croker, Colonel, 171, 190, 191

Cruizer, H.M.S., 72-74, 130

Cruttenden, Lieutenant C. J., in *Palinurus*, 20-21; expedition to Socotra, 21; visits Sana, 35; accompanies Moresby to Somali coast, 138; visits Tajjura, 140, 153; appointed Assistant Political Agent, 149; in Mocha, 165; operations in Aden, 169, 171; work in Aden, 184-185; receives Sultan Mahsin, 190; visits Lahej, 191-192; discussions with Somalis, 195; deficit in Treasury, 207-208, 210, 212, 213; at trial of Haines, 227

Curzon, Lord, 14-15

Dalhousie, Lord, 224

Damascus, 33, 34

259

Index

Damjee, Indian merchant in Aden, 48, 58, 210, 211

Danakil, people, 6, 98; negotiations with, 138–140, 149; description of, 150–151, 156

Daniell, Lieutenant, at attack on Aden, 74–75; presented Sword of Honour, 77

Denton, Commander, 65, 66

Denwah, battle at, 143

Deptford, 11

Dhu Hussain, Yemeni tribe, 97

Dhu Mohammed, Yemeni tribe, 97

Dhubee, Mohammed, murders Private Dickson, 87,

Djibouti, 138

Dobree, Lieutenant, 75

Dordogne, French warship, 135, 137

Dost Mohammed, 54, 173

Dumas, Alexandre, 157

Dunlop, J. A., member of Bombay Council, 58

Dupleix, Joseph, Governor-General of French India, 12

Duria Dowlat, plundered at Aden, 38–40, 46, 48, 49, 57, 71, 86, 210

Dutch, trade with Far East, 11

East Africa, 15, 30

East India Company, 4; formation of, 11; first factories, 11–12; charter, 12; relations with Mogul Empire, 12, 32; headquarters, 13; East India docks opened, 13; Court of Directors and Secret Committee of, 14; Government of India and the, 15–16; resists change from Cape route, 17; attitude to steam, 18, 23, 24; attempt to purchase Socotra, 21; Sultan of Lahej and the, 27; expenses, 30; rivalry with Americans, 31; on taking Aden, 40; sends gifts to Viceroy of Egypt, 136; negotiations with Somalis, 138; suppression of slave trade, 157; case against Haines, 224–229; arraigns Haines for debt, 231–238; Haines' petitions, 239

Edd, near Massawa, 143

Egypt, policy on Aden, 1–2, 4, 6; relations with East India Co., 15, 31; Bonaparte in, 17, 27, 37; claim to Yemen and Aden, 32–36, 50, 51, 56, 57, 85; troops in Syria, 33, 36, 133; Palmerston's views on, 34; captured by Selim 1, 35; relations with Sultan of Lahej, 41, 43, 45; Bombay Government and, 53; troops in Aden, 67; relations with Shaikh Sherzebee, 84; intrigues with South Arabian tribes, 110–111; troops in Yemen, 111, 129, 132, 178, 209;

rumours of war with, 129, 132; rising of Syria and Turkey against, 133, 134

Elizabeth, Queen, 11

Ellenborough, Edward Law, Earl of, succeeds Lord Auckland as Governor-General of India, 178–179; policy on Aden, 180–184; views on Mocha, 181; views on Somaliland, 182; created Earl, 224

Elphinstone, in Mocha, 130, 142; in Jedda, 132; money for, 210

Elphinstone, Lord, Governor of Bombay (1853), treatment of Haines, 212, 220, 221, 232–233, 236

Elphinstone, Mountstuart, Governor of Bombay (1823), 17

Elwon, Captain, 20

Endymion, suppressing slave trade, 163–164; in Mocha, 166–167

Eshreff Bey, 178, 181

Ethersay, Lieutenant, 130, 132

Euphrates, defending Aden, 105; blockades Shuqra, 107, 173; sent to Mocha, 130, at Tajjura, 150

Euphrates, postal route along, 17, 134; steam navigation on, 23; importance of route, 34

Europe, influence in South Arabia, 6, 7; postal route across, 17

Evans, Lieutenant, Bombay Regiment, 65, 66

Fadhl, Sir Ahmed, Sultan of Lahej, 7

Fadhl bin Mahsin, son of Sultan of Lahej, 95

Fadhli Sultan, trouble with Sultan Mahsin, 42; treaty with, 96; plan to murder Haines, 119; stirs up *jehad*, 121; murder of interpreter, 169; negotiations with, 173–174, 176; power of, 198–199, (see also Hamed bin Abdulla)

Fadhli tribe, description, 29; war with Yafa'is, 41; stipend, 95; discuss attack on Aden, 193; aggressiveness of, 198

Faki Said, Shaikh, 143

Falkland, Lord, 212

Farish, James, acting Governor of Bombay, 54; on occupation of Aden, 55–57; instructions for Haines, 57; analysis of Aden situation, 71; report on Haines, 92

Ferret, French scientist, 144

Ford, A., Midshipman in *Palinurus*, 20

Foster, Captain, engineer, repairs Aden fortifications, on Aden cantonment, 92; on Aden defences, 93, 111–114, 127

France, rivalry with Britain, 7, 51, 55, 137–138; trade with Far East, 11; rela-

Index

Index

released from prison, 240; death of, 8, 241

Hallam, Captain, in command of Aden garrison during Arab attack in July 1840, 125

Hamed, Sultan, son of Sultan Mahsin, negotiations with Haines, 40–41, 45, 60–61, 67–68, 95, 108–109, 120, 154, 189; plot to kidnap Haines, 47–50; transfer of Aden, 58–59; *Ateeh Allah*, 66; at Shaikh Othman, 96, 101–103; relations with father, 102–103, 108; murders Abdulla Khatif, 123, 174; attacks Aden, 119–127; Cruttenden calls on, 191; succeeds father, 197; agreement with Haines, 197; death, 198

Hamed ben Abdulla, Fadhli Sultan, relations with Haines, 29, 64–65; hatred of Abdalis, 65; threatens Lahej, 86; treaty with, 96; intrigues with Abdalis, 103–108; plan to murder Haines, 119; attacks Aden, 126–127

Hamerton, Captain Atkins, slavery in Zanzibar, 157, 160, 161–162

Hamilton, Lieutenant Benjamin, 41, 46, 65, 66; at capture of Aden, 75, 91; at attacks on Aden, 105, 194

Harar, 141, 159

Harris, Captain Cornwallis, mission to Abyssinia, 148–155, 186; knighted 1844 and death 1848, 155; on slavery, 158

Hastings, Warren, 12

Hatchatoor, British Agent at Tajjura, 150

Haushabi tribe, war with Abdalis, 94; treaty with, 95; liaison with, 96; refuse passage to tribes attacking Aden, 120; discuss attacking Aden, 193

Hawkins, Commander, 18, 159; his trial, note 5 (Ch. 16) p. 252

Hennell, Captain, East India Company representative in Persian Gulf, visits Boraimi, 110; slave trade, 157, 163; Governor-General's policy of non-interference, 183

Hill, Admiral de, 138

Hindus, in Aden, 97

Hisn Ghorab, description of, 24–25, note 10 (Ch. 2) p. 244–245

Hobhouse, Sir John Cam, Lord Broughton, 14

Hobson, Captain, Staff Officer Aden, 115

Hodeida, 5, 84, 209; Banians in, 30; trade in, 200

Hodges, Colonel, Consul-General in Egypt, 109–110; relations with Mohammed Ali, 129–131; 132, 133; fights with Turks against Egyptians, 134

Hogg, Sir James, Chairman of Court of Directors, 14

Holden, David, quoted, 5

Hongkong, 130

Horn of Africa, 7

Horton, Lieutenant Sidney, member of Harris mission, 148–152

House of Commons, Committees to study steam Communication with India, 23, 29

Howard, Mr., prosecutes at trial of Haines, 227–228

Hugh Lindsay, steam vessel, launched, 17; experimental voyage, 18; carries mails, 24

Hujariya, in Yemen, 84

Hulton, Dr., medical officer in *Palinurus*, 35

Hume, Joseph, 13

Hussain, Hajj, rich merchant, 45, 48

Hussain ibn Ali Hyder, Sherif of Abu Arish, buys Mocha from Egyptians and becomes Sherif of Mocha, 139; negotiations with Moresby, 141–143; intrigues with Sultan of Lahej, 165, 193; hostility to British, 167, 178; extortions of, 197, 198

Hutchinson, East India Company Agent at Mocha, 37–38

Hyder ben Mehdi, Aqrabi Sultan, attacks by Abdalis and Fadhlis, 125; Haines wants to destroy his fort, 199

Hyderabad, Nizam of, 6

Ibn Khaldun, 2

Ibrahim Pasha, son of Mohammed Ali Pasha, captures Syria from the Ottoman Empire, 34; fights in Syria against Turkish and European forces, 133–135

Ibrahim Pasha, known as 'The Little' and nephew of Mohammed Ali Pasha, informed by Haines that Aden is British, 51; Haines' instructions as to how to deal with if found that Egyptians were in Aden, 57–58; threats by to Arab chiefs proposing to visit Aden, 84; Sultan Mahsin seeks help of, 109; ordered to evacuate Yemen, 132

India, trade with Aden, 3, 6, 50; policy towards Aden, 4, 38, 40, 180–184; Arab colonies in, 6; Mogul Empire, 12; trade with London, 13; dealings with East India Company, 11, 14, 15; war in, 16; steam navigation in, 18, 24, 29; Muscat trade with, 31; Russian designs on, 34; plans for French conquest of, 37; wars fought by, 68; failure to have good relations with Yemen, 4, 112; Government of and slavery, 157, 159–160

Index

Indian Ocean, surveys in, 16, 19; Americans in, 30; French in, 137
Indians, in Aden, 26, 43, 68, 128; in Mocha, 30
Ingrams, Harold, on Arab way of life, 2–3; on British rule, 3; quoted, 8; note 4 (Introduction) p. 243
Ismail, Sayyed, 194

Jackson, Sir Charles, judge at trial of Haines, 226–228
Jacob, Colonel Harold, 4
Jacob, General John, 215
Java, Arab colonies in, 6
Jebel Hadeed, hill in Aden, 67, 122, 125, 126
Jebel Shamshan, mountain in Aden, 25, 26, 99
Jedda, Christian vessels in, 18; Banians in, 30; travellers to, 38; duties at, 85; *Elphinstone* at, 132; repercussions of events in, 183; Egyptian troops in, 209
Jenkins, Lieutenant Griffith, assistant to Political Agent, 106; at attack on Aden, 122; on sick leave and visit to Mohammed Ali Pasha, n. 133, 149
Jews, in Aden, 26, 43, 73, 80, 93, 97; in Yemen, 80
Jezret Feringee, small island, 65–66
Johnston, Sir Charles, 3, note 4 (Introduction) p. 243
Jones, Felix, Midshipman in *Palinurus*, 20
Juba river, 154

Kabul, 54, 173
Kamaran Island, 29, 208
Kandahar, 54
Karrak Island, 44
Keir, General Sir William, 160
Khormaksar, 40, 47, 63
Kilmaier, German Lieutenant, 146, 149
Kirke, Dr., member of Harris mission, 148
Knott, General Sir William, 187
Koran, 5, 158, 163, 164, 174
Krapf, John Ludwig, in Abyssinia, 144–147, 153, note 10 (Ch. 15) p. 251
Kuria Muria Islands, 30–31

La Bourdonnais, Mahé de, French admiral, 12
La Favorite, French warship, 157
Lahej, description of, 28; visited by Wellsted, 28; Sultan meets Advisers at, 45; Sultan Hamed at, 47; Hajji Hussain at, 48; treaty with, 95; Abdali and Fadhli Sultans meet at, 103, 121, 123; Haines plans expeditions against, 111, 121, 169–170
Lamb, Charles, 13

Larking, John N., British Consul in Alexandria, 135
Lefebvre, French scientist, 144
Leith, surgeon, 236
Le Mesurier, Mr., Advocate-General at Haines' trial, 226, 228, 230
Little Aden, 4
London, 13, 15, 16
Louis Philippe, King, 138, 145, 156, 157
Lowe, Commander, 59n.
Lumsden, J. G., 221, 222
Lyons, Captain, East India Company's representative in Egypt, 130, 134

Mackenzie, Captain James, reports on Egyptians in Yemen, 36, 55
Madagascar, 137
Madras, 12, 14, 16
Mahdi, Imam al, 35
Mahi, at blockade of Aden, 73–74; 77; sent to Mocha, 130
Mahmud II, Sultan, 33
Mahra tribe, Haines' negotiations with, 19, 20–21, 22
Mahra Sultan (see Omar ibn Tawari)
Mahsin, Sultan of Lahej, sale of Aden, 1, 2, 39, 45, 46; taxation by, 26; succeeds as Sultan, 27; negotiations with Haines, 28, 82, 86–87, 173–176; wealth, 28; described by Wellsted, 28; plunder of *Duria Dowlat*, 38, 39; relations with Egyptians, 41, 43, 45, 109; trouble with Fadhlis, 42, 64; treaty with Haines, 43–44, 54; plot to kidnap Haines, 47, 49–50, 57, 59; transfer of Aden, 58, 59, 62–64; makes Hamed his agent, 60–61; capture of *Ateeh Allah*, 66; submits to Haines, 77–78; relations with Bombay Government, 88–89, 188–189; attacks on Aden, 94, 103–108, 119–127, 169; treaty signed, 95–96; disagreement with son, 102–103; abdicates 1840, 108, but later takes control again, 109; plan to murder Haines, 119; relations with Sherif of Mocha, 142–143, 165, 193; intrigues with Faki Said, 143; seeks protection, 162–173; signs peace treaty, 189–191; reception in Aden, 190–191; intrigues with tribes, 193; death, 196
Maidee, Shaikh, 171–2
Main Pass or Main Gate into Crater, 83, 100, 128
Maitland, Rear Admiral Sir Frederick, 72
Malay Archipelago, 6
Malcolm, Sir Charles, 19, 24
Malcolmson, Dr., 77, 91, 207
Maria Theresa dollars, 21n., 155, 210, note 21 (Ch. 15) p. 251
Mary Ann, 141

263

Index

Index

Index

181; Richard Burton's description of, 141

Shebelli river, 154

Sherzebee, Shaikh Aoun ibn Yussuf al-, Yemeni chief, 84

Shoa, 143, 144, 167 (see also Sahela Selassie)

Shuqra, visited by Haines, 29; Sultan of, 42; blockade of, 107, 173; bombardment of, 193

Simla, 16, 94, 98

Singapore, 6, 224

Sira Island, included in territory of Aden, 40; fortifications, 62, 67, 132; attack on, 73–74, 81, 83, 91

Slavery in Mukalla, 25; in Tajjura, 140; in Abyssinia, 148, 150, 151, 154; in Zanzibar, 157; suppression of trade, 157–164, 165, 183

Smith, Captain H., R.N., in Command of attack on Aden, 72–76; at Hongkong, 130

Socotra, as coaling station, 18, 29, 38, 159; surveys of, 19, 20–21; negotiations for purchase of, 21–22, 71; description, 22; British troops in, 22–23; abandonment of, 23

Somalia, 7

Somaliland, 5, 6, 27, 98

Somalis, 15; in Aden, 43, 93

Sons of Commerce, brig, 199

Sorabjee Cowasjee, 211

South Arabia, as part of Yemen, 3; trade, 6; strategic value, 7; surveys of, 19, 24–27; intelligence agents in, 80, 185; slave trade in, 157; finance in, 210; effect of Haines' dismissal on, 214

South Pacific, 30

Speke, John Hanning, 114n.

Standen, Mr., helped defence of Haines at trial, 225

Steamer Point, district of Aden, 46; Haines' house at Tarshain on cliff over, 84, 99, 132, 212; passengers at, 184

Stovell, surgeon, 236

Subeihi tribe, 125

Suez, 6, 17, 18, 20, 29, 30; *Hugh Lindsay* at, 18; mail service, 23, 55, 132; importance of route, 34

Suez Canal, 7

Suleiman the Magnificent, 26, 35

Sultan ibn Suggur, Trucial Coast chief, 160

Sultaneh, Sultan of Muscat's ship, 160

Sumatra, Arab colonies in, 6

Sur, 177

Surat, factory in, 12; Nabob of, 41

Swan, Lieutenant, officer of the sloop *Coote*, 41, 46

Swaya Island, 65, 122, 125, 126

Syria, 33, 34

Taez, in Yemen, 85

Tajjura, negotiations at, 138–140; French in, 144; Harris mission in, 149, 150, 152; slaves in, 157, 159; murders in, 182

Tamarida, capital of Socotra, 21, 22

Tamisier, French scientist, 144

Taylor, Geoffrey, defence barrister for Haines, 225

Tehama, Egyptian troops in, 34; Cruttenden and Hulton visit, 35; control by Sherifs of Abu Arish, 139

Thames, 13

Thompson, Captain Perronet, 177

Tigre, 143; Ras of, 147

Tigris, in Zanzibar, 154, 161; in Massawa, 157

Tigris, steam navigation on, 23

Turkey (and Turks), imperialism of, 2; intrigues with Egyptians, 6; dealings with East India Company, 15; attitude to Christian vessels, 17–18; Russian pressure on, 23; capture Aden, 26; in Yemen, 26, 34, 35, 198; Palmerston's views on, 34; Convention of 1840, 133; claims to Yemen, 177–178; try to capture Mukalla, 198; war with Russia, 209 (see also Ottoman Empire)

Tyeb Ibranjee, Shaikh, accompanies Haines to Aden, 57, 63, 64, 90

Valentia, Lord, description of Aden, 25

Victoria, Queen, 8, 160

Volage, H.M.S., sent to attack Aden, 72–74, 77

Volga, steamboats on, 23

Waghorn, Thomas, raises money for steamer service, 17; arranges coal transport by camel, 23; 'on secret service' in Egypt, 134

Wahabis, 31, 139

Walpole, Sergeant, killed on Harris mission, 152

Webb, Mr., master of the *Rattler*, 168

Weiss, Sayyed Hussain, witness to Aden agreement, 45; plot to kidnap Haines, 47–50; attempts to kidnap Tyeb Ibranjee, 64; sent by Sultan Mahsin to submit to Haines, 78; accompanies Sultan Mahsin to Aden, 87; intrigues with tribes, 94; agent for Haushabis, 95; British Agent, 96, 102, 103, 107, 108, 123, 174; works against Haines, 176, 193, 198

Wellesley, Lord, Governor-General of India, 17

266

Index

Wellsted, J. R., Lieutenant in *Palinurus*, 20; surveys Socotra, 21; visits Lahej, 28; describes Sultan Mahsin, 28; opinion of camels, 176

Western, Lieutenant, with Haines in Aden, 57, 67; repairs fortifications, 82

Wilson, Corporal, killed on Harris mission, 152

Wilson, Commander John, 18

Yafa'i tribe, war with Fadhli tribe, 41; treaty with Haines, 94–95; refuses to join in attack on Aden, 120; discussions with Sultan Mahsin, 193

Yardley, Sir William, Chief Justice Bombay, 225–226, 234, 238

Yemen, Egyptians in, 1, 31, 33, 34, 51, 56, 85; trade, 2, 30, 31; birthplace of Arab race, 3; one area with South Arabia, 3–4, 51; coffee of, 6; suffering in, 7; Russians interest in, 7; towns of, 28; Turks in, 28; American trade with, 30; claimed by Egyptians, 32–36; Palmerston's views on, 34; Suleiman I captures, 35; import of arms into, 51; Jews in, 80; Shaikh Sherzebee of, 84; tribes offer territory to Britain, 97; ceding of to Egypt, 109–110; slavery in, 157; Turkey's claim to, 177

Zaidee tribes, 109

Zain ibn Aidrus, Sayyed, concerned with plot to kidnap Haines, 48–49; sends letter of truce to Haines, 67–68; helps maintain order in Aden, 91; refuses to act against Haines, 174; escorts Fadhlis, 175; escorts Cruttenden, 192

Zanzibar, Indians in, 15; American trade with, 31, French trade with, 137; *Tigris* in, 154; slavery in, 157, 159–162

Zeyla, trade with, 26, 167; East India Co. wants foothold in, 138; negotiations at, 141–142; French in, 144; slavery in, 157, 159; Sharmakay takes, 181–182

Zinjibar, in Fadhli state, 29